U0466376

海上丝绸之路的陶瓷

外销瓷如何塑造全球化的世界

[德] 吉乐（Thorsten Giehler）著

THE CERAMICS OF THE MARITIME SILK ROAD

HOW EXPORT PORCELAIN HAS SHAPED A GLOBALIZED WORLD

中国科学技术出版社
·北京·

图书在版编目（CIP）数据

海上丝绸之路的陶瓷：外销瓷如何塑造全球化的世界 /（德）吉乐著 . —北京：中国科学技术出版社，2022.9

ISBN 978–7–5046–9480–5

Ⅰ. ①海… Ⅱ. ①吉… Ⅲ. ①陶瓷—外销—研究—中国 ②陶瓷—文化史—中国 Ⅳ. ①F724.787 ② K876.34

中国版本图书馆 CIP 数据核字（2022）第 039036 号

审图号　GS 京（2022）0724 号

总 策 划	秦德继
策划编辑	申永刚　方　理
责任编辑	戚琨琨
封面设计	朱　颖
正文设计	中文天地
责任校对	焦　宁
责任印制	李晓霖

出　　版	中国科学技术出版社
发　　行	中国科学技术出版社有限公司发行部
地　　址	北京市海淀区中关村南大街16号
邮　　编	100081
发行电话	010–62173865
传　　真	010–62173081
网　　址	http://www.cspbooks.com.cn

开　　本	787mm×1092mm　1/16
字　　数	358千字
印　　张	19
版　　次	2022年9月第1版
印　　次	2022年9月第1次印刷
印　　刷	北京盛通印刷股份有限公司
书　　号	ISBN 978–7–5046–9480–5 / F・1039
定　　价	158.00元

（凡购买本社图书，如有缺页、倒页、脱页者，本社发行部负责调换）

献给我的两个欧亚混血孩子——李赞和李诺

For Lisanne and Lino, two children of Eurasia

序言

众所周知，中国瓷器是历史上最早行销全球且具有国际影响力的人工制品之一。历经几个世纪的探索，到唐朝，工匠们已经能够烧制出坯体白色、半透明的硬质瓷，其质地坚硬，易于清洁，经久耐用。白色的瓷胎表面，便利了匠人们烧制钴蓝釉下彩，或者通过釉上珐琅彩绘制各种场景和主题的图案。到13世纪的元朝，制瓷工艺进入真正成熟阶段，主要集中在江西省景德镇生产。贸易部分得益于与来自中东的穆斯林商人客户之间深入的贸易往来。

明朝前期，通过广泛的陆上和海上贸易，中国瓷器声名远扬。但直到"大航海时代"开启，西方商人将瓷器运往欧洲和美洲，它才真正具有了全球影响力。在16世纪，葡萄牙人和西班牙人最先将瓷器作为利润丰厚的商品进行贸易，荷兰人和英国人在17世纪也紧随其后。

在当时的欧洲，各地的人们都将瓷器视为一种特别而富有魅力的异域之物，但遗憾的是它只能在中国（或者说亚洲）生产。许多人都曾尝试用各种原料、各种手段烧制陶瓷，希望能够仿制出中国瓷器，但制瓷原料和工艺始终是一个谜。

18世纪初，萨克森选侯国（今属德国）中毗邻首都德累斯顿的小城迈森（一译梅森）成功烧制出了硬质瓷，这是在亚洲以外地区第一次成功地仿制出硬质瓷器，著名的迈森瓷器由此诞生。萨克森选帝侯奥古斯特二世（1670—1733年）对此功不可没。他是一位狂热的中国和日本瓷器爱好者和收藏家，鼓励并资助了化学家约翰·弗里德里希·伯特格尔（1682—1719年）和埃伦弗里德·瓦尔特·冯·奇恩豪斯（1651—1708年）进行烧制瓷器的实验。

因此可以说，瓷器成为中国和德累斯顿之间的纽带。茨温格宫瓷器收藏馆陈列的部分奥古斯特二世的瓷器藏品印证了这一点。历史上，奥古斯特二世共收藏有29 000件中国瓷器，收藏馆至今仍保存其中的8 000多件。鉴于中国瓷器的贸易历史，这些瓷器藏品都属于外销瓷，在当时被认为符合西方客户的需求。外销瓷是整个中国制瓷生产史中不可或缺的一部分，只是由于被出口，如今在中国少为人知。

有鉴于此，我对这本书的出版表示赞赏。它试图向今天的广大读者——包括学生、收藏家和爱好者——讲述有关外销至国外市场的中国瓷器的故事。这称得上是一次了不起的尝试。我相信它将帮助读者更深入地了解中国瓷器如何成为全球商品，以及它为何能在世界各地赢得无数人的赞赏和喜爱。

朱莉亚·韦伯
德累斯顿国家艺术收藏馆瓷器馆馆长

Foreword

As is well-known, Chinese porcelain was the first man-made material with global distribution and impact. After development of centuries, Chinese potters made ceramics of a hard, slightly translucent white body that was strong, easy to clean, and very durable. The white surface lent itself marvellously for decorations in cobalt-blue under the glaze or colorful scenes and motifs in enamels on the glaze. Production really started in the 13th century, during the Yuan dynasty, stimulated by contacts with Islamic customers and merchants in Persia and the Middle East. Production became concentrated in Jingdezhen, Jiangxi province.

Trade over land and by sea made porcelain known in a wide area during the first half of the Ming dynasty, but the real global influence came when Western merchants shipped porcelain to Europe and the Americas. In the 16th century, the Portuguese and the Spanish embraced porcelain as a profitable commodity, followed by the Dutch and the English in the 17th century.

Everywhere porcelain was regarded as something special and wonderful, an exotic material that could be produced only in China. Its substance and how to work it remained a mystery, although many tried to imitate it in ceramics of various materials. However, the first truly successful production of hard-paste porcelain outside Asia took place in the early 18th century in the German city of Meissen, near Dresden, the capital of the State of Saxony. Here, Elector Augustus the Strong (1670–1733), an avid collector of Chinese and Japanese porcelain himself, stimulated and financed the experiments of the chemist Johann Friedrich Böttger (1682–1719) and the natural scientist Ehrenfried Walther von Tschirnhaus (1651–1708), resulting in the birth of the famous Meissen porcelain.

China and Dresden, therefore, are connected by porcelain. This also shows in the presentation of part of the former collection of Augustus the Strong in the Porcelain Collection in the Zwinger, still housing more than 8,000 of the original 29,000 pieces from the historical holdings! Given the history of trade in porcelain, these porcelains are of the export type, regarded at the time as suitable for Western clients. They form an essential part of the assortment of Chinese production as a whole, but having been exported, they are less well known in China today.

Therefore, I applaud the publication of this book. It is a great attempt to tell the story of Chinese porcelain exported to foreign markets to a wide audience of present-day Chinese students, collectors, and enthusiasts. I am sure it will generate a deeper understanding of how Chinese porcelain became a global commodity and why it generated the appreciation and love of millions around the world.

Julia Weber
Director
Staatliche Kunstsammlungen Dresden, Porzellansammlung

陶瓷术语表

陶瓷 所有由黏土制成并通过高温烧制而成的产品的总称，包括陶器、瓷器和粗陶器。

青瓷 带绿色或青绿釉的粗陶器或瓷器，主要在中国、朝鲜、泰国和越南生产。中国将浅绿色或青绿色瓷器称为"青白瓷"。

加彩 在已经完成的陶瓷产品上添加釉面彩。镀金是通过添加金色颜料进行的一种特殊加彩形式。

米色陶器 具有不透明白色或象牙釉的白陶。

陶器 低温烧制产品，容易开裂或破碎，陶土厚重，不透明且可透水。

釉上彩 通过烧制熔化彩色粉末玻璃，并将其添加到瓷器釉彩中。这种釉彩装饰在明清时期被广泛使用，在五彩瓷和粉彩瓷中较为常见。

白锡釉陶 带白釉的棕陶。

熔块胚陶 由石英砂制成的复合材料，掺有少量细磨玻璃和一些黏土。从狭义上讲，它不是陶瓷，而是玻璃和陶瓷的混合物。

釉料 薄玻璃涂层，涂在瓷器表面使其发亮并持久着色，或涂在陶器上使其防水。釉料可以是透明、不透明或彩色的。可以在釉下（大部分是钴蓝色）或釉上（如通过釉上彩）添加颜色。

陶瓷术语表

| 开光 | 中国瓷器的传统装饰技法之一，往往在器物的某一形状（如扇形、菱形、圆形等）的空间内饰以图纹，称为开光。 |

| 珍珠色白陶 | 韦奇伍德在英国发明的带淡蓝釉的白陶。 |

| 瓷器 | 高温（1 300℃）焙烧的白色产品，透明、坚硬且不透水。制瓷黏土需含有长石岩和高岭土。 |

| 软瓷 | 中温烧制产品，透明，但不如真正的瓷器坚硬。不仅含有黏土，还如熔块胚陶一样含有石英。18世纪，当真正的陶瓷配方还不为人知时，主要在法国和英国生产。 |

| 粗陶瓷 | 高温焙烧的陶瓷产品，坚硬且不透水，但粗糙且不透明。胚体可为白色、灰色或棕色。 |

| 赤陶 | 未上釉的深色陶器。 |

| 转印技术 | 青花瓷的蓝色纹饰可以通过从手工雕刻的铜盘上的蓝色印画转印到瓷片上。 |

Glossary of Ceramic Terms

Ceramic
A general term for all products made of clay and made hard by firing at high temperature (including earthenware, porcelain, and stoneware).

Celadon
Stoneware or porcelain with a green or green-bluish glaze mainly produced in China, Korea, Thailand, and Vietnam. Light green or bluish-green porcelain items are called *Qingbai* in Chinese.

Clobbering
It means adding overglaze colors to an already finished ceramic product. Gilding is a special form of clobbering by adding gold color.

Creamware
White earthenware with an opaque white or ivory-colored glaze.

Earthenware
Low-fired products, and easily chipped or broken, heavily pottered, not translucent, and pervious to water.

Enameling
Fusing colorful powdered glass by firing and adding it on the glaze of porcelain. This overglaze decoration became widely used during the Qing dynasty and is typical for the *Famille verte* and *Famille rose* porcelains.

Faience
Brown earthenware with an opaque white cover.

Fritware
It refers to a composite material

made from quartz sand mixed with small amounts of finely ground glass and some clay; not ceramic in a narrow sense, but a mixture between glass and ceramic.

Glaze
A thin coating of glass, applied to porcelain to make it shiny and to allow durable coloring, or to earthenware to make it waterproof. Glazes may be clear, opaque, or colored. Colors can then be added under the glaze (e.g. mostly cobalt blue) or over the glaze (e.g. by enameling).

Panel
A small framed window or spot left blank (reserve) for decoration.

Pearlware
White earthenware with a shiny light bluish glaze invented in England by Wedgewood.

Porcelain
High-fired (at beyond 1,300℃) white products, translucent, hard, and impervious to water. The clay consists of felspathic rocks and kaolin.

Soft-paste porcelain
It refers to medium-fired products, translucent, but not as hard as true porcelain, which includes not only clay but also quartz. It was produced mainly in the 18th century in France and Great Britain when the formula of true porcelain was unknown.

Stoneware
High-fired ceramic products, hard and impervious to water, but coarse and not translucent. The body can be white, grey, or brown.

Terracotta
Unglazed dark earthenware.

Transfer-printing
The blue decor of blue and white ceramic is printed by transferring a blue colored print from hand-engraved copper plates, invented in Worcester in 1760.

目录 CONTENTS

导言 / 1

第一部分　外销瓷的全球之旅

第一章　早期国际贸易史上的中国陶瓷 / 12
从单色釉瓷到青花瓷 / 12
中国对亚洲邻居的影响 / 15

第二章　全球化世界的开端：欧亚贸易关系 / 32
葡萄牙人 / 32
荷兰东印度公司 / 37
荷兰人和日本外销瓷 / 45
英国人 / 48
一口通商出口热潮 / 50
广州贸易中的商品 / 55

第三章　40亿英镑的交易：瓷器贸易经济 / 98
贸易规模 / 98
贸易模式 / 102
客户 / 108
中欧瓷器贸易的终结 / 113

第四章　欧亚文化熔炉——贸易背后的故事 / 138
　　海上丝绸之路沿线的伊斯兰陶瓷 / 138
　　中国对欧洲陶瓷制造业的影响 / 143
　　模仿与创新 / 151

第二部分　收　藏

第五章　中国陶瓷 / 183
　　出口到亚洲其他国家的中国外销瓷 / 183
　　销往西方的中国外销瓷 / 196
　　销往亚洲国家的晚期外销瓷 / 229

第六章　亚洲其他国家陶瓷 / 238
　　日本陶瓷 / 238
　　越南陶瓷 / 243
　　泰国陶瓷 / 245

第七章　欧洲陶瓷 / 251
　　欧洲"青花瓷" / 251
　　欧洲"伊万里" / 266
　　欧洲"粉彩"和"五彩" / 270
　　欧洲"中国白" / 275
　　欧洲"柿右卫门"和"萨摩" / 275

图片来源 / 278
参考文献 / 281

Table of Contents

Introduction / 6

Part I   Global Journey of Export Ceramics

Chapter 1   Chinese Ceramics in the Early History of international Trade / 22
                      From Monochromatic Glazed Porcelain to Blue and White Porcelain / 22
                      Chinese Influence on Asian Neighbors / 26

Chapter 2   The Beginning of a Globalized World: European-Asian Trade Relations / 63
                      The Portuguese / 63
                      The Dutch East India Company / 69
                      The Dutch and the Export Ceramics of Japan / 78
                      The British / 81
                      The Canton-System Export Boom / 84
                      Commodities in the Canton-System / 90

Chapter 3   The Four Billion Pound Deal: The Economics of the Porcelain Trade / 117
                      The Extent of Trade / 117
                      The Patterns of Trade / 121
                      The Customers / 129
                      The End of the Chinese-European Porcelain Trade / 134

Chapter 4　The Eurasian Cultural Melting Pot — the Story after the Trade / 155
　　　　　Islamic Ceramics along the Maritime Silk Road / 155
　　　　　Europe under Chinese Influence / 161
　　　　　Imitation and Innovation / 170

Part II　The Collection

Chapter 5　Chinese Ceramics / 183
　　　　　Chinese Export Ceramics to Asian Countries / 183
　　　　　Chinese Export Porcelain to the West / 196
　　　　　Late Chinese Export Ceramics to Asian Countries / 229

Chapter 6　Ceramics of Other Asian Countries / 238
　　　　　Japanese Ceramics / 238
　　　　　Vietnamese Ceramics / 243
　　　　　Thai Ceramics / 245

Chapter 7　European Ceramics / 251
　　　　　European "Blue and White" / 251
　　　　　European "*Imari*" / 266
　　　　　European "*Famille rose*" and "*Famille verte*" / 270
　　　　　European "*Blanc-de-Chine*"/275
　　　　　European "*Kakiemon*" and "*Satsuma*" / 275

Pictures credits / 278
References / 281

导言

亚洲瓷器的历史，是一部文化交流和贸易的历史。早在2 000年前，著名的丝绸之路便成为贯通东西的桥梁（地图0.1）。尽管在形成之初，这条连接罗马帝国和中国的丝绸之路或许并非作为陶瓷贸易要道，但时至唐朝（618—907年），中国与伊斯兰国家的陶瓷贸易已相当兴盛，在丝绸之路沿线的伊朗、伊拉克和埃及，均发现了这一时期的陶瓷制品。阿拉伯帝国阿拔斯王朝（750—1258年）的哈里发哈伦·拉希德（764—809年），大约在800年已获得中国精美陶瓷，是

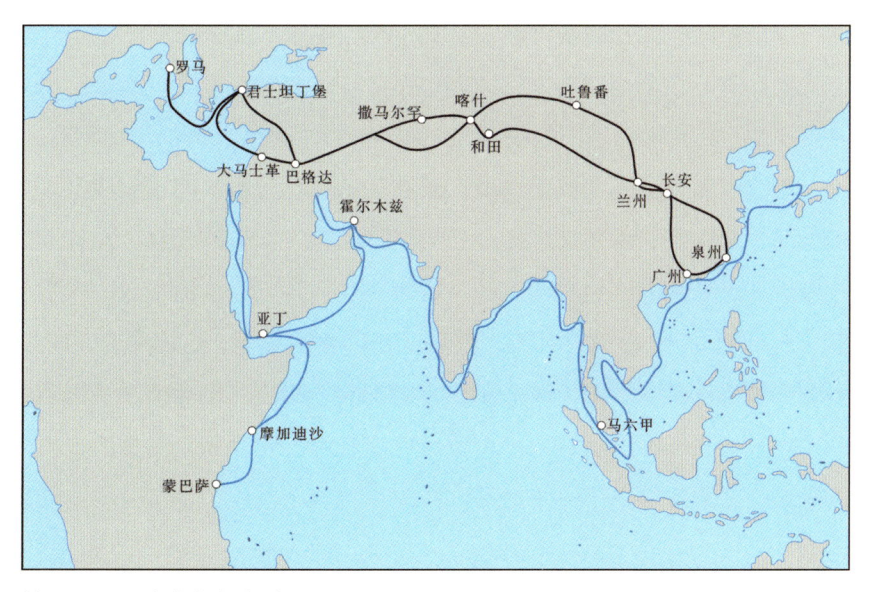

地图0.1 古代丝绸之路

已知的最早接触中国瓷的外国人之一。而终整个阿拔斯王朝，阿拉伯帝国进口了数百万件中国陶瓷，包括产自中国北方的精美白瓷和产自南方浙江省的青瓷。

上述陶瓷大部分并没有留存至今。但在一些幸运的情形下，人们在古代海上丝绸之路沿线打捞到沉船，为这些早期的全球贸易形式提供了佐证。其中最著名的莫过于阿拔斯王朝时期的一艘阿拉伯单桅三角帆船"黑石号"，它满载6万件中国长沙窑和其他瓷器驶向阿拉伯帝国的一座港口（我们至今仍不知其名称），却在今印度尼西亚的勿里洞岛附近沉没。一只从海底打捞出水的完好无损的瓷碗上刻着日期："宝历二年七月十六"，即公元826年。[①] 这些珍品瓷器目前收藏于新加坡的亚洲文明博物馆。另外，还有一艘10世纪的沉船于印度尼西亚爪哇井里汶港附近被发现，因而得名"井里汶号"，船上载有25万件中国瓷器。

唐朝之后，中西方贸易经历了几个世纪的低谷，之后再度迎来繁荣。约从1500年开始，对香料、丝绸、棉花、瓷器和茶叶等亚洲商品的需求，推动着葡萄牙人、西班牙人、荷兰人和英国人开展海外探险和发现。瓷器虽然并非他们最看重的贸易商品，却在塑造全球经济、探索新路线和海上航线方面发挥了重要作用。据估计，1550至1800年间，东亚向欧洲出口瓷器达1.86亿件。这一时期驱动中西方贸易的主要是市场供需机制，因此，地理大发现时代也是瓷器时代。

不过，比单纯的贸易关系更重要的，是陶瓷贸易过程中的文化交流。陶瓷作为一种手工艺品，其造型和纹饰多种多样，变化多端，体现出生产者和/或客户的文化传统。亚洲外销瓷便反映了上述两点。在几百年里，中国和伊斯兰世界、中国和西方以及伊斯兰世界和西方之间的文化相互交融，其影响一直延续至今。因此，"欧亚陶瓷"这一名称恰如其分，体现出连接从欧亚最西端的里斯本到最东端的东京这个广袤地区的桥梁作用。是故，我们应将它视为欧亚共同的历史和遗产。

陶瓷贸易和交流促成了造型和纹饰的跨文化发展，而这仅仅是一个起点。在许多地区，对陶瓷的强劲需求推动了当地开始生产类似的产品。公元900年后，丝绸之路或海上丝绸之路沿线的亚洲主要陶瓷生产基地，包括中东的埃及、叙利亚和波斯（今伊朗），东南亚的越南、泰国、柬埔寨和缅甸，以及东亚的朝鲜和日本，或多或少都受到了中国设计风格和工艺的影响。唐三彩也在伊斯兰国家生产，青瓷主要也在越南、泰国和朝鲜生产，青花瓷在越南、朝鲜和日本生产，类似于釉下绿彩的瓷器则在缅甸生产。

---

① 上海博物馆编：《宝历风物："黑石号"沉船出水珍品》，上海：上海书画出版社，2020。

"青花"是亚洲和欧洲最为普遍的陶瓷装饰风格。我们不仅可以在其原产地（中国江西省）发现此类瓷器，也可以在15世纪的马穆鲁克苏丹国和帖木儿帝国[①]、16世纪的奥斯曼帝国，以及直至18世纪的波斯萨非王朝的仿制品中见到其踪影。欧洲同样承其荫蔽：葡萄牙、荷兰和德国生产的白锡釉陶，其灵感便是来自中国青花瓷。德国迈森制造出的真正意义上的欧洲瓷器，其艺术设计也受到了中国设计的影响。

　　然而，所有这些制瓷中心也都逐渐形成了自己的风格。叙利亚和波斯的绿松石青瓷，朝鲜高丽王朝（918—1392年）时期的绿色镶嵌青瓷以及越南青花瓷也都漂亮精致，可与中国顶级青花瓷相媲美。如果我们将这些产品简单称为对中国陶瓷的复制，未免有失公允。它们是文化交流的产物，正是这种文化交流创造了全球流行的应用艺术品。而青花瓷便是这种欧亚文化融合的卓越代表。

　　当然，丝绸之路不仅是东西方的商业纽带，也促进了思想和宗教的传播，从而产生了新的陶瓷艺术设计、外形以及装饰图案。

　　佛教起源于印度，后来通过丝绸之路传入中亚、中国、朝鲜和日本。中国西部甘肃省敦煌莫高窟中令人叹为观止的雕塑，就是这种起源于印度的宗教信仰与中国艺术审美和纹样相互交流、融合的产物。而莲花则成为亚洲瓷器中使用最广泛的佛教装饰元素。莲花和莲花花瓣经常被以绘画、雕刻、镶嵌和压印等工艺手法装饰在瓷器上。我们经常可见陶瓷口沿、坛盖和碗盖采用荷花造型，盘子、盖碗和碗内采用莲藕和莲子纹饰。尤其是朝鲜高丽王朝信奉佛教，其御用青瓷不仅仅是艺术杰作，造型和纹饰更表达出当时人们的佛教信仰。毋庸置疑，朝鲜青瓷深受中国制瓷工艺影响，但在青瓷艺术创新方面，高丽王朝在中国制瓷的基础上完善了镶嵌法、阴刻和镂空等全新装饰技术。

　　佛教还通过斯里兰卡和印度传教士传入东南亚，被柬埔寨的高棉帝国（约400—1431年）、泰国的素可泰王国（13世纪中叶—1438年）和大城王国（1350—1767年）以及印度尼西亚的三佛齐王国（7—14世纪）所接受。

　　伊斯兰教的传播路线，陆路是以大马士革和巴格达为起点，经波斯到达印度北部，或者沿着塔克拉玛干沙漠的北线或南线到达中国西部；海路则到达马来半岛和马来群岛，或者到达北非、伊比利亚半岛和巴尔干半岛。故而，人们不仅在中国西部，而且在葡萄牙和西班牙都能找到深受伊斯兰风格影响的陶瓷。

[①] Watson 2004, p.422f.（马穆鲁克苏丹国统治埃及和叙利亚，帖木儿帝国统治中亚和西亚部分地区。——编者注）

印度小贩和商人带来的印度教和印度图案，则对柬埔寨的高棉帝国、越南南部的占城国（137—1697年）和印度尼西亚的满者伯夷国（13世纪末—15世纪）都产生了深远的影响。

欧亚大陆不仅是一个地理概念，还是一种真实的文化存在。陶瓷在统一的欧亚文化的形成和发展中发挥了重要作用。这就是青花瓷至今仍在向我们诉说的故事——一个始于中国东部地区的故事。

在中国唐朝建立海上丝绸之路的一千多年后，中国政府提出"一带一路"倡议，积极促进活跃的经济和文化间交流。"一带"指基于亚欧大陆原本的陆上丝绸之路的新丝绸之路经济带，"一路"则指为建设21世纪海上丝绸之路而创立的新欧亚海上航线。

本书试图追溯东西方文化认同的起源，通过分析文化交流、贸易路线、商人、消费者和贸易经济来阐述欧亚大陆艺术风格的发展。瓷器是文化的载体，贸易路线和船舶是传播手段，贸易本身则是跨文化交流的机制。

全书分为两部分。第一部分追溯外销瓷的全球之旅。第一章主要介绍亚洲内部贸易中的陶瓷商品，第二章阐述来自葡萄牙、荷兰、英国、瑞典等国的贸易商及其贸易路线，第三章分析瓷器的交换机制。这三章均聚焦中国，因为从公元700年至1850年，超过95%的外销瓷出自中国。但是，我们可以看到，中国在陶瓷生产过程中会不断融入世界各地的纹饰设计，并影响其他地区。第四章探讨了外销瓷对购买国的影响。在这一章中，我们将了解瓷器给欧亚艺术和文化带来的共同影响。

第二部分则为笔者个人多年来收藏的具有代表性的瓷器，按照中国陶瓷、亚洲其他国家陶瓷、欧洲陶瓷的顺序来排列。许多人都曾拥有这些瓷器——在大多数情况下，我们不知道这些人的姓名、身份、住所和所作所为。前有古人，后必有来者，我们中没有人能真正拥有这些瓷器。反之，我们只能是它们漫长历史中的过客，它们提醒我们，我们同属一个欧亚家族。①

这是一部跨学科之作，融历史、经济、应用艺术和跨文化关系于一体。依笔者拙见，跨学科思维是解决复杂问题的唯一途径。

笔者并非陶瓷专家，在著述本书的过程中吸取了很多专家的真知灼见。洛克仙妮·布朗杰出的工作和关于沉船瓷器的著作，打开了我领略南亚陶瓷之美的大门。C. J. A. 约尔格关于荷兰与亚洲陶瓷贸易的深入阐述，让我受益匪浅。G. 戈登是详细

---

① 本书前四章为中英文单独排列，从第五章开始，为便于读者阅读，采取中英文对照形式。——编者注

分析欧洲陶瓷和亚洲陶瓷关联的主要学者，给我很大启发。安德鲁·马德森和卡洛琳·怀特在确定中国外销瓷的年代历史方面做出了杰出贡献，大大有助于我鉴别自己的藏品。此外，我还要向孔茜茜女士表示诚挚的感谢，她为本书的中文翻译以及校对工作倾注了很多心血。

过去曾有许多研究人员开展过关于中国外销瓷的研究，以后还将会有更多人致力于此。本书汲取了他们的研究成果，也希望我的工作能对未来的研究工作有所帮助。这是个人的一点期许。

Introduction

The history of Asian ceramics is a history of cultural interaction and trade. The famous Silk Road (see map 0.1), already linking the East and West together 2,000 years ago, may not have been an important route for trading ceramics when it was first established between the Roman Empire and China. However, Chinese Tang dynasty (618–907) ceramics have been found along the Silk Road in Persia, Iraq, and Egypt, and one of the first known foreign recipients of exquisite chinaware was the Abbasid Caliph Harun Al-Rashid, around 800 AD. During the Tang dynasty, a vibrant trade between China and the Islamic world had started. The Abbasid Caliphate (750–1258) had already imported millions of Chinese ceramics — beautiful white monochromes from northern China and green glazed stoneware from the southern province of Zhejiang.

Most of these ceramics do not exist anymore, but in some fortunate cases, shipwrecks found along the former maritime trading routes, give us evidence of these early forms of global trade. One of the most famous discoveries was the *Belitung* shipwreck, an Arab dhow, which sailed with a cargo of 60,000 ceramics from China towards an unknown Abbasid port, but which sank near the Indonesian island of Belitung. One bowl found intact on the seabed was inscribed with a date: "16th day of the 7th month of the reign of Baoli" or 826 AD.[①] The treasure of the Yue and Changsha kilns ceramic is now displayed in the *Asian Civilisations Museum* of

---

① Shanghai Museum 2020.

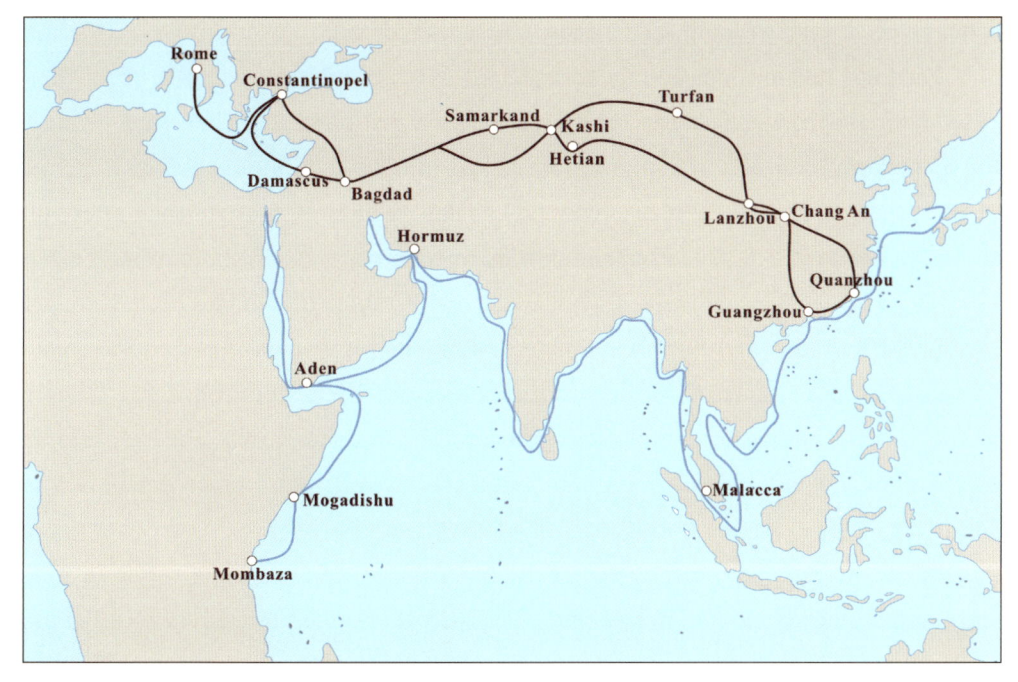

Map 0.1: The ancient Silk Roads.

Singapore. Another shipwreck of the 10th century found off the coast of Java near the port of Cirebon had a cargo of 250,000 Chinese ceramics.

This intensive trade relationship was replicated a couple of centuries later between China and the Western world. A driving force of the Portuguese, Spanish, Dutch and English expeditions and discoveries taking place from 1450 onwards was the quest for Asian commodities: spices, silk, cotton, porcelain, and tea. Porcelain — even not the most important tradeware — played its role in shaping a global economy and in exploring new roads and maritime routes. An estimated 186 million pieces of porcelain were exported from East Asia to Europe between 1550 and 1800. This period was characterized by a market mechanism of supply and demand, but not by a system of pressure, drug trafficking and war in the century that followed. The age of discovery is also the age of porcelain.

But more important than the mere trade relationships, are the cultural interactions taking place by trading ceramics. Ceramics are man-made, whose shapes and decoration vary, and they can reflect the cultural traditions of the producer and/or the client. Asian export ceramics reflect both. A joint Sino-Islamic, Sino-Western and Islamic-Western culture has been created over centuries and can still be sensed today. Therefore, it would be reasonable to call them *Eurasian* ceramics to express the culturally unifying effects they have had on the double continent stretching from Lisbon to Tokyo. Therefore, we'd better perceive them as common Eurasian history and heritage.

The trade relationships and the interactions over ceramics were jointly developing cross-cultural decors and shapes, which was only the starting point. The strong demand for porcelain prompted, in many regions, local initiatives to produce similar items. Most of the main Asian ceramic production centers, which were established after 900 along the overland Silk Road or the maritime routes, were to some extent influenced by Chinese design or techniques: Egypt, Syria, and Persia in the Middle East; Vietnam, Thailand, Cambodia, and Burma in Southeast Asia; and Korea and Japan in East Asia. The three-color ceramic of the Tang dynasty has also been produced in the Islamic world, celadon stoneware mainly in Vietnam, Thailand and Korea, underglaze blue porcelain in Vietnam, Korea and Japan, and a similar underglaze green decoration in Burma.

Moreover, the "blue and white" is the most widespread decoration style in Asia and Europe, and we can find it not only in its place of origin, in the province of Jiangxi in Southeast China; but it was also copied in Mamluk Egypt and Syria, and Timurid Persia in the 15th century[1], in the Ottoman Iznik during the 16th century, and in Safavid Persia until the 18th century. Chinese influence can also be recognized in Europe, where the production of faience in Portugal, the Netherlands and Germany was very much inspired by Chinese blue and white porcelain. It also applies to the design of the first true European porcelain produced in Meissen, Germany.

However, all these ceramic centers have developed their own styles. The turquoise celadon ware along the Silk Road in Syria and Persia, the green inlaid celadons of Korea during the Koryo dynasty (918–1392), and the Vietnamese blue and white porcelains reached a beauty and finesse able to compete with the best products of China. Thus, it would be unfair to call these ceramics simple copies of Chinese originals. They are products of cultural exchange, creating universal globalized pieces of applied art. The blue and white ceramics are particularly an expression of an amalgamated Eurasian culture.

The overland and maritime Silk Road, of course, was not only a commercial tie between the East and the West. It facilitated the expansion of thought and religions, and brought about new designs, forms and patterns.

Buddhism came to Central Asia, China, Korea and Japan, from Nepal and India via the Silk Road. The impressive clay figurines in the Mogao Caves of Dunhuang in the

---

[1] Watson 2004, p.422f.

Western Chinese province of Gansu, are evidence of the exchange of religious belief that originated in India and mixed with the artistic taste of ancient China and local design. The lotus flower became the most widely used Buddhist decoration element on Asian ceramics. Lotus flowers and petals are painted, carved, incised and imprinted on ceramics, the form of rims and covers of jars and bowls often make reference to the lotus leaf, and lotus fruits and seeds can be identified on plates, tureens and inside bowls. The royal celadon ceramics of Korea during the Buddhist Koryo dynasty are not only masterpieces of art but express by form and decoration, Buddhist belief. Korean celadons cannot deny the Chinese influence. However, it might be reasonable to say that the celadon technique was perfected in Korea. Several decoration innovations were developed or further refined such as the inlaid work (*sanggam*), engobe painting and openwork style.

Also, Buddhism reached Southeast Asia through missionaries from Sri Lanka and India, and was adopted by the Khmer, the Thai Kingdoms of Sukhothai and Ayutthaya, and the maritime power of Srivijaya.

Islam made its way from Damascus and Baghdad, via Persia, towards northern India, and along the northern or southern route of the Taklimakan desert to West China; by sea to the Malay Peninsula and the Archipelago, to North Africa, the Iberian Peninsula and the Balkans. Ceramics with Islamic-influenced motifs and decors can be found in West China, but also in Portugal and Spain.

Hinduism and its designs brought by Indian traders and businessmen influenced the Khmer Empire of Angkor, Champa in southern Vietnam, and the Majapahit kingdom of Indonesia.

The Eurasian continent is not only a geographic dimension; it is above all a cultural reality. Ceramics have always played an important role in developing and contributing to a unified Eurasian culture. This is the story blue and white porcelain still has to tell us — a story that starts in East China under the Mongolian Yuan dynasty.

More than one thousand years after the establishment of the maritime Silk Road during the Chinese Tang dynasty, the Chinese Government is linking itself to this vibrant economic and intercultural exchange by creating the Belt and Road initiative. *One belt* refers to a new economic land belt based on the original overland Silk Road from Asia to Europe and the *one road* refers to new Eurasian sea routes to build a 21st century maritime Silk Road.

The book tries to trace back the origins of a joint East and West cultural identity. It describes the development of Eurasian decor by analyzing the cultural interactions, the trading routes, the merchants, customers, and the economics of the trade. Porcelain is the carrier of culture; the trading routes and ships are the means; the trade itself is the mechanism for intercultural contacts.

The book consists of two parts. The first part traces the global journey of export porcelains. Chapter 1 is mainly dedicated to the intra-Asia trade of ceramics; Chapter 2 focuses on the agents and their routes — from Portugal, the Netherlands, the UK, Sweden, and other countries; Chapter 3 analyses the mechanism of exchange. China is in the center of these three chapters as more than 95% of all export ceramics from 700 until 1850 are of Chinese origin. However, it is shown that China, even having produced them, incorporated designs from all over the world and has vice versa influenced all regions. Chapter 4 investigates the effects the export had on the countries of destination. Here, we will understand the unifying effects of porcelain on the art and culture of Eurasia.

The second part of the book introduces some of the most typical items of my own collection, including those from China, other Asian countries and Europe. Many have owned the items before — in most cases, we do not know who they were, where they lived, and what they did. Many owners will follow in the future and nobody really owns them. Every owner is just a guest for them in their long lifespan. They own us and they remind us that Asians and Europeans belong to the same Eurasian family.[1]

This book is an interdisciplinary work. It combines history, economics, applied art and intercultural relations — which is, in my view, the only way to address complex issues.

Being far from a specialist in ceramics, I would like to express my appreciation for the work and the excellent publications on shipwreck porcelain of Roxanna Brown who has opened my eyes to the beauty of Southeast Asian ceramics. I also owe much to the work of Christiaan Jörg, who gave detailed insights into the Dutch-Asian porcelain trade and provided me with valuable comments on my earlier draft; I benefit greatly from the work of Geoffrey Godden who first analyzed in detail the linkages between European and Asian ceramics. Besides, Andrew Madsen and Carolyn White did an excellent job on dating Chinese export ceramics. Their efforts have helped me very much in identifying the items in my own collection. I owe a debt of gratitude to Ms. Kong Xixi who spent hours on careful proofreading and translating this book into Chinese.

Many researchers have worked on this topic before and many more will come afterward. We draw on their experiences and we hope that future researchers will find our work as helpful as we have found in the efforts of others.

---

[1] The first four chapters are arranged respectively in English and Chinese. From Chapter 5, both Chinese and English versions are combined for the convenience of readers. — editor

第一部分

外销瓷的全球之旅

第一章 早期国际贸易史上的中国陶瓷

从单色釉瓷到青花瓷

中国是世界上最早烧制出瓷器的国家。早在东汉末年,现今浙江地区的匠人们已经能够烧制出精美的青瓷。与陶器相比,青瓷在化学成分、烧制温度、硬度、孔隙率和吸水率方面均有显著不同,青瓷通常是半透明的,敲击时声音清脆。[①] 此后,随着生产技术的提高,到6世纪下半叶,河北生产出了广受欢迎的白瓷。

陶瓷的长途贸易始于8世纪的唐朝,与阿拉伯世界、波斯、印度、马来群岛、日本和中国之间海上航线的开拓息息相关。如今,我们将这些古代跨国贸易海上路线称为"海上丝绸之路"。

沿着海上丝绸之路,唐朝瓷器漂洋过海,出口到很多国家。其中的明星产品为越窑青瓷和长沙瓷。越窑青瓷(约700—960年)是浙江省生产的釉面青碧的瓷器,在日本、埃及、东南亚均有发现,印度尼西亚爪哇海岸挖掘出的井里汶沉船中,装载的瓷器一半为越窑青瓷。长沙瓷(约750—950年)为湖南省长沙生产的施褐彩、绿彩的乳白釉陶瓷或釉上彩陶瓷(图1.1),许多图案都深受伊斯兰教或佛教文化影响。通过海上丝绸之路,它远及越南、泰国、苏门答腊、爪哇、斯里

---

① He Li 1996, p.39.

兰卡、阿拔斯王朝乃至东非。在南海勿里洞沉船中，也发现了其身影。

此外，河北磁州窑、定窑和邢窑生产的白瓷虽然主要用于满足国内市场，但也有一些见于沉船中。

唐朝灭亡后，经过五代十国的动荡时期，宋朝建立，宋朝是一个商业相当昌盛的朝代。尤其是在南宋建立后，定都港口城市临安（今浙江杭州），靠近江西省景德镇瓷器生产中心，以海上贸易为主的出口收入成为政府主要的财政来源，外销瓷在其中起着不可忽视的作用。

宋朝出名的瓷器，包括龙泉青瓷、建窑瓷和青白瓷等。龙泉青瓷（约950—1550年）为浙江省龙泉窑生产的深绿釉陶瓷，直至14世纪中叶，一直是主要的外销瓷，并为泰国西萨查纳莱的陶瓷生产提供了灵感（图1.2）。天目瓷（约1100年—14世纪）是福建省建窑生产的深棕色和黑釉陶瓷（主要为茶碗），主要用于国内市场，也有部分出口日本。青白瓷（约1100年—14世纪）是江西省景德镇和德化瓷窑生产的青中泛白、白中透青的质地通透的细瓷。景德镇至今仍是江西省规模最大、最重要的瓷窑。

此外，还有各地民窑长期生产、出口东南亚市场的酱釉陶瓷，宋代至清末的沉船中均有发现。

外销瓷的主要目的地为日本和东南亚。这种贸易规模的庞大，可以从一条重要的沉船中窥见一斑：约1150年，满载着景德镇、德化和龙泉单色釉陶瓷的"南海1号"在广东沿海沉没。2007年，整艘船连同其上的6万多件瓷器被用特制沉箱打捞出水，运输放置在广东海上丝绸之路博物馆的巨型玻璃缸中。我们可以将其称为"东方瓦萨号"——"瓦萨号"是一艘于1628年沉没于波罗的海岸的瑞典军舰，1961年被从瑞典斯德哥尔摩附近整体打捞出来。不过，"南海1号"比"瓦萨号"早

图1.1 唐朝长沙窑瓷碗，直径16厘米，高5厘米　　图1.2 元代出口泰国的龙泉深绿青瓷罐

了近500年，见证了早期国际瓷器贸易的繁盛。

进入元朝（1271—1368年），随着指南针的发明和船舶技术的不断发展，南海的海上贸易变得更为便利，浙江瓷窑生产的单色釉青瓷出口至印度尼西亚和越南等东南亚国家。东北方的朝鲜和日本也在其辐射范围。1975年在朝鲜半岛海岸发现的"新安号"沉船，便载有近2万件来自14世纪的青瓷。辽宁省三道岗海域发现的元代"三道岗"沉船上载有约600件河北磁州窑瓷器。[①]

在这一时期，对于瓷器发展史来说最重要的事情莫过于青花瓷的发明。早在宋代，景德镇已经开始生产灰蓝或灰绿的单色釉青白瓷器，但直至约1320年，它才开始生产出胎体轻薄、釉面透亮的青花瓷。"青花瓷"意指在透明釉下白色坯体上描绘钴蓝装饰的白色瓷器（图1.3）。它的诞生意义极为重大，突破了此前只能烧制单色釉瓷的限制，形态精美，如今已经成为中国古典瓷器的代名词。

青花瓷的产生，无疑受惠于蒙古人统治下的广袤疆域，形成了欧亚以及亚洲内部的广大自由贸易区。制造青花瓷所需的重要原料钴料，便是从当时同属蒙古帝国的伊朗进口。

1330年，景德镇出口了第一件青花瓷，自此中国的外销瓷器增加了一个新的品

图1.3 元代青花赶珠龙暗龙高足杯碎片，景德镇出产

[①] 南京市博物馆、宁波博物馆、上海中国航海博物馆编：《China与世界——海上丝绸之路沉船和贸易瓷器》，北京：文物出版社，2017年，第228-238页。大部分出水物件保存在辽宁省葫芦岛博物馆。

类。在元帝国之外,世界上其他地方也出土了数以千计的元朝青花瓷碎片,例如,在叙利亚大马士革和埃及开罗发现了大约50万件瓷器碎片。[①]

在向外出口的过程中,青花瓷吸收了伊斯兰图案元素和艺术风格,满足了西亚和中东的瓷器需求。它是元代贸易往来和审美交流的产物,也是中国、伊朗和土耳其等文化相互影响的结果。

其后,在明朝永乐年间(1403—1424年),青花瓷受到皇家青睐,并在宣德年间(1426—1435年),在细腻程度和艺术造诣上达到了顶峰。明初的青花瓷造型深受中亚、波斯和阿拉伯风格的影响,反映了中国与伊斯兰世界的文化交流。品质上乘的青花瓷出口至奥斯曼帝国(1299—1923年),品质较差的则出口至东南亚。

中国对亚洲邻居的影响

不过,总体而言,从元末到明朝前期,亚洲内部以及亚欧间贸易陷入低谷。先是在1350至1360年,反元起义军与元朝统治者作战,导致陶瓷的出口严重受阻。明朝建立后,又在较长的一段时间闭关锁国:1368至1567年间,明朝禁止私人出海。即使海禁没能得到全面贯彻实施,但仍有证据表明中国陶瓷的生产量和贸易量锐减。这在国际上被称为所谓的"明朝空白期",因为中国商品很长一段时间内在出口市场上缺失。

趁此时机,东南亚两个地区得以参与到亚洲内部瓷器贸易中来。它们就是泰国的素可泰王国和越南北部的大越王国。

泰国的素可泰王国始建于13世纪中叶,1438年被大城府吞并。它主要有两个瓷窑中心。一个在素可泰城墙以北,另一个位于素可泰城以北约60千米、永河沿岸的西萨查纳莱。在14世纪,素可泰窑主要生产釉下黑彩炻瓷,如饰以游鱼图案的瓷盘。而西萨查纳莱窑生产的陶瓷产品种类则更为丰富,包括釉下黑彩炻瓷、青瓷、棕瓷以及黑白单色釉瓷。这些产品通常也被称为宋卡洛陶瓷。其釉下黑彩瓷(收藏153–155)的灵感来自中国青花瓷和越南青花瓷。青瓷则通常在半透明厚釉下雕刻花卉装饰,受到龙泉青瓷的影响很明显。

从14世纪末至1580年,西萨查纳莱的制瓷工匠抓住亚洲内部中国产品短缺机遇,不断出口陶瓷,主要出口地为印度尼西亚和菲律宾,直到泰缅战争导致该地人

---

① Carswell 2000, p.66.

口大幅减少,方才停止。西萨查纳莱青瓷盘几乎是所有15世纪中期沉船的主要货物。约1460年,一艘泰国船只"皇家南海号"装载了大量西萨查纳莱青瓷驶往爪哇岛,却沉没海底。1992年,海洋考古学家斯滕·舍斯特兰德在马来西亚东海岸发现该沉船,打捞出了21 000多件陶瓷(收藏157),现在收藏于南海海洋考古公司。

越南北部在从公元前111年至公元939年的漫长时间里都属于中国。在此期间,主要在汉朝时期(前202—220年),此地生产了大量的釉陶、无釉陶以及一些中国风格的炻瓷。939年越南独立,建立大瞿越王朝,1054年后正式使用国号"大越"。13世纪末或14世纪初,大越王国开始了陶瓷出口贸易。通过海上丝绸之路,越南港口与中国港口、印度、阿拉伯国家和波斯连接起来,开展香料、纺织品、金属以及陶瓷贸易。定居在沿海一带的阿拉伯商人常常参与开展贸易。

1407年至1427年的短暂时间,越南北部再次归属中国管辖,当时活跃于中国南部的阿拉伯商人,大大促进了越南青花瓷的发展。越南可能是第一个受中国影响而在本国生产青花瓷的国家。

15世纪越南外销陶瓷大多是青花瓷。它们在装饰上与中国的青花有着强烈的相似性,但坯体往往是灰色的,釉面不透明。另外一个典型的特点是底座上的巧克力棕色装饰和内部未上釉的堆火圈(图1.4)。伊斯坦布尔的托普卡帕宫博物馆现在保存着一件1450年越南出口的陶瓷珍品。这种釉下蓝与釉下红、绿釉彩相结合的独特技术主要应用于瓷盘,但也应用于量产的蓝色釉下彩带盖盒。

1993年,越南会安渔民发现了"会安号"沉船。该船沉没于约1450年,船上装载有15万余件越南青花瓷珍品,包括瓷盘、壶、瓶、罐、杯、碗、瓷像和盒,瓷器上均饰以神话动物或风景画图案。这是迄今关于15世纪后期越南陶瓷的最重要的

图1.4 16世纪越南巧克力底青花瓷盘

发现（收藏 149），其规模及品质证明了河内附近的北方瓷窑迅速扩张。

越南南部在历史上既不隶属于中国，也不属于大越王国，而是属于占族建立的占婆王国。他们也生产和出口陶瓷。15 世纪的"潘达南号"沉船便装载着数以千计的占族单色釉陶瓷。

在 14 至 16 世纪，主要在印度尼西亚、菲律宾市场，当然也包括西亚市场，泰国和越南的陶瓷取代了中国陶瓷。它们部分弥补了中国陶瓷对东南亚市场出口量的下降。"就 14 世纪末至 16 世纪初的沉船而言，每艘船上的东南亚陶瓷比例达到 60％ 至 99％。而在早期贸易期间，中国商品则占 100％。这充分说明了中国商品的短缺。"[1]

然而，即使在"明朝空白期"，中国对东南亚的瓷器出口也并未完全陷入停滞。定都伊斯坦布尔的奥斯曼帝国是青花瓷最忠实的买家，苏丹的托普卡帕宫是世界上收藏中国陶瓷最多的地方。1500 年左右，装有景德镇青花瓷的"利纳号"戎克船（中国大帆船）在菲律宾布桑加岛附近沉没。[2] 该船的目的地可能就是奥斯曼帝国或菲律宾群岛的某个苏丹国。这很好地说明了当时中国会迎合伊斯兰或西亚的品位生产瓷器。

除了江西景德镇，中国重要的外销瓷产地还有福建漳州。漳州窑瓷器（图 1.5）通过附近的厦门，大量出口至东南亚和马来群岛，主要为漳州青花瓷，也包括红色和绿色釉瓷器。和景德镇为伊斯兰宫廷生产的精致瓷器相比，漳州窑青花瓷瓷胎略显粗糙，釉下蓝彩绘看起来更像赶工之作，通常为简单的线条或汉字，或自由奔放地绘以花卉鸟类和其他动物。当然，这种纹饰是否具有美感就见仁见智了（收藏 17–31）。

漳州瓷窑在对东南亚瓷器出口中的重要性，基本相当于景德镇瓷窑在对欧瓷器出口中的重要性。时至今日，在马来群岛或南海仍可发现许多漳州窑瓷器。2001 年在越南海岸发现的"平顺"号沉船，载有数千件明代漳州陶器，很可能是在约 1608 年前往马来半岛的途中沉没（收藏 18 和 19）。2007 年，另一艘载有漳州瓷器的沉船——南澳 1 号在广东汕头附近海域被发现。

1567 年明朝海禁解除后，国际瓷器贸易又活跃起来。但是，陶瓷贸易的商品构成发生了变化。早期占主导地位的白釉、浅绿色釉、绿色釉以及棕色釉等单色釉瓷的出口量不断下降，青花瓷取而代之（图 1.6）。

---

[1] Brown 2009, pp.27–28.

[2] Goddio 1997, pp.79–101.

图 1.5　明代漳州窑立凤盘　　　　　图 1.6　明代或清初沉船青花瓷，损坏并附着沉积物

综上所述，早期以单色釉瓷为主的亚洲内部瓷器贸易延续了 8 个世纪，包括唐、五代、宋、元和明朝前中期，且随着 16 世纪明朝海禁解除而宣告终结。中国在这数百年里出口到亚洲其他地区的陶瓷数量不详。目前，从海底发掘出的瓷器不足 100 万件，未来有可能还会发掘出数百万件。

在结束对早期亚洲内部贸易的回顾前，我们不妨看看每个朝代的代表性沉船（地图 1.1 和表 1.1）。

表 1.1　亚洲内部贸易载有中国陶瓷的重要沉船

朝代	沉船	陶瓷
唐朝（618—907 年）	黑石号	湖南长沙瓷
五代（907—960 年）	井里汶号	浙江越窑青瓷
宋朝（960—1279 年）	南海 1 号	江西德化和景德镇窑青白瓷，福建龙泉窑青瓷
	华光礁 1 号	福建、广东和江西烧制的单色釉陶瓷
	半洋礁 1 号	福建建窑烧制的黑釉瓷
元朝（1271—1368 年）	新安号，大练岛沉船	福建龙泉青瓷
	三道岗	河北磁州窑烧制的白底黑花瓷
明朝（1368—1644 年）	利纳号 南澳 1 号，平顺号，圣伊西德罗号	江西景德镇青花瓷 福建漳州窑青花瓷

1550 年左右，国际陶瓷贸易开启了新的篇章。随着葡萄牙人发现了欧亚之间的海上新航线，可以经过好望角和印度洋通往印度尼西亚、菲律宾和中国，中国在对欧瓷器出口贸易中开始扮演重要角色。葡萄牙人以及随后的荷兰人、英国人源源不

断地将瓷器运输至欧洲，不过，直到17世纪中叶之前，亚洲内部贸易仍占中国瓷器出口额的80%以上。此外，欧洲船只，包括最初的葡萄牙船只以及后来的荷兰东印度公司船只，利用澳门、台湾岛、日本出岛和爪哇岛的巴达维亚（今雅加达），极大地促进了中日贸易。这标志着全球化世界的开始。

地图 1.1　有重要瓷器出水的亚洲沉船遗址

Part I

Global Journey of Export Ceramics

Chapter 1

Chinese Ceramics in the Early History of International Trade

From Monochrome Glazed Porcelain to Blue and White Porcelain

China was the first porcelain producer in the world. Porcelain originated in Zhejiang province during the late Eastern Han dynasty. The characteristics in comparison to earthenware include aspects of the chemical composition, the temperature at which it is fired, the hardness, the porosity, and the absorbency of water. Porcelain is usually translucent and resonant when it is struck.[①] White translucent porcelain — a feature appreciated most in Europe — has been first produced in the second half of the 6th century at kilns in Hebei province.

The long-distance trade of ceramics began in the 8th century during the Chinese Tang dynasty. It is closely linked with the establishment of the maritime routes between the Arab world, Persia, India, the Malay Archipelago, Japan, and China. Referring to the ancient overland trade by caravans, we call these routes the "Maritime Silk Road".

Ceramics for export purposes have been produced in various Chinese provinces and kiln sites. Among all the products, *Changsha ware* and *Yue celadon* are the earliest. *Yue celadon* stoneware (c. 700−960) is green or celadon-colored stoneware from Zhejiang province. It has been excavated,

---

① He Li 1996, p.39.

for example, in Japan and Egypt, and found in the shipwreck of the *Cirebon* off the Java coast. More than half of the *Cirebon* ship was laden with *Yue celadon*. *Changsha ware* (c. 750–950) are ceramics with polychrome brown or green painting under a milky glaze or with overglaze painting (pic. 1.1). The kilns were located in Changsha in Hunan province. Many motifs have Islamic or Buddhist influences. *Changsha wares* traveled along the South China Sea maritime trade routes from China to Vietnam, Siam, Sumatra, Java, Sri Lanka, the Abbasid Caliphate, and even East Africa. *Changsha ware* was discovered as a load in the *Belitung* shipwreck in the South China Sea.

Besides, white porcelain produced in the Cizhou, Xing, and Ding kilns in Hebei was mainly for domestic purposes but has also been excavated from early shipwrecks.

After the perish of the Tang dynasty and decades of turmoil, the Song dynasty was established. Later it moved the capital from Kaifeng in the north to the port city of Hangzhou near the production centers of porcelain. Export, mainly by sea, became a notably important source of income for the government, in which export porcelains played an indispensable role.

Some famous porcelains for export include *Lonquan celadon* stoneware, *Jian Yao*, and *Qingbai* porcelain and stoneware. The dark green glazed stonewares from the Longquan kilns in Zhejiang province were the major export ceramics until the mid-14th century, and inspired the Thai ceramic production of Si Sachanalai (pic. 1.2). *Jian Yao* (or Temmoku) stoneware (c. 1100–1350) were dark brown and black glazed stoneware (mainly tea bowls) produced during the Song dynasty at the Jian kiln in Fujian province for domestic use and export to Japan (plate 2.2). *Qingbai* porcelain and stoneware (c. 1100–14th century) were fine and translucent porcelain or stoneware with a pale bluish or greenish white glaze. They were mainly produced during the Song dynasty in the

Pic. 1.1: Tang dynasty *Changsha ware* bowl, Diameter 16 cm, height 5 cm.

Pic. 1.2: Yuan dynasty dark green celadon jar from the Longquan kiln exported to Siam.

kilns of Jingdezhen and Dehua (plates 1 and 5).

Besides, coarse brown-glazed ceramics have been produced for a long period in provincial kilns for the markets in Southeast Asia and were discovered in many shipwrecks from the Song to the late Qing dynasty.

Japan and Southeast Asia were the most relevant destinations for export ceramics. An important shipwreck gives evidence of the Song dynasty trade. The *Nanhai No. 1* ship was fully laden with monochrome ceramics from Jingdezhen, Dehua, and Longquan when it sank in the late 12th century off the Guangdong coast. The whole ship together with more than 60,000 pieces of porcelain has been raised from the seabed and transported in 2007 using a kind of enormous water cage and placed in a pool in the newly established *Guangdong Maritime Silk Road Museum*. It is now the "*Vasa* of the East" — referring to the Swedish warship of 1628 which has been lifted almost completely in 1961 out of the Baltic Sea water of Stockholm. However, the *Nanhai No. 1* is almost 500 years older than the *Vasa,* and is a reference for the early international trade in ceramics.

During the Mongolian Yuan dynasty which ruled China from 1279 to 1368, the monochrome celadon ceramics were exported from kilns in Zhejiang province to West and Southeast Asian countries, such as Indonesia and Vietnam. Maritime trade in the waters of China was eased by the invention of the compass and better ship technology. The *Sinan* shipwreck, discovered in 1975 off the Korean coast, had a cargo of almost 20,000 14th century Yuan dynasty celadons mainly from Zhejiang. The *Sandaogang* shipwreck, discovered off the coast of Liaoning, had a cargo of approximately 600 items from the Cizhou kiln.[①]

The fundamental improvement in the history of porcelain is the invention of blue and white porcelain. The kilns of Jingdezhen — the famous capital of porcelain — in Jiangxi province in Southeast China started producing monochrome pale blue or pale green ware (*Qingbai*) during the Song and Yuan dynasties. However, the production of the so-called blue and white porcelain did not start until around 1320. The term "blue and white porcelain" stands for white porcelain with a cobalt blue decoration on the white shard under a transparent glaze (pic. 1.3). Its creation was so significant that broke the myth that only monochrome wares can be produced.

The Mongolians who created under their reign a huge Asian-European and intra-

---

[①] Nanjing City Museum, 2017, pp.228–238, Most of the items discovered are in the *Huludao Museum* in Liaoning province.

Pic. 1.3: Yuan dynasty blue and white shard from a stem cup made in Jingdezhen.

Asian free-trade area enabled the emergence of blue and white porcelain by the import of cobalt from Persia to China — both part of their empire.

A decade later, the export of the first Chinese blue and white porcelain started from Jingdezhen. They catered to the demand for porcelain in West Asia and the Middle East by adopting Islamic motifs and artworks. Outside the empire, thousands of blue and white shards from the Yuan dynasty have been excavated, for example, in Damascus, and about half a million broken pieces have been found in Cairo.[1] By and large, blue and white porcelain, a synonym of classical Chinese porcelain, is in the end a result of trade relations and the exchange of tastes during the Yuan dynasty. This itself is a result of mixing Chinese, Persian and Turkish cultural influences.

At the beginning of the 15th century, blue and white porcelain gained appreciation by the imperial court (first in the Yongle period from 1403–1424) and it is said that the blue and white ware in the Xuande period (1426–1435) reached its peak in terms of fineness and art but also reflected the interaction with the Islamic world. The porcelain

---

[1] Carswell 2000, p.66.

vessel shapes of the early Chinese Ming dynasty show strong Central Asian, Persian, and Arabic influences. High-quality blue and white porcelains were imported by the Ottoman Sultanate and lower-quality products found their way to Southeast Asia.

Chinese Influence on Asian Neighbors

Initiatives in other regions to produce porcelain have partly been fostered by the distortion of the intra-Asian and Asian-European trade due to the domestic circumstances of China. The export of Chinese ceramics was hampered from 1350–1360 when the soldiers of the later Ming dynasty were fighting against Mongolian rule. With the establishment of the Ming dynasty, the open and cosmopolitan attitude of the Mongolian dynasty towards trade was replaced by close-door politics: officially the Ming banned private maritime export from 1368 until 1567. And even when this sea ban could not be fully enforced, there is clear evidence of a sharp reduction in production and trading in Chinese ceramics. The so-called "Ming gap" describes the fact that Chinese commodities were missing in the export markets for a substantial period.

During the Ming ban, two regions in Southeast Asia used the opportunity of the shortage of Chinese ceramics and entered the intra-Asian ceramic trade: the Thai Kingdom of Sukhothai and the Empire of Dai Viet in nowadays Northern Vietnam.

The Thai Kingdom of Sukhothai was founded in the mid-13th century and annexed by the Thai Kingdom of Ayutthaya in 1438. There are two important old kiln centers in the former Thai Kingdom of Sukhothai. One center is just north of the city wall of Sukhothai, the other center is located some 60 km north of Sukhothai in Si Satchanalai along the banks of the Yom River. The Sukhothai kilns produced in the 14th century mainly underglaze iron (black) decorated stoneware, such as plates with a fish motive. By comparison, in Si Satchanalai, the second Thai kiln center, the variety of ceramic products is bigger than in Sukhothai: potters produced underglaze iron decorated stoneware, celadons, brown, white and black monochromes. Generally, these products are also named Swankhalok ware. The underglaze black ceramics (plates 153–155) were inspired by blue and white porcelains from China and Vietnam. However, the influences of Chinese celadons from Longquan on the Thai celadons from Si Satchanalai are much more obvious.

When the Ming ban came into effect, the potters of Si Satchanalai took advantage of the shortage of Chinese products in the intra-Asian market. The kilns of Si Satchanalai exported ceramics continuously — mainly to Indonesia and the Philippines — from sometime in the late 14th century until about 1580 when the area was depopulated under the impact of wars with Burma. Si Satchanalai celadon plates comprised the primary cargo for practically all the middle 15th century shipwrecks. At that time the area belonged to the Siamese Kingdom of Ayutthaya. The *Royal Nanhai*, a Siamese junk on the way to Java, that sank in around 1460 had a big cargo of Si Satchanalai celadons. More than 21,000 items were recovered in 1992 by the maritime archaeologist Sten Sjostrand (plate 157).

In the 15th century, Vietnamese ceramics partly substituted the missing blue and white products from China. North Vietnam (Dai Viet) was part of the Chinese empire for about 1,000 years, from about 111 BC until 939 AD, and again for a brief period between 1407 and 1427. In 939 the region gained independence. In the late 13th or early 14th centuries, Dai Viet entered the ceramic export trade. The Maritime Silk Road, linking Chinese ports, ports in the Vietnamese Red River Delta, and ports of the Kingdom of Champa in Southern Vietnam with India, Arab countries and Persia, was used for trading spices, textiles, metals and ceramics, often with the assistance of Muslim merchants who had settled along the coast.

China occupied Dai Viet again from 1407 to 1427. The presence of Muslim traders in South China and Vietnam, and the Chinese occupation, were a major stimulus for the development of Vietnamese blue and white export porcelain. Vietnam was probably the first country where Chinese-inspired locally produced blue and white ceramics emerged.

The products from Vietnam traded in the 15th century were mostly blue and white ware. While showing strong similarities to Chinese blue and white in decor, Vietnamese export ceramic bodies tended to be greyer and non–translucently glazed. Other typical features are the chocolate-brown dressing on the base and unglazed stack-firing circles in the interior (pic. 1.4). One of the most important pieces dated 1450 is preserved in the *Topkapi Museum* in Istanbul. The unique combination of underglaze blue with overglaze red and green enamels was used mainly on plates but also on covered boxes which were produced in underglaze blue in big volumes.

The *Hoi An* shipwreck discovered in 1993 off the Vietnamese coastal city of Hoi An is the most important found of Vietnamese ceramics of the late 15th century. The *Hoi An* shipwreck, contained a precious cargo of over 150,000 Vietnamese blue and white ceramics. The cargo included dishes, pouring vessels, bottles, jars, cups, bowls, figural ceramics and boxes — all painted with mythological animals or landscape

Pic. 1.4: Two Vietnamese blue and white bowls with chocolate base, 16th century.

scenes. The size and fine quality of the cargo are evidence that the northern kilns near modern-day Hanoi quickly expanded to meet the great demand in Southeast Asian markets for high-quality ceramics (plate 149).

The South of Vietnam has historically not been part of China or the Empire of Dai Viet but belonged to the independent Hindu Kingdom of Champa. They also produced and exported ceramics. The *Pandanan* shipwreck of the 15th century carried thousands of Cham monochrome ceramics.

During the 14th and 16th centuries, Thai and Vietnamese ceramics have partly compensated the shrinking export volumes of Chinese ceramics in the Southeast Asian markets. "The mere presence of Southeast Asian ceramics at every maritime shipwreck site from the late 14th century to the beginning of the 16th century in proportions of 60 to 90 percent, as opposed to 100 percent Chinese trade ware at earlier sites, is itself evidence of a Chinese shortage."[1]

However, even during the Ming gap, export to Southeast Asia never came to a complete standstill. The best customer of Yuan and Ming blue and white ceramics was the Ottoman court in Istanbul. The Topkapi Palace holds the biggest collection of Chinese ceramics in the world. The *Lena* junk with blue and white porcelain from the period of the Ming Emperor Hongzhi sank around 1500 off the Philippine Island of Busuanga.[2] The cargo from Jingdezhen was probably on its way to the Ottoman

---

[1] Brown 2009, pp.27–28.
[2] Goddio 1997, pp.79–101.

Empire or a Sultanate in the Archipelago and is a very good example of porcelain made according to the Islamic or West Asian taste.

In addition to Jingdezhen, another important ceramics-producing region in China was Zhangzhou (pic. 1.5). From Zhangzhou, located in Fujian Province near Xiamen, ceramics formerly termed *Swatow* wares were shipped in big numbers to neighboring countries. The Zhangzhou ware is predominantly blue and white porcelain for mainland Southeast Asia and the Malay Archipelago. Compared to ceramics from Jingdezhen, the shard is coarse, and the underglaze blue painting looks done in a hasty way in comparison to the high-end products of Jingdezhen made for Muslim courts. However, the beauty of the decoration lies in the eyes of the observer (plates 17–30).

For trade with Southeast Asia, the kilns of Fujian province were as important as the Jingdezhen kilns in Jiangxi for export products to Europe. Even today, many Zhangzhou pieces are unearthed in the Malay Archipelago or the South China Sea. *Bin Thuan* shipwreck, discovered in 2001 off the Vietnamese coast, had a cargo of thousands of Ming dynasty Zhangzhou ware and probably got lost around 1608 on its way to the Malay Peninsula (plates 18–19). In 2007, another shipwreck with Zhangzhou porcelain — the *Nan'ao No. 1* was discovered off the Guangdong coast nearby Shantou.

When the Ming ban was lifted in 1567 the international trade in porcelain took off again. However, the composition of trade ceramics has changed. Less and less monochrome white, pale green, green and brown ceramics were exported. Instead blue and white porcelain has substituted the products of the early trade (pic. 1.6).

In summary, the early intra-Asian trade in mainly monochrome ceramics stretched over eight centuries and covered the Tang dynasty, the period of the Five Dynasties

Pic. 1.5: Ming dynasty *Swatow* dish with a standing phoenix.

Pic. 1.6: Ming or early Qing dynasty blue and white shipwreck porcelain damaged and with encrustations.

and Ten Kingdoms, the Song dynasty, the Yuan dynasty, and half of the Ming dynasty, ended during the Ming ban in the 16th century. The number of ceramics exported from China to other Asian regions from the 8th century to the 15th century is unknown. Less than one million pieces have been discovered on the seabed. Another million others may be unearthed in the future. An emblematic shipwreck found stands for each dynasty until the end of the early intra-Asian trade (map 1.1 and table 1.1).

Table 1.1: Important Shipwreck Discoveries with Chinese Ceramics for the Intra-Asian Trade

Dynasty	Shipwrecks	Ceramics
Tang dynasty (618–907)	*Belitung*	*Changsha ware*
Five dynasties and Ten Kingdoms (907–960)	*Cirebon*	*Yue celadon* from Zhejiang
Song dynasty (960–1279)	*Nanhai No. 1*	*Qingbai* from Dehua and Jingdezhen, celadon from Longquan
	Huaguang Jiao No.1	Monochromes from Fujian, Guangdong and Jingdezhen
	Banyang Jiao No.1	*Jian Yao* stoneware from Fujian
Yuan dynasty (1279–1368)	*Sinan, Dalian Dao*	*Longquan celadon*
	Sandaogang	White-glazed black painted stoneware from Hebei (Cizhou kiln)
Ming dynasty (1368–1644)	*Lena*	Jingdezhen Blue and White
	Nan'ao No.1, Bin Thuan, San Isidro	Zhangzhou Blue and White

Approximately 1550 was the start of the second chapter of the international ceramic trade. It marked the beginning of a globalized world. The period from 1550–1800 saw a massive expansion in the numbers of traded ceramics due to better ship technology, additional traders and new customers. After the Portuguese discovered new sea routes passing the Cape of Good Hope and the Indian Ocean towards not only the Malay Archipelago but also the Philippines and China, the export of porcelains to Europe started to play an important role. And even when the Portuguese and later the Dutch shipped and imported porcelain to Europe, the intra-Asian trade continued and probably made up more than 80% of the Chinese ceramic exports until the middle of the 17th century. Moreover, European ships, first Portuguese and later the Dutch East India Company, played an increasing role in facilitating the intra-Asian trade between China and Japan through Macao, and later through the Dutch entrepots on

Taiwan, Dejima Island in Japan, and Batavia (Jakarta) on Java Island. The process of globalization finally started.

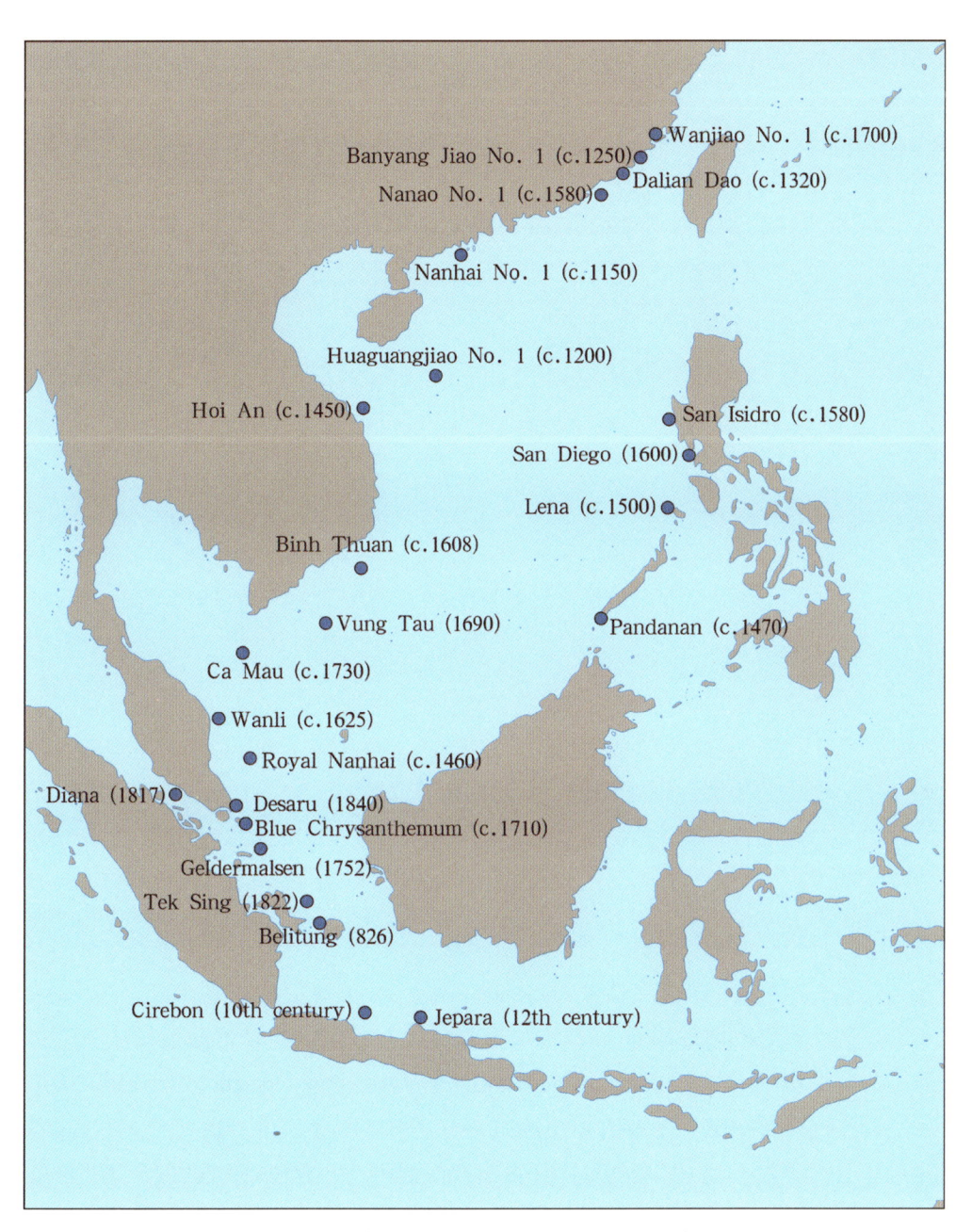

Map 1.1: Shipwreck sites in Asia with important porcelain discoveries.

第二章 全球化世界的开端：欧亚贸易关系

葡萄牙人

欧洲商人到 16 世纪才开始接触中国瓷器。由于瓷器重量大且易破损，不适合进行陆路长途运输，因此，直到欧亚开通海上丝绸之路，陶瓷贸易才正式开启。

在欧洲到亚洲的海上通道发现之前，欧亚之间的贸易要么通过陆上的传统丝绸之路进行，要么通过"半海半陆"的组合路线进行（地图 0.1）。前者被阿拉伯商人所把持，后者以印度洋为核心的部分也掌握在阿拉伯商人手里，西方的威尼斯和热那亚共和国则垄断了组合路线的欧洲部分。来自这些意大利城邦的商人将远道而来的亚洲商品转运到欧洲销售，利润滚滚。

然而，随着 1299 年奥斯曼帝国的兴起，以及 1453 年君士坦丁堡被奥斯曼帝国所攻陷（后改名为伊斯坦布尔），传统欧亚贸易的利润率急剧下降。奥斯曼帝国成为一个占统治地位的海上强国，封锁了通往黑海的通道，控制了地中海的大部分地区，其中包括丝绸和香料的重要贸易港口。国际力量对比的转变，以及当时欧洲造船、航海和制图技术的进步，促成了"大航海时代"的到来。西方人前赴后继地想要寻找替代的、能够直接联结东西方之间的海上航线。

1498 年，葡萄牙人瓦斯科·达·伽马（图 2.1）沿着海路抵达印度的卡利卡特，成为通过海路抵达亚洲的第一人。25 年后，葡萄牙人费迪南德·麦哲伦和西班牙人胡安·塞巴斯蒂安·埃尔卡诺才完成了途经南美洲、菲律宾和印度尼西亚的第一次环球航行。

不过，当欧亚大陆两端的商人们通过海路建立起直接联系，最受欧洲人青睐的并非瓷器，而是香料。"起初是香料。"奥地利小说家斯蒂芬·茨威格的著作《麦哲伦传记》开篇如是写道。当时欧洲香料异常紧俏，人们愿意为香料豪掷千金。经营香料因此成为有重利可图的行业。在金钱的驱使下，商人们长途奔波，将印度马拉巴尔海岸和苏门答腊岛的胡椒、印度尼西亚摩鹿加群岛（又称香料群岛）的肉豆蔻和丁香等珍奇香料运送欧洲。

图 2.1 瓦斯科·达·伽马，葡萄牙探险家、航海家（约 1469—1524 年）

翻看欧亚海上航线开通后 350 年间的历史，我们能看到欧洲列强为了能在利润丰厚的亚洲产品贸易中分得一杯羹而相互混战。葡萄牙、荷兰和英国在建设和完成海上丝绸之路的西方航线中扮演主要角色。当然，西班牙、法国、瑞典、丹麦以及其他国家也参与其中。

然而，这些西方国家进入的并非是未被开发的市场。如前所述，从阿拉伯海、波斯、印度、锡兰一直延伸到东南亚海岸和南海，这条海上贸易线路生机勃勃，历史悠久。在欧洲船只出现在此区域之前，阿拉伯三角帆船、中国戎克船，以及印度、印度尼西亚、亚美尼亚和伊朗等的船只千帆竞渡，有力推动了印度的棉花和胡椒，伊朗的丝绸，中国的黄金、丝绸和陶瓷，印度尼西亚的香料，日本的银器和漆器的贸易。一套复杂的贸易体系和对外关系体系已经存在了数百年。

中国在这套体系中扮演核心角色，但是对其邻国来说却不是一个简单的贸易伙伴。那些想要与中国进行贸易的国家不得不派遣朝贡使团觐见中国皇帝，并承认中国的文化优越地位。从 11 到 14 世纪，南海的海上交通的繁忙程度并不亚于欧洲的波罗的海和地中海。位于南海东北角、濒临台湾海峡的泉州，是当时最为繁忙的港口。明朝时期，越南、朝鲜、日本、马六甲苏丹国、爪哇岛、泰国、斯里兰卡甚至印度各邦都接受了朝贡关系。由于禁止私人贸易，官方的朝贡贸易是商品交易的主要形式。但是，朝贡国并非殖民地，而是在互利互惠基础上建立的经济关系。

因此，15 世纪，在葡萄牙人到来之前，马六甲已经是最重要的中转港和贸易集散地之一。来自亚洲各地的商人都在马六甲设立仓库。马六甲海峡的建立充分利用了其战略地理位置优势和马六甲苏丹国的开明态度，它连接了南海和印度洋，至今仍是世界上最重要的航道之一。今天的欧亚海上丝绸之路主体仍然包括马六甲海峡（但新加坡取代马六甲成为主要中转港）、霍尔木兹海峡和苏伊士运河。

伴随欧洲人的航海大发现而来的是殖民步伐。1510 年，葡萄牙占领印度西海岸的果阿，这是它在印度的第一个贸易基地和防御工事，未来的葡属印度殖民地的首府。不久，为了控制马六甲并夺取香料贸易路线，葡萄牙人进一步向东南挺进。1511 年，在阿方索·德·阿尔布克尔克的指挥下，葡萄牙舰队征服了马六甲，从而在非洲和东亚之间建立了新的中转港，以促进葡萄牙的欧亚贸易。1513 年，乔治·欧维士通过海路抵达中国，成为首个通过海上航线抵达中国的欧洲人。首个葡萄牙人抵达日本则发生在 1543 年。

葡萄牙人在印度站稳脚跟后，建立起从里斯本到印度（途经非洲和阿拉伯海岸），从马六甲到东印度群岛，从澳门到长崎的贸易航线，在沿线建立了若干中转港。这个贸易网络（地图 2.1）在 16 世纪为葡萄牙带来了滚滚财富。

地图 2.1　1550—1685 年间主要瓷器贸易路线

尽管葡萄牙通过军事力量强行进入既有的亚洲内部贸易体系，却无法改变其商业规则。亚洲出产的香料、纺织品、陶瓷等都是欧洲的紧俏商品，但由于葡萄牙没有太多可以与亚洲商人交易的商品，他们不得不用白银支付。

葡萄牙人的优势集中在海上。他们拥有比亚洲竞争对手规模更大、速度更快、装备精良、全副武装的船只，控制了阿曼的马斯喀特、伊朗的霍尔木兹等咽喉要道，以及印度古吉拉特邦北部和马拉巴尔海岸南部的一些港口，拥有巨大的海上航线优势。依托于此，他们不仅能把商品从一个港口运至另一个港口，还向其他船只征收保护费——"卡塔兹"。航线上的每艘商船都必须购买卡塔兹，才能获得贸易和运输许可，葡萄牙则保护其免受海盗和其他国家威胁。果阿、第乌、霍尔木兹和马六甲是收取卡塔兹的主要关卡。[1]

然而，葡萄牙对陆上的印度莫卧儿王朝、中国明朝或日本德川幕府的影响都微不足道。尤其是中国和日本，注重陆上情况或把精力专注于国内，并不在意其狭长沿海地区发生的事件，只开放小型口岸开展有限的贸易活动：1557年，中国明朝政府允许葡萄牙人租借珠江三角洲的澳门半岛，但要交纳租金。同年，日本允许葡萄牙在长崎附近的平户建立起小型商馆。在长达一个多世纪的时间里，澳门是中国主要的官方对欧贸易口岸，直到17世纪广州正式开放中欧海上贸易。

葡萄牙船只开展中国瓷器贸易，要稍早于租借澳门半岛。1550年左右，葡萄牙人可能是在亚洲内部的转口港购买了首批中国瓷器：当时，中国戎克船会停靠在马来半岛的马六甲或大泥、大城府[2]、苏门答腊岛、爪哇岛或苏拉威西岛等转口港，用丝绸、铜、黄金和瓷器换取香料、锡和白银。

1567年，明朝海禁正式结束，陶瓷贸易得以迅速发展。自此，葡萄牙商人既可以正式在澳门、广州交易会购买瓷器，也可以从停靠在南海转口港的中国戎克船那里购买瓷器。英国人和荷兰人后来将景德镇青花瓷称为"克拉克瓷"，因为它们最初是由葡萄牙克拉克帆船运至欧洲（图2.2）。[3]

葡萄牙人还利用澳门和长崎之间的海上航线，攫取巨额利润。由于明朝在解除海禁后依然禁止与日本的私人海上贸易，葡萄牙的船只得以取代中国戎克船，将中国的丝绸和陶瓷运往日本，换取日本白银，这些白银不仅在中国需求旺盛，也给葡萄牙带来额外交换资本，可以用来在印度尼西亚购买香料或纺织品。直到17

---

[1] Feldbauer 2005, p.129.
[2] Garnier 2004, pp.66–75.
[3] Mostert 2015, p.38.

图2.2 明万历克拉克瓷盘，瓷盘饰以鸟和岩石图案，为中国外销荷兰的瓷器

世纪，丝绸换白银都是最有利可图的套利交易之一。

然而，在16世纪，瓷器在对欧贸易中无足轻重，只是作为压舱物的次要商品，与其他更重要和珍贵的贸易商品如胡椒、香料和植物、丝绸和棉花等一道被运往里斯本。16世纪的船载货物清单便是证明：1587—1588年间，胡椒占货物重量的68%，生姜占3.7%，肉桂占6.3%，棉花和丝绸占10.5%，靛蓝染料占8.4%，包括瓷器在内的其他物品占1.5%。①

2004年，南海海洋考古公司的海洋考古学家斯滕·肖斯特兰德在马来西亚丹绒加拉海岸以外6海里海域发现了"万历号"沉船。它可能为一艘受葡萄牙指挥的中国戎克船，装载了大约3.7万件景德镇青花瓷，约在1625年从澳门驶向马六甲，在葡荷海战中沉没。② 船上的货物很好地展示了早期欧洲与明朝的瓷器贸易（收藏33）。其中两件瓷器商品是早期"中国订单瓷器"的典范——由欧洲客户订购，中国制作，瓷器以釉下彩的方式绘出客户家族的徽章图案。

1580年，西班牙国王、哈布斯堡家族的腓力二世合并葡萄牙，称为伊比利亚联盟。此前，野心勃勃的两国在教皇的主持下，先后于1494年签订《托尔德西里亚斯条约》，1529年签订《萨拉戈萨条约》，将全球视为自己的囊中之物予以分割。根据该协议，印度洋属于葡萄牙势力范围，西班牙不得进入。但合并后，西班牙也可以通过菲律宾和墨西哥介入亚洲贸易了。

西班牙于16世纪初征服了墨西哥的阿兹特克帝国，建立起新西班牙总督辖区，这为西班牙向亚太地区进一步扩张奠定了基础。不过，尽管麦哲伦于1521年环球航行期间就已抵达菲律宾，西班牙直到1571年才征服了马尼拉，将其作为西属东印度群岛的首府。米格尔·洛佩斯·德莱加斯皮（1502—1572年）担任首任总督。

1565年，西班牙马尼拉大帆船航线开启，并一直持续到1815年。这条线路从马尼拉穿越太平洋，经墨西哥回到西班牙，不过大部分进口货物并非运往西班

---

① Feldbauer 2005, p.144.

② Sjostrand 2007, pp.44-45.

牙，而是停留在墨西哥。"这些船只在 250 年里往返于马尼拉和（墨西哥）阿卡普尔科，将陶瓷、香料、丝绸、象牙、翡翠和其他奢侈品从中国运到墨西哥，以换取新大陆（美洲）的白银。"① 从每年 12 月到次年 4 月，数以百计的中国戎克船来往于中国海岸和马尼拉之间，马尼拉因此成为经墨西哥进行中欧贸易的重要转口港。②

1991 年，海洋考古学家弗兰克·戈迪奥在马尼拉湾附近发现了西班牙帆船"圣地亚哥号"。1600 年它因与两艘荷兰船只作战而沉没，船上载有中国景德镇克拉克青花瓷和漳州窑青花瓷。无独有偶，2016 年，考古学家在墨西哥阿卡普尔科大教堂附近地下 1.5 米处发现了数千块明代瓷器碎片。这无疑是中国与西属菲律宾、西属墨西哥之间密切贸易关系的证明。

荷兰东印度公司

葡萄牙船只在欧亚海上长途贸易中的垄断地位持续了近一百年之久。当时，只有西班牙的马尼拉大帆船才敢挑战这种垄断霸权。不过自 1580 年两国合并后，葡萄牙在亚洲海域不得不面对一个强大对手，也就是荷兰。

荷兰于 1482 年臣服于哈布斯堡王朝，1556 年被纳入西班牙帝国的版图。自 1568 年起，荷兰为摆脱西班牙统治开始了长达 80 年的独立战争，在西葡合并后，则演变为荷葡战争。

1596 年，第一批荷兰船只抵达印度尼西亚爪哇岛。1598 年，荷兰人在雅各布·科内利松·范·内克的指挥下，发起了对印度尼西亚群岛的第二次探险，随行的还有极地探险家雅各布·范·海姆斯凯尔克，以及澳大利亚的发现者威廉·杨松·布劳。此次探险给荷兰人带来了非常大的利润，促成了 1602 年荷兰东印度公司的诞生，也使得原本发生在欧洲的宗教和政治冲突蔓延至亚洲。

荷兰东印度公司（图 2.3）是世界上第一家股份制公司。1602 至 1796 年间，该公司派遣了近 100 万名欧洲人在 4 785 艘从事亚洲贸易的船舶上工作，辛勤运送了超过

---

① Ganse 2008, p.37.

② Goddio 1996, p.100.

图 2.3　荷兰东印度公司的旗帜

250万吨的亚洲贸易商品，从而成为欧亚之间最重要的贸易商和运输商。荷兰东印度公司可能是第一家真正意义上的跨国企业，拥有来自不同国家的股东，以及欧洲和东亚各地的员工。其总部，建于1606年的东印度公司大楼，至今仍屹立在阿姆斯特丹，现属于阿姆斯特丹大学所有。

荷兰东印度公司在非洲、中东、南亚、东南亚和东亚地区拥有贸易垄断权，其贸易地位与葡萄牙相当。1610年，它在印度尼西亚的安汶岛建立了第一个亚洲总部，尝试种植原产于特尔纳特岛（属摩鹿加群岛）的丁香。1619年，该公司将总部迁至由荷属东印度群岛第四任总督简·皮特斯佐恩·科恩（图2.4）创建的城市巴达维亚，即今天的雅加达。之后荷兰人征服了附近盛产肉豆蔻的班达群岛，垄断了肉豆蔻的生产和贸易。荷兰人对岛上土著进行屠杀，这揭露了荷兰在东印度群岛统治期间最黑暗残忍的一面。1621年，岛上15 000名居民几乎全部被杀害，幸存的班达人也被当作奴隶运往巴达维亚。

图2.4 简·皮特斯佐恩·科恩（1587—1629年）

1627年，荷兰和葡萄牙在澳门首次交战，以荷兰水手的伤亡而告终。作为反击，荷兰军舰对西班牙和葡萄牙的船只展开袭击，将其击沉或俘获。其中一个战利品就是满载丝绸、麝香和瓷器的葡萄牙"圣卡塔琳娜号"帆船，它在如今的新加坡海岸附近被俘获，船上装载的货物在阿姆斯特丹被出售，这是在北欧举行的首场大型中国瓷器拍卖会。

与葡萄牙人一样，荷兰人的势力起初也不足以改变亚洲原有的贸易规则，因此被迫与爪哇岛、苏门答腊岛、苏拉威西岛以及印度东西海岸的伊斯兰政权达成协议。此外，他们还必须与来自中国、印度、伊朗、奥斯曼帝国、泰国、葡萄牙和英国的商人共享海上航行沿线的中转港。印度的苏拉特、苏门答腊岛的占碑、爪哇岛的万丹、马来半岛的大泥和苏拉威西岛的望加锡是当时各种亚洲奢侈品的国际集散地。这些地区的统治者多信奉伊斯兰教，主张开放自由的贸易环境和氛围。

荷兰用了数十年时间，才最终将对手葡萄牙从大多数亚洲贸易中转港（表2.1）

赶走。1648年荷葡战争结束，葡萄牙将印度沿海的安汶、马六甲、锡兰（今斯里兰卡）和科钦转让给荷兰东印度公司军队。1669年，荷兰人占领了黄金、钻石、象牙、檀香木、珍珠和香料中转港望加锡。1682年，拥有人数众多的华商社区以及荷兰、英国、葡萄牙和丹麦贸易基地的胡椒集散地万丹将独家贸易权授予荷兰。从此，巴达维亚成为亚洲内部贸易的中转港、荷兰东印度公司货船的始发港。这些货船经斯里兰卡或印度经开普敦，驶往荷兰首都阿姆斯特丹。

表2.1　1550—1842年瓷器海上贸易路线，包括始发港、转口港和目的地

出口港	中转港	进口港
中国： 　– 漳州 　– 广州 　– 澳门 　– 厦门 　– 舟山 　– 福州 　– 宁波 日本： 　– 伊万里 　– 平户 　– 长崎 越南： 　– 东京（河内古称） 　– 会安	中国： 　– 澎湖列岛 　– 台湾安平 东南亚： 　– 万丹 　– 占碑 　– 巨港 　– 巴达维亚 　– 望加锡 　– 马尼拉 　– 大城府 　– 大泥 　– 马六甲 印度： 　– 果阿 　– 苏拉特 　– 加尔各答 　– 科钦 波斯（今伊朗）： 　– 霍尔木兹海峡 　– 阿巴斯 斯里兰卡： 　– 锡兰	东南亚： 　– 万丹 　– 巴达维亚 　– 望加锡 　– 大城府 　– 东京（今河内） 　– 洛越 　– 马尼拉 欧洲： 　– 里斯本 　– 阿姆斯特丹，米德尔堡 　– 伦敦 　– 洛里昂 　– 哥德堡 　– 哥本哈根 　– 奥斯坦德 美洲： 　– 阿卡普尔科 　– 塞勒姆和波士顿，马萨诸塞 波斯（今伊朗）： 　– 阿巴斯 奥斯曼帝国： 　– 摩卡 　– 巴士拉 非洲： 　– 开普敦

荷兰东印度公司复制并完善了葡萄牙人开创的经济模式，使其达到了前所未有的规模。它不仅通过亚欧长途贸易，而且通过亚洲内部贸易获得丰厚利润，还利用亚洲不同区域之间产品价格差进行套利交易。尤其因为当时日本闭关锁国，对葡萄牙船只关闭口岸，荷兰东印度公司借此对日本开展白银换丝绸的贸易，获利丰厚。荷属东印度群岛总督简·皮特斯佐恩·科恩在给荷兰东印度公司董事会的一封信中描述道：

> 我们可用从古吉拉特邦运来的布匹（指棉花）交换苏门答腊岛的胡椒和黄金。[……]我们可用檀香木、胡椒粉和里亚尔（西班牙银圆）交换中国商品和黄金；我们可用中国商品从日本换取白银；用科罗曼德海岸的布匹交换中国的香料、其他商品和黄金；用苏拉特布匹交换香料；用阿拉伯半岛的其他商品和里亚尔交换香料和其他普通商品，环环相扣。所有贸易无须荷兰投入任何资金，只需船只便可完成。[……]我们已经拥有最重要的香料。[……]因此，先生们，尊敬的董事们，没有什么可以阻止公司开展世界上利润最为丰厚的贸易。①

荷兰东印度公司介入中国瓷器贸易是在1604年。在17世纪前20年里，荷兰从万通和大泥购买中国的丝绸和瓷器，通过在那里的华人社区建立起印度、东南亚香料和其他商品的帆船贸易。

1622年，荷兰东印度公司占领中国澎湖列岛，两年后占领台湾南部，并建造安平古堡（图2.5）。荷兰人统治台湾南部长达38年，并凭借邻近中国大陆（福州和厦门）的距离优势，频繁进行帆船贸易，或直接航行至漳州（荷兰东印度公司文件中称之为"漳州河"）。

占领台湾为荷兰东印度公司在亚洲带来了丰厚的利润。公司主要通过安平古堡进口中国瓷器，然后经由巴达维亚运往阿姆斯特丹。另外，公司还参与了亚洲内部贸易市场：瓷器与其他商品一起，被运至荷兰东印度公司在波斯阿巴斯港、印度苏拉特、奥斯曼帝国、泰国大城府和曼谷、越南东京（今河内）或会安，以及柬埔寨首都洛韦的商馆（地图2.1）。在贸易最初的50年间，荷兰东印度公司运往欧洲的陶瓷数量逾300万件。

---

① Frank 1998, pp.281–282.

图 2.5　荷兰在中国台湾建造的安平古堡，铜版画，约翰·布劳绘

从荷兰东印度公司官员的日志中，我们可以看到详细的关于荷兰东印度公司在巴达维亚、台湾、平户（长崎附近）、大城府和东京等商馆的商业活动。例如，巴达维亚总督在 1644 年 12 月 12 日的日志中提到，来自台湾、装载 202~332 件各式瓷器的荷兰东印度公司"赛尔号"抵达港口。[①] 船舶发货清单清晰地列出了所有瓷器的种类和外形，包括细颈瓶、花盆、酒坛、直筒花瓶、芥末罐、碟、杯、碗、盘、大平盘等，并且记录了准确数据，如 9 070 只克拉克碗（收藏 34）、10 485 只碗、15 695 只盘子、33 020 只红茶杯等，价格总计 37 987 荷兰盾（弗罗林），平均每件价格为 0.18 荷兰盾。当时一枚荷兰盾约为 10.8 克白银，即 0.29 两（以白银为基础的中国货币），整船瓷器价值相当于 410 千克白银。这份清单表明，大部分货物都是日用瓷器。碟子和盘子有不同规格，直径分别为 50 厘米、29~36 厘米（收藏 32）和 21~23 厘米，我们在 17 世纪早期荷兰和佛兰德静物画（图 2.6）中可看到这种盘子。[②]

1653 年，因中国国内动荡，中荷瓷器贸易中断，荷兰商人开始努力寻找替代品。当时有两种选择：第一，寻找可以替代中国的亚洲瓷器生产商；第二，在荷兰国内生产。荷兰人对两种方法都进行了尝试。一方面，他们鼓励日本陶瓷坊仿制中国克

---

① Volker 1954, pp.51–52.

② Ketel, p.10.

图2.6 荷兰静物画中的中国克拉克瓷，弗洛里斯·范·戴克（1575—1651年）绘

拉克瓷（收藏138和139）。另一方面，荷兰南部的代尔夫特陶瓷商抓住这一商机建造新的陶瓷厂。代尔夫特34家工厂中有17家是在1653至1662年的10年间建立的，这是对中国进口瓷器的短缺采取的直接应对措施。代尔夫特陶瓷远看起来像是瓷器，但实际上是锡釉陶。这种陶器既不像瓷器那样通透，也不像瓷器那样耐用。

为了维护其贸易地位，荷兰于1655年派遣官方使团，觐见年轻的顺治皇帝。此行的主要目的是说服中国统治者允许荷兰人直接进入中国市场，并提出帮助清政府对抗福建沿海的郑成功势力。该使团于1655年7月从巴达维亚启程，9月乘船抵达广州。

1656年3月，荷兰东印度公司使团从广州启程，主要经河道行驶，于7月抵达北京，停留至10月。此次出使本身并未实现出使目的，可以说以失败告终。顺治皇帝将此行视为朝贡，只答应每8年授予一次极其有限的直接贸易权。然而另一方面，该使团对中欧关系产生了重大影响。使团成员、荷兰作家和旅行家约翰·尼霍夫（1618—1672年）就这次中国之旅撰写了一部著作《荷兰东印度公司使节团访华纪实》，内含145幅铜版画。该书于1665年出版荷兰语和法语版，1669年出版英语版。它奠定了欧洲对中国一百多年的印象。直至18世纪中期，西方人对中国的描述仍然与这些古老的铜版画（图2.7）如出一辙。

我们可以想象，在这种情况下，欧洲人非常渴望深入了解这个向他们出口丝绸和瓷器珍宝的国家。尼霍夫的游记，以及之后荷兰人欧弗特·达佩尔（1636—1689年）就1667年荷兰使团第二次出访清廷所著游记中塑造的中国形象，在欧洲持续了很长一段时间，并掀起了延续近两个世纪的中国风潮。①

① Ulrichs 2003.

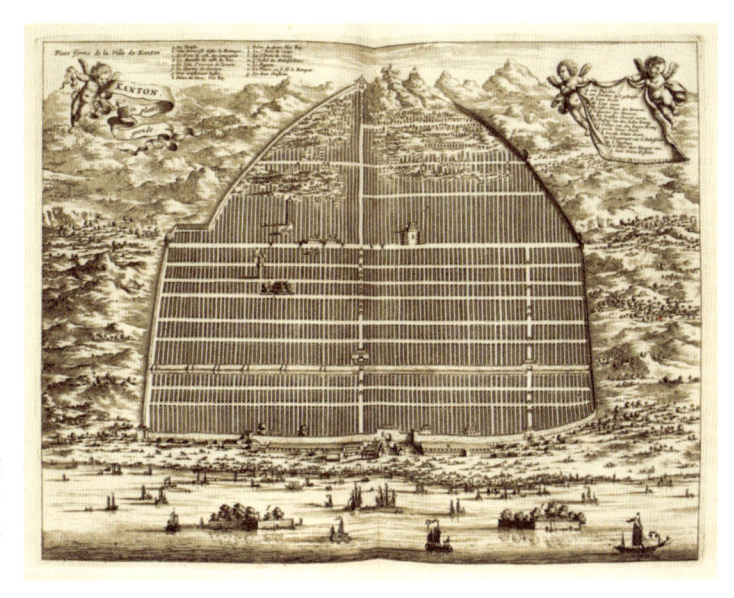

图 2.7 荷兰东印度公司使团首次觐见顺治皇帝时西方绘制的广州地图，出版于 1665 年

这些版画展现了中国的城市、植物、动物和日常生活场景。特别值得一提的是，这些版画塑造了一种积极的中国形象，展示了一个统治者智慧过人，人民文明有素且崇尚音乐、绘画和诗歌的理想国度。然而，真实的情况并非如此。只是由于当时欧洲正饱受战争之苦，从"八十年战争"（包括"三十年战争"）到英荷战争和西班牙王位继承战争，连绵不绝，以至于欧洲人幻想异邦为太平盛世之国。

荷兰人出使北京失败，未能与中国建立直接贸易关系。1662 年，郑成功收复台湾[①]，1683 年康熙皇帝（图2.8）统一台湾。此后中国再次成为世界上最大的瓷器生产国和出口国。

荷兰东印度公司在中国丧失了有利的地理位置，便转而利用来往于巴达维亚的中国商船进行贸易。在荷兰人被禁止前往中国期间，他们邀请中国人来到其位于爪哇岛的大本营。平均每年有 14 只商船装

图 2.8 清朝康熙皇帝（1654—1722 年）

① Andrade 2011.

载根据客户品位定制的康熙青花瓷（收藏 35-48）、五彩瓷（收藏 52-55）和被称为巴达维亚瓷的棕釉瓷器（收藏 56-58）抵达巴达维亚。①

从 1683 年起，荷兰陶瓷贸易进入一个新阶段，荷兰东印度公司本身几乎不再从事陶瓷贸易，而是将贸易权转交给私营贸易商，他们作为承运人，利用荷兰东印度公司的船只将瓷器运往欧洲。遗憾的是，这一时期的史料记载已经丢失，或者交易信息没有被认真记录在案。

这一时期中国出口欧洲的瓷器种类和质量都比战前的克拉克瓷有所提高。青花瓷品质上乘，瓷片洁白如雪、晶莹剔透，釉下蓝绘精致美观。尤其是康熙统治时期所生产的外销瓷（图 2.9），从外观和质量来看均为最上乘之作。

如今中国收藏家一致认为外销瓷品质低下。但实际上民窑出身的外销瓷与国内官窑瓷器差别并不大。如果要拿《故宫博物院藏文物珍品全集》中收录的约 80 件品质一流的康熙御用瓷器② 与外销瓷进行比较，那未免有失公允。但我们仍然可以总体上对康熙时期出口的外销瓷与内销瓷进行比较。首先，二者在用料品质上并无差别。其次，外销瓷和内销瓷的造型相似，但尺寸不同。二者最大的区别在于釉下蓝绘的细腻程度不同。

图 2.9　清康熙荷兰银镶嵌青花茶壶

① Jörg 1982, p.20.
② Frank 1998.

1729 至 1799 年是荷兰第三个瓷器进口时期，C. J. A. 约尔格完整记录并分析了这个时期。[1] 当时荷兰东印度公司决定通过中国官方唯一开放口岸——广州港开展贸易。然而，彼时瓷器已不再是荷兰人需求的重点，而被一种新产品所取代。这种新产品不仅吸引了新的欧洲对手，而且改变了 19 世纪中国与西方的势力平衡——茶叶。后文将做详述。

荷兰人和日本外销瓷

日本最初是中国、越南和泰国外销陶瓷的主要输入国。17 世纪初，九州岛发现了瓷土原料，建立起有田窑。日本掌握制瓷工艺，是受到朝鲜制瓷工匠的影响，这比中国晚几个世纪，但比欧洲约早 100 年。

日本陶瓷制品在亚洲陶瓷史上风格独树一帜，但其国内生产规模有限。传统的日本国产茶陶在一定程度上确实无法与周边国家的产品相媲美。这些产品乍看起来简单、胎厚、釉质不均，甚至有一点原始之味，却充满自然美感，用手触摸令人心情愉悦。每件作品都与众不同，外观质朴，折射出日本人的哲学和禅宗佛教思想，但是当然不太适合外销。外销瓷与日本传统审美迥异，西方客户，尤其是荷兰人在其造型和纹绘确定过程中发挥了重要作用。

日本与欧洲人的接触，始于 1543 年葡萄牙人门德斯·平托偶然抵达日本海岸。在接下来的 60 年里，葡萄牙传教士试图使日本人皈依天主教，并促进了中日贸易。通过在平户和澳门的商馆，葡萄牙人大大促进了中日丝绸和白银贸易。[2] 日本利用葡萄牙造船专业知识建立了商船舰队，在"朱印"体系下运行。所谓朱印，是指日本商船需持有日本政府颁发的朱红印执照，方可从事海外贸易。从 1592 到 1635 年，大约有 350 艘"朱印船"航行至越南、菲律宾、台湾岛和泰国，主要从事以银换丝绸、糖以及陶瓷的贸易。

荷兰人对日本的经营也不落人后。1609 年，荷兰东印度公司在平户开始了与日本的贸易活动，1637 年从葡萄牙手中接管了长崎附近的一个小型商馆，距离有田仅 75 千米。

不过，从 1633 年起，日本针对外国人和当地国际商人的优惠政策发生了变化。掌权的德川幕府多次发布锁国令，开启了一段闭关锁国时期，类似于明朝时期的中

---

[1] Jörg 1982.
[2] Ptak 2007, p.286.

国。只有一个港口对外国开放，即位于长崎湾的人工岛出岛（图2.10），荷兰东印度公司成为唯一获准与日本交易的欧洲贸易商。直到19世纪中期，日本都禁止外国人进入日本或与日本人进行接触。荷兰东印度公司员工不得不在出岛上与日本开展了200多年的贸易，却不被允许踏上日本本土半步。

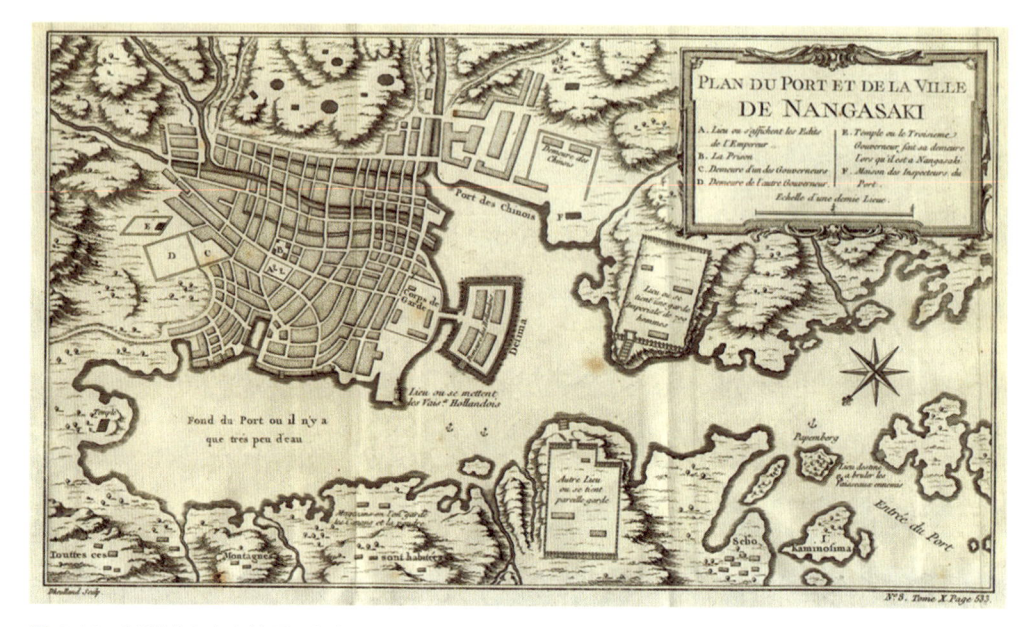

图2.10 长崎港和出岛地图，铜版画，贝林绘，1764年

17世纪50年代，中国瓷器出口因为内乱而停滞期间，荷兰人将目光转向了日本。1659年，荷兰人首批订购的3.5万件日本有田烧被投放奥斯曼帝国穆哈市场。[①] 1660年，日本瓷器首次进入欧洲。直到18世纪中期，荷兰人推动了有田烧的对欧出口，并与中国帆船商共同促进了亚洲内部的有田烧贸易。[②]

有田烧青花瓷（日本陶瓷界称为"染付"，见收藏138）在很大程度上受到中国景德镇瓷器的影响。荷兰商人明确要求日本生产中国克拉克风格的瓷器（图2.11），他们将中国克拉克瓷或者荷兰代

图2.11 带有荷兰东印度公司徽章的日本克拉克风格瓷盘

---

① Volker 1954, p.130.

② Shono 1973, p.11f.

尔夫特白锡釉陶提供给日本陶瓷作坊作为参考进行复制。

荷日瓷器贸易开始并不顺利。T. 沃尔克认为，从1660到1683年中国市场重新对外开放，共有19万件日本陶瓷被运往欧洲。但是考虑到日本在这20多年间实际上垄断了亚洲陶瓷市场，这个数量便不值一提。荷兰客户似乎对其代尔夫特陶瓷感到满意，即使这些陶瓷并非硬质的半透明陶瓷，而是柔软、粗糙和易碎的白色陶器。由于代尔夫特锡釉陶是对中国明清瓷器的仿制，因此我们实际上可将一些日本青花瓷称为中国产瓷器的二代衍生品。

有田烧的第二种样式风格即柿右卫门样式也广受欢迎，并出口到欧洲（收藏144）。柿右卫门意指使用彩釉（橙色、红色、绿色和其他色彩）装饰的简约风格，通常为不对称设计，没有边框。

伊万里烧同样受到荷兰人的青睐。伊万里烧是日本瓷器工匠于17世纪发明的一种釉下蓝彩陶瓷，饰以釉上红彩或金彩（图2.12）。伊万里这个名字来自伊万里镇，一个靠近有田窑的港口城市。

这种产品大获成功，甚至中国康熙年间的瓷器工坊也开始对其进行仿制（图2.13）。荷兰和德国，尤其是英国生产商也仿制伊万里烧。他们有时候仿制日本伊万里烧，有时仿制中国伊万里瓷器。因此很难确定现存的欧洲伊万里瓷器是日本伊万里烧初代，还是其第二代衍生品。

随着中国于1683年重新开始出口瓷器，以及18世纪欧洲瓷器和白釉陶器的出现，日本外销到欧洲的瓷器数量越来越少。

1854年，美国海军司令佩里率领军队强行闯入东京湾，在横滨与日本谈判达成一项条约，闭关锁国政策就此终结。

与中国、越南和泰国相比，日本涉足陶瓷外销市场的时间很晚。不过，在1873

图2.12　日本江户时期伊万里瓷盘（1700—1730年）　　图2.13　清乾隆中国伊万里瓷盘（约1750年）

到1940年间，日本成为亚洲最有影响力的陶瓷出口国。

英国人

大英帝国是历史上最大的帝国，不仅在印度，也在马来群岛和中国等亚洲其他地区留下了足迹。然而，第一批英国船只在16世纪才开启印度洋和太平洋海上航线，因此我们不应过高估计英国在这一时期对亚洲的作用和影响。

"伦敦商人在东印度的贸易公司"，简称英国东印度公司，是世界上最古老的东印度公司（图2.14），1600年获得英国女王伊丽莎白一世的许可状，早于之前提到的荷兰东印度公司（1602年成立）、法国东印度公司（1664年成立）、瑞典东印度公司（1731年成立）等。皇家许可状授予了英国东印度公司与亚洲（包括印度、东南亚和东亚）开展英格兰及后来大不列颠贸易的独家经营权。但是这种垄断一直备受争议，直至1698年另一家可与其竞争的东亚公司"英国东印度贸易公司"成立。

图2.14 英国东印度公司徽章

然而，英国东印度公司在亚洲的活动开局并不顺利。17世纪，它不得不与强大的荷兰东印度公司在经济和军事方面展开激烈竞争。1652至1674年间三次英荷战争，均以荷兰的胜利告终。因此，英国东印度公司很难将香料从马来群岛运到欧洲客户手中，而且在东南亚贸易中也一直屈居第三，名列中国帆船贸易商和荷兰东印度公司之后。

与葡萄牙和荷兰一样，英国东印度公司也在大泥、大城府、万丹、安汶、望加锡和平户建立了小型商馆和防御工事，但未能控制或垄断任何欧亚贸易商品。英荷战争后，英国东印度公司和葡萄牙人一样，不得不撤出东亚地区。英国在爪哇岛上最重要的香料据点万丹商馆，1682年被荷兰人占领。英国人花了一个多世纪的时间才在东印度群岛建立起据点：1786年英国正式占领槟城岛后，主要在马来半岛建立了据点；1819年占领新加坡后建立据点。

不过，英国东印度公司并非一家纯粹的贸易垄断公司。1757年在普拉西战役中，英国东印度公司的军队打败了印度孟加拉邦的地方统治者，占领了孟加拉邦全境。

自此不断扩张，将整个印度纳入大英帝国版图。印度东印度公司是广袤的英国亚洲殖民地的最高统治者，在这些区域拥有庞大的军事力量和征税权。尤其印度出产的棉花，对英国东印度公司来说具有重要的经济意义，在与中国开展茶叶、丝绸和陶瓷贸易中发挥着重要的作用。

出于多种原因，英国东印度公司是东印度公司与中国建立直接贸易关系的成功典范，这与本书的主题"瓷器贸易"息息相关。继葡萄牙在澳门建立殖民地后，英国成为第二个在中国大陆与中国开展直接贸易的欧洲国家。英国成为中国商品出口欧洲最重要的运输国，成功超越了荷兰东印度公司以及其他所有欧洲国家的总和。有关英国东印度公司的文献著述很多，印度历史学家和经济学家乔杜里[①]的著作尤其值得研读。然而，关于英国东印度公司瓷器贸易的相关数量和特点等详细信息却鲜有记载。

1672年，英国东印度公司在台湾建立了商馆。1678年，英国东印度公司在厦门建立了一个小型商馆[②]，可以用白银购买丝绸、茶叶和瓷器。之后，它在浙江宁波对面的舟山岛也建立了一个商馆。

1683年清朝收复台湾后，一度开放海禁，设立广州、宁波、泉州、松江四大海关进行中欧贸易，不过后来政策日渐收紧，以至于只有广州保持开放。仅在1699年，英国东印度公司进口瓷器就达到了约120万件，价值超过了15 000英镑，合4.5万两白银（一两白银为37.5克）[③]，相当于近1.7吨白银。从1699年开始至1791年的近百年时间里，英国东印度公司在广州购买的年均瓷器价值为6 000英镑。这意味着东印度公司每年进口50万件，合计进口4 500万件瓷器，并将其运往伦敦。

1791年英国东印度公司正式结束瓷器进口贸易。此后，英国私营贸易商——大多为英国东印度公司商船上的船员——继续从广州进口中国瓷器。但是，直到1810年的20年间，总进口金额降至大约每年1 500英镑。[④]

1793年，当英国第一个外交使团，即著名的马戛尔尼使团觐见中国乾隆皇帝时，欧亚瓷器贸易几乎已经终结。该使团的使命是为中英茶叶贸易打开新的贸易港口。正如140年前的荷兰使团觐见顺治皇帝一样，这次出使也同样遭遇失败的窘境。这次使团出使是一个跨文化误解的案例。马戛尔尼使团的使者拒绝在觐见中国帝王

---

① Chaudhuri 1978.

② Pitcher 1893, p.30.

③ Chaudhuri 1978, p.519.

④ Madsen 2011, p.42.

时三跪九叩，而乾隆皇帝也不愿意接见一个代表外国国王的外交使团，只是把这次访问理解为一次朝贡觐见。这次出使的结果后来常常被当作清朝故步自封、孤芳自赏的例证，因为半个世纪后中国就面临丧权辱国、备受欺凌的局面。然而，这也被视为一个具有象征意义的事件——当欧洲不尊重中国的历史和文化成就时，在中国会面临何种境地。

1793年的使团来访也标志着西方优越感的开始——200多年后的今天，欧洲仍须努力克服这种优越感。随着瓷器贸易的结束，平等的跨文化交流也不复存在。在21世纪的今天，我们深切缅怀那个时代。那时，欧洲被中国深深吸引甚至被打动，模仿中国的习惯和产品，有时甚至在脑海中描述一个中国风的理想国。

一口通商出口热潮

中欧之间的间接贸易在上述中国以外的转口港开展。18世纪，中国与欧洲的直接贸易大半集中在广州。尤其是在1757年乾隆皇帝关闭广州以外的三大海关，直到1842年第一次鸦片战争结束前，广州成为唯一对欧洲商人开放的口岸。从中国运往欧洲的瓷器大部分从广州发出。这就是"一口通商"体系。

"一口通商"是规范中国和西方世界对外贸易的体系。外国人只能在每年交易季，通过广州的垄断代理机构"十三行"开展贸易，不得与"十三行"以外的中国人接触。在交易季以外，外国公司的员工不得不南下澳门。此举主要旨在满足清廷的愿望并消除其担忧——实施文化保护，孤立外国在华利益，确保税收和关税。"公行"的存在是"一口通商"的核心特征。"公行"是由特许行商组成的垄断行会，代表中国政府与外国公司进行官方贸易，并收取所有税费。

与中国其他港口城市相比，广州（图2.15）具备很多优势，因此能够和西方东印度公司开展垄断贸易。首先，就地理位置而言，广州位于南海北部，中国大陆部分的最南端，来自印度洋的船只容易抵达。广州毗邻中国的茶叶产区，通过水路运输也相对容易抵达江西省景德镇。其次，因为广州位于珠江内河而非公海，这有助于控制外国船只航行。只有当江水涨潮，较大型船只才可航行。而且珠江三角洲支流、沙洲和小岛星罗棋布，中国船长可利用地形优势，控制进出船只。[①] 再次，广州毗邻澳门半岛，有利于找到翻译人员、经验丰富的中国商人，也更容易解决港口

---

① Van Dyke 2007, p.35.

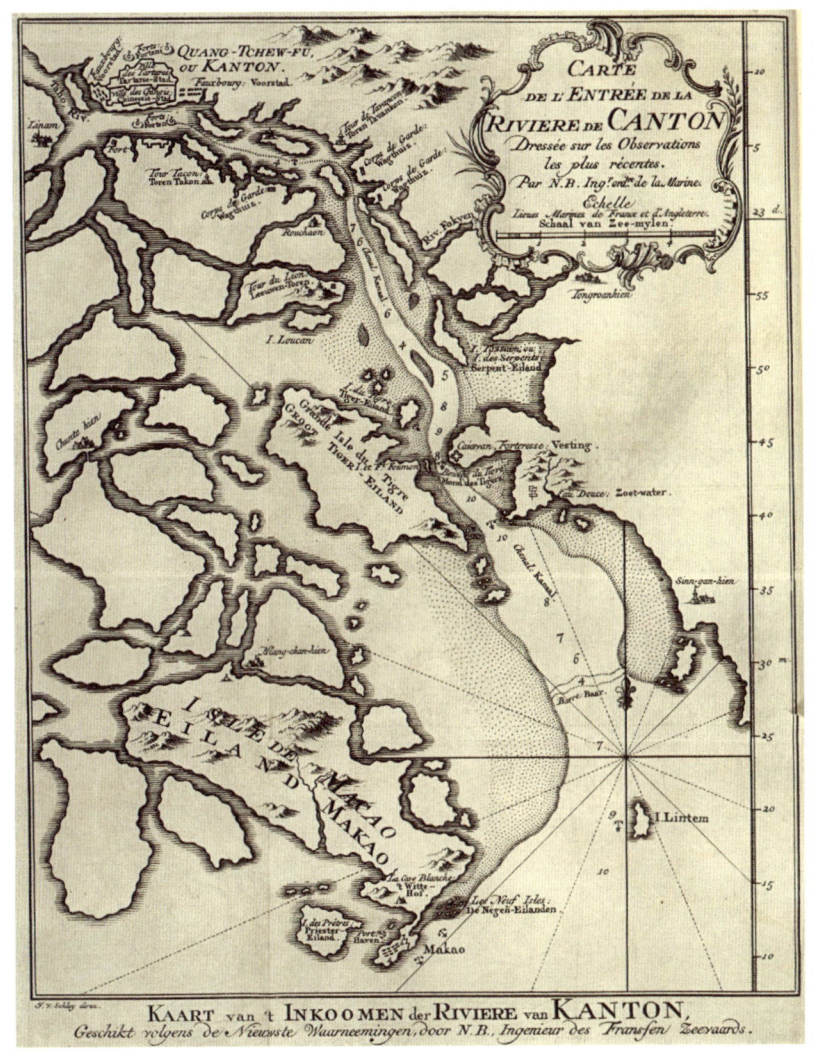

图 2.15　广州、澳门和珠江口地图，铜版画，贝林绘

税费等问题。

在中国船长的带领下，东印度公司商人沿着珠江逆流而上，抵达城市东部仅数千米之外的黄埔（琶洲）装卸货物。东印度公司的进出口业务掌握在所谓的"大班"（即船长）手中。他们代表中国政府和行商开展公司业务。

十三行区位于城墙外的西南河岸。外国公司可在此租用房舍，但不能进入城市。这些建筑与珠江至十三行中间的两条（后来是三条）街道构成的区域，在某种程度上与长崎附近人工岛出岛如出一辙。如今，人们可将十三行区视为自由贸易区或自由港。许多图片（图 2.16）展现了当时商馆的情景，门前的旗杆显示外籍员工

图 2.16　佚名画家绘制的广州十三行，19 世纪

是否在十三行区。

在 18 世纪的中欧直接贸易中，英国无疑占据最重要的地位。1698 年，"英国东印度贸易公司"成立，成为英国东印度公司的竞争对手。该公司旗下的"麦克斯菲尔德号"于 1699 年抵达广州。这是第一艘获得清廷批准、从事中英官方直接贸易的船只。1708 年，两家英国东印度公司合并成为"英国商人东印度联合公司"，1715 年在广州租用了其中一处永久性商馆。

广州不仅吸引了英国东印度公司，而且吸引了其他所有的欧洲东印度公司：1699 年，法国东印度公司在广州建立了商馆；1732 年，瑞典东印度公司建立了商馆；1734 年，丹麦亚洲公司建立了商馆。此外，奥斯坦德公司、普鲁士王国亚洲公司以及西班牙皇家菲律宾公司等小型公司也在广州租用了商馆。

法国这个欧陆强国从未在中欧贸易中扮演重要角色。1664 年，法国便成立了法国东印度公司，拥有从好望角到麦哲伦海峡之间的贸易特权，其首任主席是路易十四时期的财政部部长。1699 年，第一艘法国船只"安菲特里忒号"到达广州。然而，法国和其他国家之间旷日持久的战争，阻碍了它海上贸易的进一步发展。当时法国在印度东海岸的本地治里附近拥有大量殖民地。但为了避免其他国家对法国东印度公司的船只采取敌对行动，法国不得不在数年中多次中断贸易。法国东印度公司的总部位于洛里昂港（地图4.1），但公司通常在法国南特拍卖中国或印度商品。1719年起改称法国印度公司。1722至1723年间，法国船只的瓷器运输量较大，一共拍卖了68.3万余件商品。① 其他主要的货物运输分别发生在17世纪30年代、60年代和70年代。② 该公司于1790年清算停业。

瑞典东印度公司（图2.17）从某种意义上说，是欧亚贸易中的一个特例。1731年瑞典政府授予该公司皇家特许权，享有好望角以东所有瑞典贸易和航运垄断权，以后又4次重新授予。但瑞典不像英国、荷兰和法国东印度公司一样拥有殖民地或飞地。瑞典东印度公司在广州的英国商馆旁租借了一间商馆以开展贸易。在广州十三行的油画上，我们可以看到瑞典国旗位于英国商馆西边，位于1784年成立的美国商馆东边。

1732年3月7日，瑞典东印度公司的第一艘商船"菲特列国王号"从哥德堡启航，于9月19日抵达广州，停留至1733年1月16日，并于1733年9月7日返回

图 2.17　挂着瑞典东印度公司旗帜的帆船

① Beurdeley 1962, p.43.
② Wellington 2006, pp.131–206.

哥德堡。此次航行共计 550 天。

一直到 1806 年最后一艘商船返回哥德堡，瑞典东印度公司共进行了 132 次航行，其中 129 次从哥德堡经加的斯抵达广州，再返回瑞典。瑞典东印度公司在加的斯购买西班牙银圆——这是中国商人唯一能接受的货币。大多数航行都是直接从加的斯经好望角，穿过马达加斯加以东的印度洋，以及苏门答腊岛和爪哇岛之间的巽他海峡到达广州。只有 3 次航行直接驶往孟加拉邦，而不是中国。

这段时期总共可分为以下几个阶段：1731—1766 年派 61 艘船驶往亚洲，1766—1786 年派 39 艘船，1786—1806 年则有 32 艘船驶往亚洲。

在这 70 多年里，共有 7 艘瑞典东印度公司船只失事。最著名的事故发生于 1745 年，即哥德堡号第三次中国之旅期间。该船 1743 年 3 月 14 日驶离瑞典，1744 年夏天抵达中国海岸。1745 年 1 月 10 日从广州出发返航，9 月 12 日在距离哥德堡几千米之外的海域沉没。"哥德堡号"装载约 366 吨茶叶，100 吨瓷器（大约 30 万件）、丝绸和香料。部分货物后来被打捞出来，包括几千件瓷器和一些瓷器碎片（收藏 94）。关于航行时间和路线的详细信息，可查阅附录 C.科尼克斯的分析以及 J.F.尼斯特勒穆的著作。[①] 尽管瑞典东印度公司成立较晚，却在中欧瓷器贸易中发挥着重要作用。

丹麦亚洲公司（图 2.18）规模较小，是丹麦政府第三次尝试建立可持续赢利的贸易公司。1731 年，第一艘丹麦船只抵达澳门和广州。1732 年，丹麦亚洲公司成立，主要从事广州贸易，还在印度东海岸的特兰奎巴设立了基地。1734 年，第一艘丹麦亚洲公司船只——"石勒苏益格号"抵达广州。丹麦亚洲公司共 120 次派遣船只前往广州，大部分从哥本哈根直抵中国，有几次在印度科罗曼德海岸的商馆停留。和瑞典东印度公司一样，丹麦亚洲公司主要进口茶叶和瓷器，供国内使用或走私到英国。

图 2.18　丹麦亚洲公司位于哥本哈根的总部，彼得森（1861—1926 年）绘

[①] Nyström 1883, pp.154–161.

奥斯坦德公司的历史较为短暂，却收获了更大的经济利益。1714年，西班牙王位继承战争结束，尼德兰（今比利时和卢森堡）成为奥地利哈布斯堡王朝的领地。1715年哈布斯堡王朝成立了奥斯坦德公司，总部在比利时的安特卫普，16世纪早期葡萄牙香料贸易的主要集散地。1722年公司派遣第一艘商船，从拥有得天独厚条件的深海港奥斯坦德扬帆启航，前往广州。在公司存在短短10年间，共有21艘船被派往广州和印度。[1] 奥斯坦德公司的贸易以茶叶为主，进口到欧洲的瓷器数据不详。

由于奥斯坦德公司在经济上大获成功，英国、荷兰和法国大力施压令其关闭。为确保女儿玛丽亚·特蕾莎的王位继承权，哈布斯堡王朝统治者查理六世于1732年下令关闭奥斯坦德公司。他的女儿，未来的奥地利女大公，尽管失去了东印度公司，却成为中国和日本瓷器收藏家。她在维也纳的美泉宫有两间瓷器间，一间为椭圆形，另一间为圆形，共珍藏了252件瓷器。这足以证明女皇对瓷器收藏的热爱。[2]

总部位于埃姆登的普鲁士王国亚洲公司（1751—1757年）的瓷器进口数据同样没有详细记载。这家存续时间很短的公司仅6次派遣船只驶往广东，就因为七年战争（1756—1763年）而被迫中断业务。

西班牙通过1785年成立的皇家菲律宾公司开展业务。皇家菲律宾公司有权开展菲律宾-中国-西班牙间贸易，其航线沿着西班牙加的斯、广州并绕过非洲好望角返回西班牙。这条航线是对马尼拉大帆船航线的补充。1814年该公司解散。

美国商人也利用广州在中国和波斯之间开展贸易。1784年，"中国皇后号"帆船于纽约启航并抵达广州。

荷兰东印度公司较晚才开设商馆，因为阿姆斯特丹与巴达维亚就在广东开设商馆是否会损害巴达维亚作为中国帆船贸易转口港的地位长期争论不休。由于中国商船将中国商品运往巴达维亚，荷兰东印度公司并不急于在广州进行直接贸易。1729年，第一艘荷兰东印度公司商船"科斯霍恩号"抵达广州。此后，每年有4到5艘、总计200余艘荷兰东印度公司船只停靠广州。

广州贸易中的商品

瓷器并非广州中欧贸易中最昂贵或最炙手可热的商品。大多数船只会装载瓷器，要么是为了追求瓷器带来的利润，要么是将瓷器作为压舱物，保护茶叶和丝绸

---

[1] Picard 1966, p.150.

[2] Gawronski 2012, p.90.

等货物不受海水侵蚀。从广州开港开始,茶叶就成为最受西方公司青睐的单一中国商品,其货物价值占比也不断攀升。

各个东印度公司之间的产品构成也不相同,英国东印度公司和荷兰东印度公司的差距尤其明显。

据统计,1765 至 1769 年,茶叶占英国东印度公司进口总额的 73.5%,丝绸占 20.9%,包括瓷器在内的其他物品只占 5.4%。[1] 英国东印度公司每年进口瓷器的数量几乎不超过 50 万件,尽管其派往广州的船只数量大大超过荷兰东印度公司的船只数量。荷兰东印度公司同期比例构成大致相同,尽管其绝对进口数量较少。但从 1728 至 1793 年整体来看,瓷器对荷兰东印度公司的重要性似乎高于英国东印度公司。尤其是在 1769 到 1774 年间,荷兰瓷器贸易绝对数量达到顶峰,每年进口的瓷器价值超过 10 万弗罗林(约白银 3 万两),大致相当于 100 万件瓷器的购买价格。

另外,英国东印度公司关于瓷器的统计数据比较粗略,仅罗列箱子的数量和采购价格,而非确切的件数。相比之下,荷兰东印度公司(图 2.19)的瓷器进口统计数据非常详细。这也反映出瓷器进口对荷兰东印度公司比对英国东印度公司更为重要。

图 2.19　荷兰东印度公司船只东来,佚名,1762 年

---

[1]　Yang-Chien Tsai 2003, p.82.

荷兰东印度公司的统计数据从某种程度上讲也具有艺术历史价值。该数据不仅准确记录了瓷器数量，还详细记录了其造型、用途和纹饰。1770 年，5 艘荷兰东印度公司船只"威廉五世号""橙色王子号""博特号""年轻的赫林曼号"和"博格号"从广东进口的商品见下表 2.2[①]。

表2.2　5 艘荷兰东印度公司船只进口瓷器[②]

名称	数量
青花瓷啤酒杯	1 854
釉上彩啤酒杯	1 600
青花瓷瓶	6 070
青花瓷小碗	8 260
带祥龙图案的青花瓷小碗	2 030
中国伊万里小碗	4 305
巴达维亚棕釉小碗，内饰青花图案	3 760
巴达维亚棕釉小碗，内饰釉上彩	1 575
釉上彩小碗	4 285
白釉小碗	3 395
无茶碟半品脱[②]小茶碗	42 000
无茶碟四分之一品脱小茶碗	21 355
带茶碟小茶碗	15 848
青花圆形黄油盘，带盖和支架	997
黄油碟	18 379
青花瓷夜壶	348
带碟巧克力杯	35 959
带碟无柄咖啡杯	367 678
青花咖啡壶	195
中国伊万里咖啡壶	199
釉上彩咖啡壶	339
五件式瓷罐橱柜饰品	2 516
青花痰盂	387
小餐盘	62 364

---

① Jörg 1982, pp.226–306.
② 品脱为容积单位，半品脱约为 250 毫升。——编者注

续表

名称	数量
青花色瓷器餐具套装	215
圆盘	8 640
鱼盘	240
青花牛奶杯	420
牛奶壶	3 151
摩尔杯	53 165
潘趣酒碗	7 323
沙拉碗	1 709
椭圆形剃须碗	175
汤盘	12 851
糖碗	7 014
无柄茶杯和茶碟	219 141
茶壶	934
茶具和咖啡器具套装	821
青花盖碗	338
	总计：921 835 件

如果单将杯和碟拿出来统计，二者总数约为 160 万。如果要更加精确计算，甚至可以精确到每个瓷器套装或五件式瓷罐橱柜饰品中的单件物品。这样来看，准确估计出口瓷器件数是有难度的。

C. 科尼克斯将每个杯子和碟子单独计数，估计瑞典东印度公司 1732—1766 年间进口瓷器数量高达 3 380 万件[①]，1766—1786 年间进口瓷器数量达 1 130 万件[②]。

由于统计数据不完整，或采用的计量方式不同（采购金额、销售价格、重量、件数或套数、箱或桶等都被当作计量标准），因此试图得出精确数据只是徒劳。根据经验估计，3 000 两银子（112 千克纯银或 1 000 英镑）大约相当于 10 万件瓷器的价值。荷兰东印度公司和英国东印度船只每次大约将 20 万件运回欧洲，而瑞典东印度公司和丹麦的船只比荷兰和英国东印度公司的船只庞大，船只运载量也会更大。

东印度公司的货物清单还让我们能够有机会了解出口瓷器的不同种类、造型和纹饰。大多数出口商品是批量生产的青花餐具，但也可根据西方品位定制特殊商

---

① Koninckx 1980, p.220.

② Kjellberg 1974, pp.233–234.

品，即所谓的"中国订单瓷器"。例如，可定制带有家族徽章的彩绘图案（收藏 83–84），也可定制当时在英格兰非常流行的名字首字母图案。[①] 另一种广受青睐的定制商品是五件式瓷罐橱柜饰品——五个一套用于摆设的花瓶——以及造型和纹饰协调一致的茶具套装和餐具套装。中国少见的带柄杯，系根据欧洲人的品位和饮食习惯定制，多用于喝茶、咖啡、热巧克力以及啤酒。

风格各异的瓷器被出口到欧洲、西属菲律宾和美洲：象牙白和中国白釉瓷、釉上彩瓷器（五彩和粉彩、纹章瓷和玫瑰奖章），南京式样瓷，广东式样瓷，菲次休青花瓷，外棕釉巴达维亚瓷（图 2.20），复制日本伊万里烧的中国伊万里瓷器，以及江苏省宜兴窑生产的紫砂瓷。

图 2.20 清乾隆巴达维亚牛奶壶，施以粉彩釉

在广东外销的瓷器，99% 产自江西省景德镇。只有白色或象牙色中国白瓷（收藏 219）主要产自福建省德化和江苏省宜兴。景德镇瓷窑在烧制瓷器时只施加釉下蓝彩，但瓷器的釉上彩通常在广东完成，以便根据西方客户提供的定制图案或者客户家族徽章，对"中国订单瓷器"进行釉上彩加工。

数以百万计的陶瓷从景德镇运到广州，然后运至欧洲和美国客户手中。瓷器在中国境内的主要运输方式为船舶运输，穿越江西省和广东省多条河流。"这条路线始于鄱阳湖，沿赣江到达南昌。之后，瓷器被装上较小的内河船只，逆流而上运往赣州。货船沿着小河继续前行，最终到达江西省南部。接下来，这些瓷器只能靠人

---

① Ganse 2008, pp.140–145.

力搬运出梅岭山口。梅岭山口绵延约 30 千米，海拔约 275 米。从梅岭山出来后，瓷器被重新装上小船，在蜿蜒狭窄的北江上游航行，直至抵达广州。"①

纹绘设计影响是双向的，有时也相互渗透。中国外销瓷的造型可能以东印度公司带来的金属、玻璃和木材样品为模型，并且制瓷工匠以客户带来的图纸为样板进行纹绘设计。例如许多明代青花瓷均模仿阿拉伯黄铜器皿，该器皿装饰则可能也是模仿中国、日本、西方风格，或将上述风格融为一体。

下面介绍一下销往欧洲的中国外销瓷的主要标准图案：

> 克拉克瓷（1550—1645 年出口）：景德镇、漳州等地生产的釉下青花瓷，瓷胎薄透，内壁有开光装饰，围绕盘中心还有一圈传统装饰，常用寓意吉祥的动物和佛教吉祥物作为装饰。② 主要产于明朝万历年间（收藏 32-34）。
>
> 明末清初青花瓷（1620—1670 年出口）：明末清初，景德镇的皇家订单量减少。瓷器生产商开始根据欧洲和亚洲客户的需求定制生产青花瓷器，以寻求新的市场机遇。这期间出现了新的器型和装饰，制瓷工匠也更具创造力。在此时期末期，景德镇瓷窑受到了战争影响并被摧毁。
>
> 中国白（1620—1800 年出口）：福建德化窑生产的未加装饰的白色或象牙色瓷器，通常是小雕像和杯子（收藏 219）。
>
> 康乾时期青花瓷（1683—1760 年出口）：清代康熙、雍正、乾隆年间主要出口到荷兰的景德镇高品质釉下蓝瓷，饰以丰富多彩的形象和风景（收藏 35-51）。
>
> 五彩瓷（1685—1730 年出口）：五彩瓷是釉面颜色鲜艳的瓷器，只有康熙、雍正时期景德镇烧制的五彩才作为外销瓷销往欧洲（收藏 52-55）。③
>
> 中国伊万里瓷（1695—1760 年出口）：这种陶瓷结合釉上红彩和釉下蓝彩，通常采用镀金工艺，因此更加华丽。它模仿日本有田烧制的釉下蓝彩陶瓷，饰以釉上红彩或金彩的伊万里烧（收藏 59-66）。中国的伊万里瓷器只用于外销，没有出现在国内市场上。
>
> 巴达维亚瓷（1695—1790 年出口）：此种外销瓷外施酱釉，内壁绘青花，有些内壁带有开光纹饰。它以当时荷兰东印度公司东南亚贸易中心巴达维亚

---

① Sjostrand 2007, p.64.
② Wu Ruoming, 2014.
③ Jörg Christiaan J. A., 2011: Famille Verte: Chinese porcelain in green enamels.

命名，即今天的雅加达（收藏56-58）。①

粉彩瓷（1720—1800年出口）：景德镇出产的粉色和玫瑰色釉上彩瓷器，其所采用的不透明和半透明瓷釉技术可能是受到法国的影响，添加白色可使色度和色差产生渐变（图2.21和收藏70-82）。

纹章瓷和墨彩（1720—1820年出口）：中国根据欧洲人的需求生产的瓷器，通常带有其家族徽章，瓷器中央饰以彩绘。装饰彰显了欧洲人的品位，通常没有中国风的韵味。一般会在景德镇烧制好白胎瓷，然后运往广州进行彩绘烧制（收藏83-85）。

南京式样瓷器（1760—1820年出口）：景德镇出产的各种釉下青花瓷，带有特定的边框装饰，多为亭、寺、河、树景色（图2.22和收藏86-104）。这种装饰与英国的中国风装饰相互影响。原材料的质量略逊于康熙青花瓷。其中一部分南京式样瓷器在英国镀金（收藏98），或者在荷兰进行釉上彩绘（"加彩"，收藏67-69）。

菲次休瓷（1780—1820年出口）：景德镇出产的优质釉下青花瓷，四组花卉或植物均匀围绕盘中心的主图案分布，主要出口美国（收藏105）。

广东式样瓷器（1785—1853年出口）：景德镇出产的品质稍逊的釉下青花瓷，主要出口至美国，与南京式样瓷器类似，饰以中国河流和凉亭图案（收藏107-109）。

图2.21　清乾隆粉彩瓷盘（约1750年）　　图2.22　清乾隆南京式样青花瓷盘（1760—1780年），饰以亭子和蝴蝶纹饰

---

① 关于巴达维亚瓷器的起源和特征的研究并不多，见：Li, Baoping, 2012 and Holley, Andrew and Jean Martin: *Illustrated Catalogue of Colonel William Thomlinson's Collection of Chinese 18th Century Export Porcelain. 'Batavian' Style and other Brown Glazed Wares,* Hartlepool。

广彩：玫瑰奖章样式和大奖章样式（1860—1911年出口）：广州织金彩瓷（简称"广彩"），指广州烧制的织金及其采用的低温釉上彩装饰技法，色彩炫彩华丽。其中，玫瑰奖章样式的特点为四个面板图案交替围绕盘心奖章圆圈，主要出口美国；[1] 大奖章样式主要描绘中国人（中国风）的日常生活场景（收藏110-113）。

---

[1] 关于中国向美国出口瓷器的最详细研究是：Schiffer, Herbert, Schiffer, Peter and Schiffer, Nancy: Chinese Export Porcelain。

Chapter 2

The Beginning of a Globalized World: European-Asian Trade Relations

The Portuguese

Europe came into contact with Chinese porcelain rather late in the 16th century. Porcelain was never transported long distances overland due to its weight and fragility. Therefore, the trade could only take place after the discovery of the Atlantic part of the Maritime Silk Road between Europe and Asia.

Before the discovery of the seaways from Europe to Asia, the Asian-European trade used either the land-based traditional Silk Road or the combined "half maritime-half land" routes (see map 0.1). Muslim traders dominated the Silk Road and the Indian Ocean-based maritime routes. In the West, the Mediterranean republics Venice and Genova had a monopoly on the European part of the Eurasian trade. Merchants from these Italian cities distributed the Asian commodities in Europe and became incredibly rich.

With the rise of the Ottoman Empire and the fall of Constantinople in 1453, this trade and the profit margins declined sharply. The Ottoman Empire became a dominant naval power, blocked access to the Black Sea, and controlled much of the Mediterranean Sea including the crucial trading harbors for silk and spices. These shifts in power and the improvements in shipbuilding, navigation and cartography led to the "Age of Discovery". The Portuguese sent out expedition after expedition to find out alternatives to the land routes, which had linked East Asia, India, the

Pic. 2.1: Vasco da Gama, Explorer and Viceroy of Portuguese India (c. 1469–1524).

Arab world, and the Mediterranean Sea for centuries.

It was only in 1498 that the first European, Vasco da Gama (pic. 2.1), reached Calicut in India on a seaway and it still took another 25 years before a mission led by the Portuguese Ferdinand Magellan and the Spaniard Juan Sebastian Elcano completed the first circumnavigation of the earth, passing by South America, the Philippines and Indonesia.

However, it was not porcelain that attracted Europeans most, but spices. "*Im Anfang war das Gewürz*" (*In the beginning was the spice*), was how the Austrian novelist Stefan Zweig began his biography on Magellan. Spices were very much in demand in Europe and people were willing to pay very high prices, giving traders good margins: Pepper from the Indian western Malabar Coast and Sumatra, and more exotic spices such as nutmeg and cloves from the Indonesian Spice Islands or the Moluccas between the Philippines and Australia.

In the 350 years following the discovery of the seaways to Asia, we saw a battle between various European powers to get their share in the lucrative trade of Asian products. Portugal, the Netherlands and Great Britain were the main actors to build and complete the western part of the Maritime Silk Road. Besides, Spain, France, Sweden, Denmark and some others have played a role as well.

However, all these seafaring countries did not enter an untouched market. As described above, a vibrant trade stretching from the Arabian Sea along the coast of Persia, India, and Ceylon towards the Southeast Asian coasts and the South China Sea had been established and working for centuries. Arab dhows, Thai and Chinese junks, Muslim traders from Gujarat, Armenian and Persian merchants, and ships of the Buddhist kingdom of Srivijaya facilitated the exchange of Indian cotton and pepper, Persian silk, Chinese gold, silk and ceramics, Indonesian spices, Japanese silver, and lacquer ware long before any European ship appeared. A complex system of trading and foreign relations had been in place for centuries.

China had a crucial role in the eastern part of the Maritime Silk Road but was not an easy trading partner for its neighbors. Countries with a craving for trade with China had to send tribute missions to the Chinese Emperor, to acknowledge the cultural superiority of the "Middle Kingdom". From the 11th to the 14th century, the South China Sea saw an intensity of maritime traffic as in the Baltic or the Mediterranean Sea in Europe. Quanzhou, beside the Taiwan Strait and at the northeast corner of the South China Sea, was the most relevant port during that time. During the Ming dynasty, countries such as Dai Viet (northern Vietnam), Champa (southern Vietnam), Korea, Japan, the Sultanate of Malacca, Java, Sukhothai, Ceylon, and even Indian provinces accepted the tributary relationship. Official tributary trade was the predominant form of commodity exchange since private trading was banned. However, being a tributary state of China did not imply a colonial status, it established an economic relationship based on mutual benefit.

Malacca was one of the most important entrepots and trading hubs in the 15th century before the Portuguese arrived. Traders from all parts of Asia built their warehouses in Malacca — a city taking advantage of its strategic geographic location and the cosmopolitan attitude of the Malacca Sultanate. The Malacca strait linking the South China Sea with the Indian Ocean is still today one of the most important shipping routes in the world. The main maritime Eurasian Silk Road of today still includes the Strait of Malacca (but with Singapore instead of Malacca as the main entrepot), the Strait of Hormuz, and the Suez Canal.

Colonialization followed the Big Discovery. Soon after having established the first trading posts (so-called *factories*) and fortifications in India, the Portuguese headed further southeast in order to gain control of Malacca and to get access to the trading routes for spices. A Portuguese fleet under the command of Alfonso de Albuquerque conquered Malacca in 1511 and established various new entrepots on the way between Africa and East Asia to facilitate Asian-European trade. Goa on the Indian west coast became the capital of the Portuguese *Estado da India*. Jorge Alvares was then the first European who reached China by sea in 1513, and the first contact with Japan took place in 1543.

The Portuguese *Estado* created entrepots along the trading route from Lisbon to India via the African and Arab coasts, from Malacca to the Spice Islands, and from Macao to Nagasaki. The commercial network (map 2.1) brought Portugal great wealth during the 16th century. However, even though they forced (by executing military force) their way into the existing Asian trading system, Portugal was not able to alter the commercial rules. Spices, textiles, porcelain, and other commodities highly in demand in Europe had to be paid for. And since Portugal did not have much to barter,

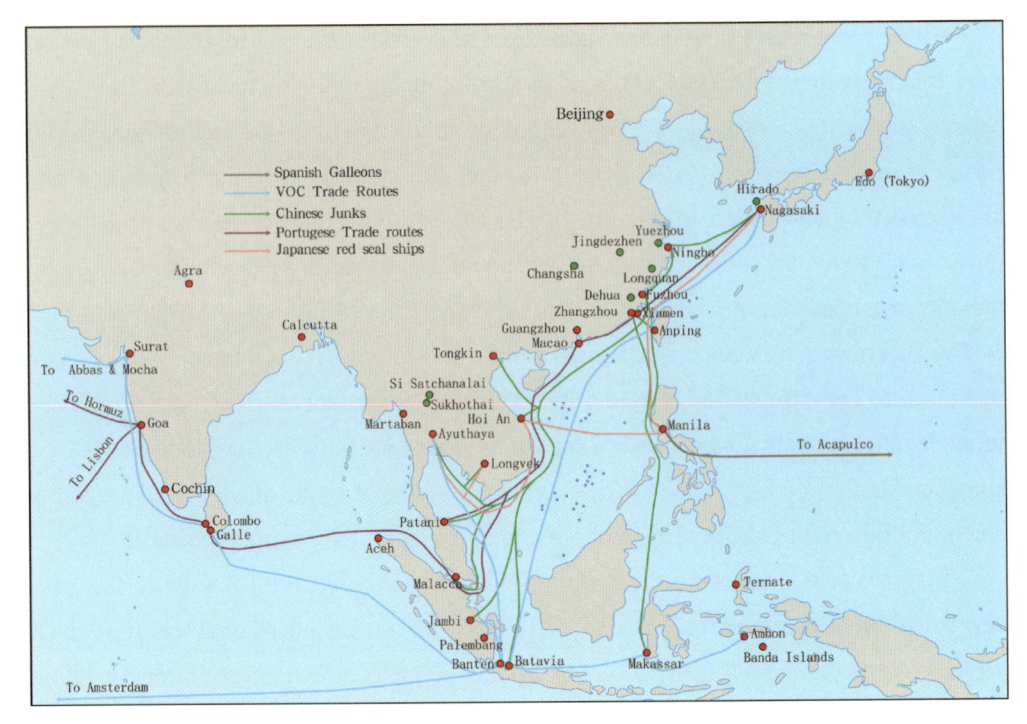

Map 2.1: Major porcelain trading routes (1550–1685).

the commodities had to be paid for in silver.

Portugal's power was offshore. Highly armed ships, bigger and faster than any Asian competitor, and the control of various important entrepots such as Muscat, Hormuz, and some Indian ports in northern Gujarat and at the southern Malabar Coast, gave them many advantages on the sea routes. They not only shipped commodities from one port to the other, but they were also able to tax other ships with the so-called "*cartaz*" fee. The *cartaz* had to be bought by every merchant ship in the region as a license to trade and transport, and it granted the buyer Portuguese protection against pirates and other states. Goa, Diu, Hormuz, and Malacca were the most important customs offices to charge the *cartaz* fee.[①]

Onshore, however, the influence of the *Estado da India* on Mughal India, Ming China, or the Japanese Tokugawa Shogunate was negligible. These land-based or inland-oriented empires did not really take notice of what happened in their narrow coastal strips or — like China and Japan — opened only a very tiny window for some very restricted trading activities: The Chinese Emperor gave permission in 1557 to the Portuguese to lease the Macao peninsula in the Pearl River Delta for an annual tribute.

---

① Feldbauer 2005, p.129.

The same year in Japan the *Estado* was allowed to open a small trading post in Hirado, near Nagasaki. Over more than a century, Macao was the only official port opened to Europe until Guangzhou was allowed for Sino-Europe maritime trade in 1699.

The import of Chinese porcelain by Portuguese ships started around 1550. Since direct trade was not possible until the establishment of a trading post in Macao was endorsed, Portuguese traders may have purchased the first pieces of porcelain in one of the intra-Asian entrepots: in Malacca or Patani on the Malayan Peninsula, in the Thai capital Ayutthaya[①] or on Sumatra, Java or Sulawesi — places where Chinese junks stopped to barter silk, copper, gold, and ceramics for spices, tin, and silver.

In 1567 the Ming ban officially ended, and one can see the expansion of the ceramic trade. Portuguese traders were now able to buy porcelain both officially in Macao, at the Canton fair, and from Chinese junks at any entrepot in the South China Sea. The British and Dutch called the blue and white porcelain from Jingdezhen "*Kraak*", since it had first been shipped to Europe by Portuguese carracks (pic. 2.2).[②]

Pic. 2.2: Late Ming dynasty (Wanli period) Chinese *Kraak* plate with bird and rock decoration — Chinese export porcelain to the Netherlands.

And it was the sea route between Macao and Nagasaki, that produced the highest profit for the Portuguese traders. Even after the ban was removed in 1567, the Ming dynasty still forbade private maritime trade with Japan. Portuguese ships were, therefore, able to substitute Chinese junks in shipping Chinese silk and porcelain to Japan in exchange for Japanese silver, which was highly in demand in China, and which gave Portugal additional means to purchase spices or textiles in Indonesia and India. The *silk for silver* trade was one of the most lucrative arbitrage trades until the 17th century.

However, porcelain was a minor commodity and served also as necessary ship ballast and a supplement to the other more relevant and precious trading goods heading to Lisbon such as pepper, other spices and plants, silk and cotton. It did not play a crucial role in trade with Europe until 1600. Cargo lists from the 16th century give evidence: in the years 1587–1588 around 68% of the cargo weight was pepper, 3.7%

---

① Garnier 2004, pp.66–75.
② Mostert 2015, p.38.

ginger, 6.3% cinnamon, 10.5% cotton and silk, 8.4% indigo dye, and 1.5% others including porcelain.[①]

The *Wanli,* discovered by Sten Sjostrand in 2004 off the east coast of Malaysia, was probably a ship under the Portuguese flag sent to the ground in a battle with the Dutch around 1625. It had a porcelain cargo of approximately 37,000 blue and white porcelains from Jingdezhen[②] and it was on a voyage from Macao to Malacca. The cargo gives a good overview of the early Eurasian trade with Ming porcelain (plate 33). Two items are examples of an early *chine de commande* — ordered by its European customers with underglaze images of the coat of arms of the families who ordered them.

Between 1580 and 1640 Portugal and Spain were unified under the Spanish monarchs forming a huge empire including the Iberian Peninsula, the Low Countries, and other Spanish Habsburg territories in Europe, the Viceroyalties of the Americas, and all the Portuguese and Spanish possessions and factories in Africa and Asia. Spain, so far banned from the Indian Ocean by the treaties of Tordesillas and Zaragoza, earlier arrangements with the Portuguese, had organized Asian-European trade via the Philippines and Mexico.

After the Spanish conquest of the Aztec Empire in Mexico, the new Viceroyalty of New Spain served as a basis for further Spanish expansion toward Asia across the Pacific. Magellan had reached the Philippines in 1521 during his circumnavigation of the earth but it still took several decades until a colonial rule was established — the first European colonization in Asia. Manila became the capital of the Spanish East Indies in 1571 and the archipelago was named after Philip II of Spain. The colony was administered through the Viceroyalty of New Spain in Mexico. Miguel López de Legazpi (1502–1572) was the first Governor-General of the Spanish East Indies including Guam and the Mariana Islands which were important resting points for the Spanish galleons sailing between the Philippines and Mexico.

The Manila galleon route was established in 1565 and lasted until 1815. "The galleons, which sailed the oceans between Manila and Acapulco for about 250 years, brought porcelain, spices, silk, ivory, jade and other luxuries from China to Mexico in exchange for New World silver."[③] Spain did not have much to offer to China in exchange for the Asian products in demand, except silver from the Americas. Hundreds of Chinese junks sailed every year (during the season December to April each year)

---

① Feldbauer 2005, p.144.
② Sjostrand 2007, pp.44–45.
③ Ganse 2008, p.37.

between the Chinese coasts and Manila, which became an important entrepot for Chinese-European trade via Mexico.①

The *San Diego* — a Spanish galleon sunk in 1600 in a battle with two Dutch ships near Manila Bay — was discovered in 1991 by the maritime archaeologist Franck Goddio. The Dutch independence war against Habsburg Spain took place not only in Europe but even far away from home in Asian waters. Goddio has excavated from the seabed Chinese blue and white *Kraak* porcelain from Jingdezhen and blue and white *Swatow* porcelain from Zhangzhou as examples of the intensive trade relations between China and the Spanish Philippines and Spanish Mexico. In 2016, thousands of Ming dynasty porcelain shards were found in Mexico a meter and a half underground nearby Acapulco's Cathedral.

The Dutch East India Company

For almost one hundred years the ships of the *Estado da India* had a monopoly in the maritime long-distance trade between Europe and Asia, only challenged by the Spanish galleons sailing from Manila to Acapulco and from Veracruz towards Cadiz or Sevilla. However, the formation of the Iberian Union by Spain and Portugal in 1580 created a critical competitor for Portugal that was able to destroy almost all its possessions in Asia—the Netherlands.

The Low Countries came under Habsburg rule in 1482 and became part of the Spanish Empire in 1556. The Dutch Eighty Years' War for independence from Spain starting in 1568 turned also into a Dutch-Portuguese war after the integration of Spain and Portugal.

The first Dutch ships reached the Indonesian Island of Java in 1596. In 1598, they dispatched the second Dutch expedition to the Indonesian Archipelago, under the command of Jacob Corneliszoon van Neck, and with the polar explorer Jacob van Heemskerk and the discoverer of Australia Willem Janszoon. This expedition had been extraordinarily profitable. This led to the creation of the Dutch East India Company (*Vereenigde Oost-Indische Compagnie*, VOC), established as the first joint stock company in 1602. The religious and political conflicts of Europe were exported to Asia then.

Between 1602 and 1796 the VOC sent almost a million Europeans to work in the Asia trade on 4,785 ships, and netted for their efforts more than 2.5 million tons of Asian trade

---

① Goddio 1996, p.100.

Pic. 2.3: Flag of the Dutch East India company VOC.

Pic. 2.4: Jan Pieterszoon Coen (1587–1629), Governor-General of the Dutch East Indies.

goods, making them the most important trader and carrier between Asia and Europe. The VOC (pic. 2.3) was probably the first truly multinational company with shareholders from various countries and workers from Europe to East Asia. The headquarters, the *Oost Indisch Huis* built in 1606 was in Amsterdam and still exists today, belonging now to the University of Amsterdam.

The VOC maintained trading posts in Africa, the Middle East, South Asia, mainland Southeast Asia, maritime Southeast Asia, and the Far East. The VOC established its first Asian headquarters on Ambon Island in Indonesia in 1610 where it tried to start the production of cloves originally from Ternate in the Moluccas. They moved their headquarters in 1619 to Batavia, today's Jakarta, founded by Jan Pieterszoon Coen (pic. 2.4) — the 4th Governor-General of the Dutch East Indies. The Banda Islands, home of nutmeg cultivation, became the first colonial possession of the Dutch in Asia, giving them a monopoly over nutmeg production and trade. The massacre of the indigenous population of the Islands is one of the darkest sides of the Dutch rule in the Archipelago. In 1621, almost all the 15,000 inhabitants of the Islands were killed and the surviving Bandanese were sent as slaves to Batavia.

The encounters between the Dutch and the Portuguese in the early 17th century in Macao ended fatally for the protestant sailors. In response, Spanish and Portuguese ships were attacked by Dutch warships, and sunk or taken as a prize. The Portuguese carrack *Santa Catarina* fully laden with silk, musk and porcelain, was captured near the shores of present-day Singapore, and the cargo was sold in Amsterdam — this was the first big auction of Chinese porcelain in northern Europe.

Like the Portuguese in India and China, the Dutch also were not strong enough in the beginning to alter the established trade rules in Asia, and they had to find arrangements with the various Muslim Sultanates on Java, Sumatra and Sulawesi, and on the Indian east and west coast. In addition, they had to share the trading posts along the spice, textile and porcelain routes with other traders from China, India, Persia, the Ottoman Empire, Siam, Portugal and England. Surat in India, Jambi on Sumatra, Banten on Java, Patani at the Malayan Peninsula, and Makassar on Sulawesi are fascinating examples of cosmopolitan entrepots for all kinds of Asian luxury goods where mainly Muslim rulers have created an open attitude and atmosphere.

It took approximately 60 years until the Dutch had pushed out the Portuguese competition from most of the Asian trading entrepots (see table 2.1). At the end of the Dutch-Portuguese war, Portugal lost Ambon, Malacca, Ceylon and Cochin on the Indian Malabar coast to the forces of the VOC. Makassar — the entrepot for gold,

Table 2.1: The Porcelain Trading Routes of the Maritime Silk Road Including Ports of Origin, Entrepots and Destinations from 1550 to 1842

Export Harbors	Entrepots	Import Harbors
China:	China:	Southeast Asia:
– Zhangzhou	– Pescadores Islands	– Banten
– Guangzhou (Canton)	– Anping, Taiwan	– Jakarta (Batavia)
– Macao	Malay Archipelago:	– Makassar
– Xiamen (Amoy)	– Banten (Bantam)	– Ayutthaya
– Zhoushan (Chusan)	– Jambi	– Tonkin, Vietnam
– Fuzhou	– Palembang	– Longvek, Cambodia
– Ningbo	– Jakarta (Batavia)	– Manila
Japan:	– Makassar	Europe:
– Imari	– Manila	– Lisbon
– Hirado	Mainland Southeast Asia:	– Amsterdam and Middelburg
– Nagasaki (Dejima)	– Ayutthaya, Thailand	– London
Vietnam:	– Patani, Thailand	– Lorient
– Tongkin	– Malacca, Malaysia	– Gothenburg
– Hoi An	– Martaban, Myanmar	– Copenhagen
	India:	– Ostend
	– Goa	Americas:
	– Surat	– Acapulco
	– Calcutta	– Salem and Boston, Massachusetts
	– Cochin	Persia:
	Persia:	– Bandar Abbas
	– Hormuz	Ottoman Empire:
	– Bandar Abbas	– Mocha
	Sri Lanka	– Basra
		Africa:
		– Cape Town

diamonds, ivory, sandalwood, pearls and spices had been captured in 1669 by the Dutch. Banten, the center of pepper trade with a strong Chinese trading community and with Dutch, English, Portuguese and Danish trading posts, provided exclusive trading rights to the Dutch in 1682. By then, Batavia, the capital of the Dutch East Indies, became the top intra-Asian entrepot and the point of origin for the cargo of the VOC fleet to Europe via Sri Lanka, India and Cape Town, to Amsterdam.

The VOC realized profits not only from the long-distance trade between Asia and Europe but also from intra-Asian trade and the arbitrage between product prices in different regions of Asia. In this sense, the Dutch East Asia Company copied an economic pattern the Portuguese had already started — but they improved it and brought it to a scale never seen before. Jan Pieterszoon Coen has described this in a letter to the VOC board:

> *"Piece goods [means cotton] from Gujarat we can barter for pepper and gold on the coast of Sumatra. [...] Sandalwood, pepper, and rials we can barter for Chinese goods and Chinese gold; we can extract silver from Japan with Chinese goods; piece goods from Coromandel coast in exchange for spices, other goods, and gold from China; piece goods from Surat for spices; other goods and rials from Arabia for spices and various other trifles - one thing leads to another. And all of it can be done without any money from the Netherlands and with ships alone. [...] We have the most important spices already. [...] Hence gentlemen and good administrators, there is nothing to prevent the Company from acquiring the richest trade in the world."*[1]

Nevertheless, the VOC had difficulties accessing the Chinese market directly. They finally had to rely on Chinese middlemen in the above-mentioned entrepots. During the first two decades of the 17th century, Chinese silk and porcelain were acquired in Banten and Patani where Chinese migrant communities established the junk trade for spices and other goods from India and Southeast Asia. The first VOC import of Chinese porcelain took place in 1604.

In 1622, the VOC settled near the Chinese coast on the Pescadores Islands (Penghu) in the Taiwan Strait and moved two years later to Taiwan where they build Fort Zeelandia (pic. 2.5). The Dutch ruled the southern part of Taiwan for 38 years and took

---

[1] Frank 1998, pp.281–282.

Pic. 2.5: The Dutch Fort Zeelandia on Taiwan, copper engraving by Joan Blaeu.

advantage of the short distance to mainland China (Fuzhou and Xiamen) enabling a vibrant junk trade or sailing directly to Zhangzhou (called "River of Chincheuw" in the original documents of the VOC).

The possession of Taiwan was one of the most profitable for the VOC in Asia. From there the VOC organized the silver-silk trade with Japan when Japan closed its ports to Portuguese vessels. Most of the Chinese porcelain imports of the VOC were handled through Zeelandia and then sent via Batavia towards Amsterdam. Alternatively, Asian markets were addressed: Porcelain next to other commodities was shipped to VOC trading posts in Persia (Bandar Abbas), to Surat in India, to the Ottoman Mocha on the Arab peninsula, to Ayutthaya (capital of Siam), to Tongkin or Hoi An (Quinam) in Vietnam and to Longvek—the capital of the Khmer (see map 2.1). In the first 50 years, until the 1650s when the export of Chinese porcelain came to a standstill, the VOC shipped more than three million pieces to Europe.

The daily reports (Dagh-Registers) of the VOC officers give us a detailed overview of the trading activities between the various VOC factories in Batavia, Taiwan, Hirado (near Nagasaki), Ayutthaya and Tongkin. The daily report of the Governor in Batavia on December 12th 1644, for example, mentions the arrival of the VOC ship *Saayer* from Taiwan with 202,332 pieces of miscellaneous porcelain.[①] The invoice of the ship

---

① Volker 1954, pp.51–52.

lists accurately all types and shapes of porcelain including flasks, flower pots, wine jugs, beakers, mustard pots, saucers, cups, bowls, dishes, platters, etc., and even gives the exact number such as 9,070 klapmutsen (the Dutch name for bowls, see plate 34), 10,485 bowls, 15,695 dishes, 33,020 red tea-cups and so on. In total, the price was 37,987 Dutch guilders (florin fl.) resulting in an average of about 0.18 fl. per piece. One Dutch guilder at that time was approximately 10.8 g silver or 0.29 tael — the Chinese silver-based currency — which brings the porcelain cargo to an equivalent of 410 kg of silver. The list indicates clearly that most of the cargo was porcelain for daily use and most of it got broken and/or lost in Europe over the centuries. The dishes and platters came in different sizes from 50 cm in diameter (*hele schotel*) and 29-36 cm (see plate 32) (*halve schotel*) to 21-23 cm (*een-derde*), and can be found depicted in the early 17th century Dutch and Flemish still life paintings (Pic. 2.6).[①]

Pic. 2.6: Dutch still life painting with Chinese *Kraak* porcelain by Floris van Dyck (1575-1651).

In 1653, the shipment of Chinese porcelain to the Netherlands came to an end because of the civil war, and Dutch customers were desperately looking for alternatives. Two options existed: first, to find another Asian producer who could provide a substitute for Chinese porcelain; second, to produce it domestically. The Dutch tried both. Japanese potters were encouraged to copy Chinese *Kraak* porcelain (plates 138-139). And the potters from Delft in South Holland were businessmen enough to take a chance by establishing new pottery companies. Out of the 34 factories in Delft, 17 were established within the ten years between 1653 and 1662 as a direct response to the shortage of Chinese imports. Dutch Delft ceramic is not porcelain but faience —

---

① Ketel, p.10.

earthenware with a white tin glaze, which looks like porcelain, but only from a distance (plate 166). It is neither as translucent nor as durable as porcelain. It still took the Europeans about 50 years before they were able to produce real porcelain.

In order to improve their position, the Dutch sent an official delegation to the young Qing Emperor Shunzhi in 1655. Their main purpose was to convince the Chinese ruler to grant the Dutch direct access to the Chinese market, and to offer support against the Ming rebels who controlled the coastal area of Fujian. The journey started in July 1655 in Batavia reaching Canton by ship in September.

The VOC embassy travelled mainly along the rivers from March 1656 and reached Beijing in July where they stayed until October. The embassy itself was a failure and the aims could not be realized. The Emperor perceived it as a tributary mission and granted only very limited direct trade every eight years. However, for another reason, the delegation was remarkable for Sino-European relations. Member of the delegation was the Dutch author and traveler Johan Nieuhof (born 1618 in Ülsen and died 1672 in Madagascar) who wrote a book about the journey through China with 145 copper engravings on the basis of his drawings: *An embassy from the East-India Company of the United-provinces to the Grand Tartar Cham Emperor of China,* published in 1665 in Dutch and French and 1669 in English. The book and these pictures built up the European image of China for more than a hundred years and it was amazing that even in the mid-18th century most depictions of China were mere copies of these old copper engravings (pic. 2.7).

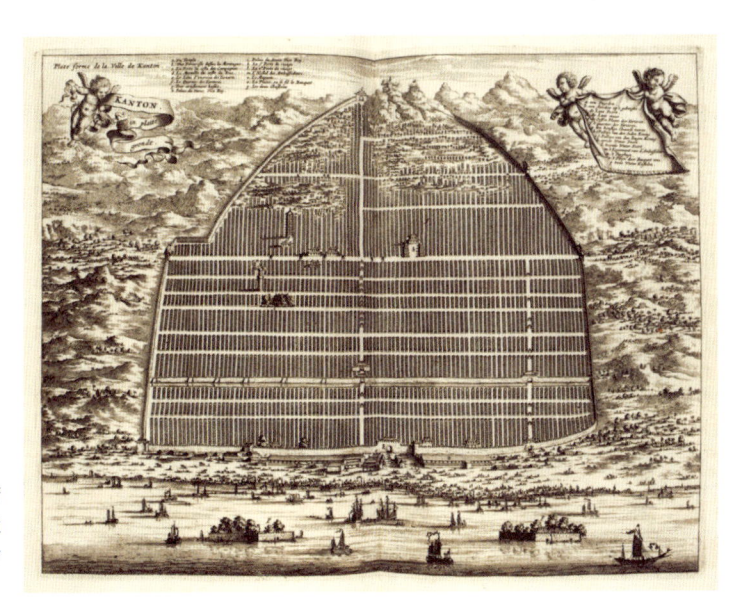

Pic. 2.7: Western map of Canton at the time of the first VOC embassy to Emperor Shunzhi, published 1665.

People in Europe were very curious to learn more about the country from where silk and porcelain were imported and treasured. The Nieuhof travel report and a second report compiled by the Dutch Olfert Dapper (1636–1689) have shaped the image of China in Europe for a long time and have created a "Chinoiserie fashion" for almost two centuries.[①]

The engravings show cities, plants, animals and scenes of everyday life in China. Specifically, the pictures of these scenes created a positive attitude towards China — a kind of dreamland with wise rulers and cultivated people devoting their life to music, painting and poetry. In a country suffering from decades of civil war, in the south against rebels and in the north against nomad tribes, the reality, however, was very different. Nevertheless, Europe and the Netherlands also suffered from war — from the Eighty Years' War, including the Thirty Years' War, to the Anglo-Dutch wars and the War of Spanish Succession. There was reason enough to dream of a country of peace and harmony.

In 1662 during the Chinese civil war, the Ming loyalist Zheng Chenggong led his Chinese troops from the mainland coast and won Taiwan.[②] Taiwan got captured in 1683 by the Qing Emperor Kangxi (pic. 2.8). With this event the civil war came to an end and China again became the world's biggest porcelain producer and exporter.

After unsuccessful missions to Beijing and being unable to establish direct trade, the Dutch again made use of the Chinese junk traffic with Batavia. When the Dutch were not allowed to go to China, they invited the Chinese to come to their headquarters on Java Island. On average 14 junks arrived every year in Batavia[③] carrying *Kangxi blue and white* porcelain (plates 35–48), *Famille verte* porcelain (plates 52–55), and the brown glazed so-called *Batavia* porcelain

Pic. 2.8: Emperor Kangxi (1654–1722) of the Qing dynasty.

---

① Ulrichs 2003.
② Andrade 2011.
③ Jörg 1982, p.20.

(plates 56–58) according to the taste of their customers from far away.

From 1683 to 1728 the VOC hardly did the porcelain trade by herself but left it to private traders who then used the VOC ships as carriers to Europe. Unfortunately, the documents for this period got lost or the trade was not carefully documented.

The variety and quality of porcelain exported to Europe had increased in the after-war period in comparison to the pre-war *Kraak* ware. The blue and white ware was of good quality with a very white and translucent shard and careful underglaze blue painting. *Kangxi* export porcelain (pic. 2.9) matched the quality of high-end domestic porcelain.

Pic. 2.9: Blue and white Kangxi period Dutch silver-mounted teapot.

The difference between the high-quality porcelain for the Emperor and the export ware was not big even though these days the prejudice toward low export quality still dominates the perception of Chinese collectors. Around 80 pieces of first-rate imperial *Kangxi* porcelain are listed in the *Complete Collection of Treasures of the Palace Museum*.[①] Actually, it is not fair to compare applied art for export purposes with *guanyao* fine arts made for the Emperor. What were the main differences between the *Kangxi* export porcelains and the imperial ware? First, it is not the quality of the material. Second, the shapes of export ware and domestic ware are similar but differ in size. The biggest difference, however, is in the finesse of the blue underglaze painting.

Two shipwrecks discovered in the South China Sea were laden with Kangxi blue and white porcelain for export purposes: the *Wanjiao No. 1* and the *Vung Tau* (see map 0.1). The cargo of the *Vung Tau* shipwreck is a good example of what was demanded

---

① Frank 1998.

by Europeans during that time (plate 41). The ship sunk on its way to Batavia in 1690. Most of the 48,000 recovered items are small vases with or without covers, for display only and often arranged as garnitures.

The main shapes and subsequently also the usage of imported porcelain changed in Europe during the first quarter of the 18th century. Vases became much less popular, and tableware including plates, teacups and saucers started to dominate the shipments. Plates were still used for decoration, but more and more like the cups used as tableware and for drinking tea and coffee.

The indirect China trade via Batavia lasted until 1729 when the VOC decided to make use of the only officially open window of China, the harbor of Canton. The third and last import period of the Dutch from 1729 to 1795 is almost perfectly documented and analyzed by C.J.A.Jörg.[1] However, at that time porcelain was not the center of Dutch demand, it had been overtaken by a new product, which not only attracted a new European competitor but also would change the course of the 19th century balance of power between China and the West: tea.

The Dutch and the Export Ceramics of Japan

Before, Japan was a major destination for Chinese, Vietnamese and Thai export ceramics itself. At the beginning of the 17th century, Kaolin raw material was discovered on the island of Kyushu. Japanese producers influenced by Korean potters discovered the art of porcelain making, many centuries after the Chinese potters and only about 100 years before it was discovered in Europe.

For Japan, domestic production was not sufficient, even though the products made in Japan have a unique standing in the Asian tradition of pottery. Indeed, traditional Japanese domestic tea ceramics are to some extent not comparable with the products of the neighboring countries. They are at the first sight simple, thick, uneven and even somehow primitive. However, the beauty lies in its proximity to nature, and in the way it pleases the hand touching it; every piece is different and has its own natural appearance very much linked to Japanese philosophy and Zen Buddhism, but of course, it is also not very suited to export purposes. The difference between Japanese domestic ceramics and ceramics made for export purposes seems to be much wider than in the case of China. Western customers, especially the Dutch, played a critical role in its design.

---

[1] Jörg 1982.

It was in 1543 when the first European — the Portuguese Mendez Pinto — landed accidentally on the shores of Japan. Over the following six decades Portuguese missionaries tried to convert the Japanese to Catholicism, and trade between China and Japan was facilitated. The Portuguese played a crucial role in the silk and silver trade between China and Japan through their hubs in Hirado, near Nagasaki, and Macao.[①] Portuguese shipbuilding know-how also supported the creation of a Japanese merchant fleet operating under the "Red Seal" system. During the early decades of the *Tokugawa Shogunate* between 1592 and 1635 approximately 350 so-called Japanese Red Seal ships — licensed by the Japanese Government — sailed to Dai Viet, the Philippines, Taiwan island and Siam, trading mainly silver for silk and sugar but also ceramics (see map 2.1). Vietnamese ceramics found their way on Red Seal ships to Japan.

The VOC had already established trading activities with Japan in 1609 in Hirado and took over a small trading hub from the Portuguese near Nagasaki in 1637 — only 75 km away from Arita.

However, in 1633 the favorable policies towards foreigners and local international merchants changed and a period of self-isolationism (*sakoku* means "closed country") started. Only one port was left open to European traders — the artificial tiny Dejima Island in the bay of Nagasaki (pic. 2.10), a trading post of the Dutch VOC. It was forbidden to enter the country or have contact with the Japanese until the mid-19th century.

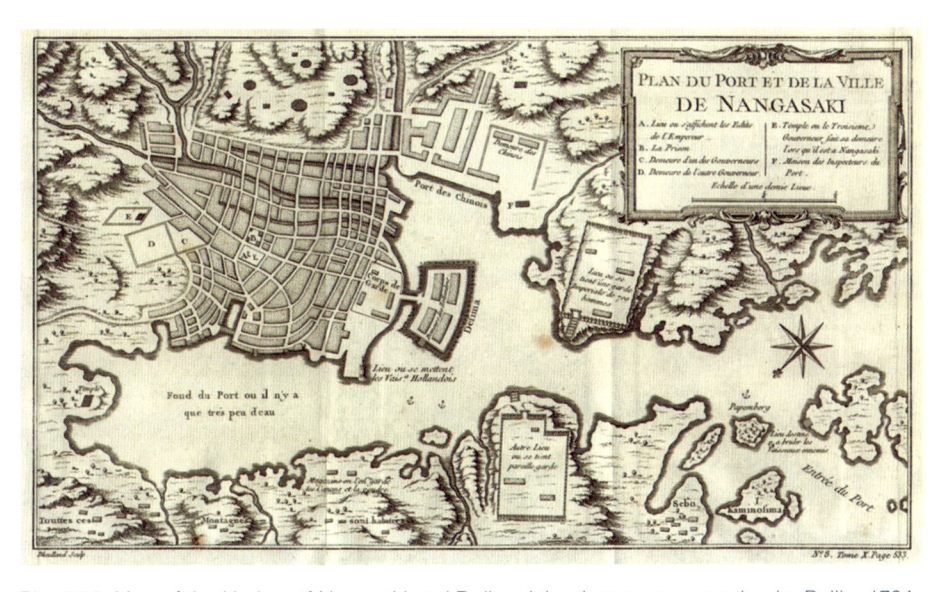

Pic. 2.10: Map of the Harbor of Nagasaki and Dejima Island, copper engraving by Bellin, 1764.

---

① Ptak 2007, p.286.

In the 1650s, during the Chinese civil war, when Chinese porcelain exports came to a standstill, the Dutch East India Company searched for new sources of porcelain in Japan.

The Dutch, from 1659 to the mid-18th century, facilitated the trade of Arita porcelain to Europe and together with Chinese junks also within Asia.[①] The first Dutch order of 35,000 pieces of Japanese porcelain was for the Ottoman marketplace in Mocha.[②] The first import to Europe took place in 1660.

And indeed, the Arita blue and white porcelain (called *"sometsuke"* in Japanese, see plate 138) was very much influenced by Chinese products from Jingdezhen. Dutch traders were explicitly asking for porcelain in the Chinese *Kraak* style (pic. 2.11). The Dutch sent Chinese *Kraak* or Delft faiences to the Japanese potters in Arita as reference pieces for their work.

Pic. 2.11: Japanese *Kraak* style plate with the VOC coat of arms.

The beginning of the Dutch-Japanese porcelain trade was not very successful: according to T. Volker, a total of 190,000 pieces were shipped to Europe from 1660 until 1683 when China came to the market again. Taking into consideration the monopoly the Japanese had on Asian ceramics for these two and a half decades, this was a small number of pieces. It seems that the Dutch customers were somehow comparably satisfied with their Delft products — even not being the hard and translucent porcelain they knew but soft, coarse and easy breakable white-covered earthenware.

A second decoration style and kiln in Arita — *Kakiemon* — became popular as well and was exported to Europe (plate 144). *Kakiemon* refers to a scheme of decoration, which comprises sparse design in colored enamels (orange, red, green and others), usually asymmetrically placed and without a framework as the border.

For fairness, one has to mention that the same indirect intercultural influence also took place with the Japanese *Imari* porcelain. The *Imari* ware (called *"kinrande"* in Japanese) is an underglaze blue decorated porcelain with overglaze red and gold invented by Japanese potters in the mid-17th century (pic. 2.12). The name *Imari* comes from the town Imari — a harbor city nearby the Arita kilns on the southern Island of Kyushu.

---

① Shono 1973, p.11f.
② Volker 1954, p.130.

The products became so successful that even Chinese producers started to imitate them during the reign of Emperor Kangxi (pic. 2.13). The Dutch and German, but above all English producers copied *Imari* ware as well: in some cases, according to the Japanese originals, in some cases according to *Chinese Imari*. It is not easy to say whether the European *Imari* is the first or the second cultural derivation of the Japanese object.

Pic. 2.12: Edo period Japanese *Imari* porcelain plate (1700–1730).

Pic. 2.13: Qianlong period *Chinese Imari* plate (c. 1750).

When Chinese producers restarted porcelain exports during the Kangxi period, and due to the emergence of European porcelain and white glazed earthenware in the mid-18th century, Japanese exports to Europe became less and less.

The closed-door politics came to an unintended end when the US navy commander Perry was able to negotiate in 1854 a treaty with Japan in Yokohama.

Japan entered the ceramic export market at a very late point in time compared with China, Vietnam and Thailand. However, Japan became in the last quarter of the 19th century the most influential Asian ceramic exporter, keeping that position until the 1930s.

The British

The British Empire was the largest empire in history and left its footprints not only in India but also in other regions of Asia including the Malay Archipelago and China. However, we should be careful not to overestimate its role and influence on Asia at a time when the first English ships started to discover the seaways of the Indian and Pacific Oceans in the 16th century.

The *Company of Merchants of London Trading into the East Indies* or short the *British East India Company* (EIC, pic. 2.14) got its charter from Elizabeth I, Queen of

Pic. 2.14: Coat of arms of the British East India Company.

England in 1600 which makes it the oldest East India Company in a row of others, such as the already mentioned Dutch VOC (established in 1602), the French *Compagnie française pour le commerce des Indes orientales* (1664), and various Danish East India companies, including the *Asiatisk Kompagni* (DAK in 1732) and the Swedish *Svenska Ostindiska Companiet* (SOIC in 1731). The royal charter granted the EIC the exclusivity of the English and later the British trade with Asia, including India, Southeast Asia and East Asia, even though the monopoly was debated significantly until a competing East Asia company was established in 1698.

However, the beginning of the EIC activities in Asia was not very successful. During the 17th century it had to face the strong economic and military rivalry of the powerful Dutch VOC. Three Anglo-Dutch wars between 1652 and 1674 were fought and ended in favor of the Dutch States. The EIC therefore could hardly deliver the spices from the Malay Archipelago to its customers in Europe and was always number three in maritime Southeast Asia after the Chinese junk traders and the VOC.

Similar to the Portuguese and the Dutch, the EIC also established small trade factories and fortifications in Patani, Ayutthaya, Banten, Ambon, Makassar and Hirado, but were not able to take control or monopolize the Eurasian trade for any of the commodities. After the Anglo-Dutch wars, the EIC — like the Portuguese — had to withdraw from the East Asian region. The factory in Banten — the most important one for the English spice trade on Java Island — was lost to the Dutch in 1682. It took more than a century before the British were able to get strongholds in the East Indies — mainly on the Malay Peninsula when they took formal possession of Penang Island in 1786, and with the foundation of colonial Singapore in 1819.

In addition to the trade monopolies, the EIC became, during the 18th century, a sovereign ruler of Asian territories such as Bengal in India with its capital Calcutta and Penang Island off the coast of Peninsular Malaysia. The EIC had a huge military force and the right of taxation within these territories. Troops of the EIC defeated the Indian ruler of Bengal in the Battle of Plassey in 1757. Calcutta, and later the whole of Bengal, was captured by the EIC. This marked the beginning of British rule in India which lasted for almost two centuries and which was part of the formation of a global empire. Bengal — the major production area of cotton — was the wealthiest state of the Indian Mughal Empire and soon became economically as important to the EIC.

For several reasons, the EIC was the most successful East Indian company to establish a direct trade relationship with China — crucial for the porcelain trade being the subject of this book. England became the second European nation to open direct trade with China in Mainland China — after the establishment of Portuguese Macao in 1557. The British became by far the most relevant carrier of Chinese goods to Europe, surpassing the successful VOC and all other European nations combined. The literature on the EIC is abundant and the works of the Indian historian and economist K. N. Chaudhuri[1] are worth studying. Much less documented, however, are the details of the volume and the characteristics of the EIC's porcelain trade.

Contact with the Qing government was gradually built. In 1672, a small post was established in Taiwan; later the EIC built a small trading post in Xiamen (Amoy) in 1678[2], and was able to purchase silk, tea and porcelain in exchange for silver. Zhoushan Island opposite Ningbo in Zhejiang province was another trading post of the EIC.

After the Qing dynasty recaptured Taiwan in 1683, four customs were officially set in Canton, Ningbo, Zhangzhou and Shanghai. But only Canton was left open later as the place where most of the Sino-Western trade should be carried out. In 1699 the EIC alone imported porcelain to the value of more than £15,000 or 45,000 Chinese tael — a silver unit of 37.5 g.[3] This amounts to almost 1.7 tons of silver and must have been around 1.2 million pieces of imported porcelain for this specific year alone. From 1699 until the official porcelain imports of the EIC came to an end in 1791, porcelain to the value of an average of £6,000 annually was purchased in Canton. This is a rough equivalent of 500,000 pieces per year and in total, around 45 million pieces have been imported and shipped to London by the EIC alone.

After 1791 British private traders — in most cases, the crewmembers of the EIC vessels — continued importing Chinese porcelain from Canton. However, the amount probably came down to £1,500 annually[4] during the two decades until 1810.

When the first British diplomatic mission — the famous Macartney Embassy — to the Chinese Emperor Qianlong took place in 1793, the Eurasian porcelain trade was

---

[1] Chaudhuri 1978.
[2] Pitcher 1893, p.30.
[3] Chaudhuri 1978, p.519.
[4] Madsen 2011, p.42.

almost over. The mission goal was to open new harbors for the Sino-British tea trade. It was a failure like the Dutch mission to Emperor Shunzhi 140 years before. The mission is an example of intercultural misunderstandings. Macartney refused to stick to the official imperial procedures and Emperor Qianlong was not willing to receive a diplomatic mission representing a foreign king of a powerful nation but interpreted the visit as a tributary mission. The mission outcome was later often taken as evidence of an inflexible and self-isolating China: a China defeated and humiliated half a century later. However, it could also be understood as a symbolic event — what might happen when Europe does not pay respect to the historic and cultural achievements of China.

The 1793 mission marks also the beginning of the Western feeling of superiority — a state of mind Europe is learning to overcome now more than two centuries later. When the porcelain trade ended, equal intercultural interaction ended. Now, in the 21st century, we can link ourselves back to this period of equality when Europe was fascinated and sometimes overwhelmed by China — imitating its habits and products and sometimes even painting a Chinoiserie dreamland in its mind.

The Canton-System Export Boom

The indirect Chinese-European trade took place outside China in the various entrepots already mentioned above. The direct Chinese trade with Europe in the 18th century (especially after the closure of three other customs under Emperor Qianlong's command in 1757) took place almost exclusively in Canton — the only port open to European traders until the end of the first Opium War in 1842. Most of the porcelain that went from China to Europe was shipped from Canton.

The so-called "Canton System" was a system of regulating foreign trade between China and the Western world. Foreigners were confined to small commercial districts or agencies called "thirteen factories" (*thirteen Hongs*) located at the Pearl River. Within these factories, foreigners were prohibited from outside contact with Chinese nationals. Outside the trading season, staff of the foreign companies had to move downstream to Macao. Essentially, this was to meet the desire of the Qing court and their concern with cultural protection, isolation of foreign interest in China, and also the secured collection of necessary taxes and duties. A central feature of the Canton System was the existence of the "*Cohong*", a monopolistic guild of licensed *Hong* merchants who officially traded with foreign companies and charged all taxes and fees on behalf of the Chinese government.

Canton (pic. 2.15) had several advantages in comparison to other Chinese harbor cities, which finally led to its trading monopoly with the East India companies from the west. First, geographically it was easy to reach for ships coming from the Indian Ocean being in the far South of China at the northern rim of the South China Sea. Also, it was not too far away from the tea-growing areas of China and relatively easy to reach by river transport from Jingdezhen in Jiangxi province. Second, foreign ship traffic was easy to control as it did not face the open sea but lay inland at the Pearl River. The river could only be used by bigger vessels with the ebb and flow of the tide. In addition, the Pearl River Delta forms a labyrinth of water arms, sandbanks, and small islands, which makes the use of Chinese pilots necessary acting as another way to control in

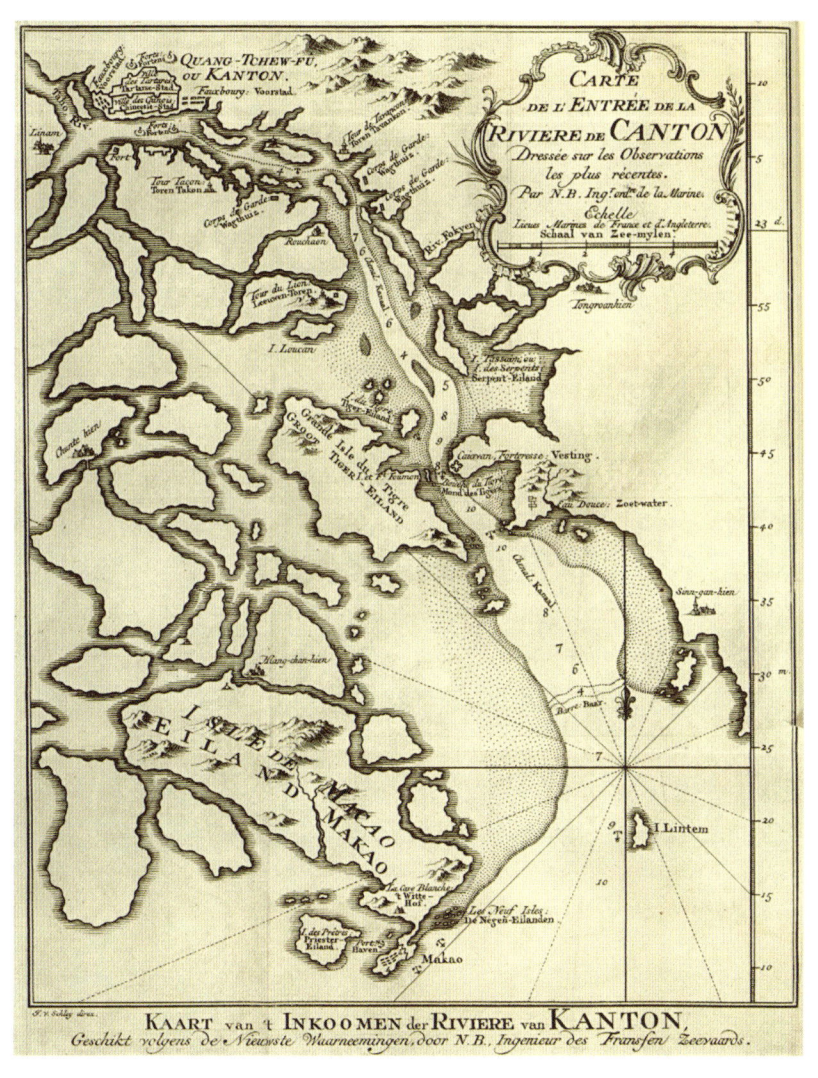

Pic. 2.15 Map of Canton, Macao and the mouth of the Pearl River, copper engraving by Bellin.

and outgoing ships.[①] Third, the proximity of the Macao Peninsula — the Portuguese settlement since 1557—was an advantage for finding translators and experienced Chinese merchants, and for settling port fees and duties.

The *East Indiamen*, as the big European sailing ships were called, were guided upstream along the Pearl River by Chinese pilots to the Island of Whampoa (*Pazhou*) just a couple of kilometers to the east of the city where their cargo was unloaded and loaded. The import-export business of the East India companies was in the hands of so-called "supercargoes". They represented the company to the Chinese authorities and the *Hong* merchants.

The *thirteen-factory district* was outside the city walls, to the southwest along the Pearl River. The foreign companies were allowed to rent the buildings but not allowed to enter the city itself. To some extent, this arrangement is comparable with the artificial Dejima Island next to Nagasaki, where the Dutch VOC staff trading with Japan had to live in isolation for more than 200 years. Nowadays one would rather compare the thirteen *factory district* with a free-trade area or a free-port terminal. Many illustrations (pic. 2.16) show the layout of the factories with flag poles at the front of the buildings indicating whether the foreign staff is present or absent.

Pic. 2.16: Thirteen factories in Canton by an unknown painter, 19th century.

In the direct Sino-European trade during the 18th century, Britain, with no doubt, played the most significant role. The *Macclesfield,* owned by the *English Company*

---

① Van Dyke 2007, p.35.

Trading to the East Indies, established in 1698 as a competitor to the *Company of Merchants of London Trading into the East Indies,* reached Canton in 1699. This was the first English ship that got approval from the Chinese central authorities to start official direct trade between England and China. In 1708 both English East India companies merged as the *United Company of Merchants of England Trading to the East Indies*. The new EIC started renting one of the permanent factories in Canton in 1715.

Canton had not only attracted the British EIC but also every other European East India company which had been established during the 17th and 18th centuries: The French *Compagnie française pour le commerce des Indes orientales* built its trading post in Canton in 1699, the Swedish *Svenska Ostindiska Companiet* (SOIC) in 1732, the Danish *Asiatisk Kompagni* (DAK) in 1734. Also, smaller companies, such as the Habsburg *Ostend Company* or the Spanish Company of the Viceroyalty of New Spain in America, leased factory buildings in Canton.

France never played a big role in the Sino-European trade. In fact, France had already established in 1664 an East India company with trade privileges between the Cape of Good Hope and the Strait of Magellan, and its first president was the Minister of Finance of Louis XIV. However, the numerous and long-lasting wars against England, the Dutch and the Habsburg Monarchy, impeded any bigger engagement in sea-borne trade. The War of Austrian Succession and the Seven Years' War between France and Great Britain even found battlefields in India, where France had a big colonial possession around Pondichéry on the east coast of India. Even though the first French ship, the *Amphitrite*, had already reached Canton in 1699, trade had to be suspended various times, for several years, in order to avoid hostile action of European powers against the ships of the *Compagnie des Indes* (CDI). The CDI had its headquarters in the harbor of Lorient but usually auctioned Chinese or Indian commodities in Nantes. Bigger porcelain shipments took place in the years 1722–1723. More than 683,000 pieces were auctioned.[1] Other major shipments took place in the 1730s, the 1760s and the 1770s.[2] The Company was liquidated by 1790.

The Swedish SOIC (pic. 2.17) is somehow a special case in Eurasian trade. It was established in 1731, enjoying the Swedish monopoly for all trade and shipping east of the Cape of Good Hop, and the privileges granted in 1731 (Royal Charter) were renewed by the Swedish Government four times. However, the Swedish had no colonial possession or enclave like all the other East India companies, especially the

---

[1] Beurdeley 1962, p.43.
[2] Wellington 2006, pp.131–206.

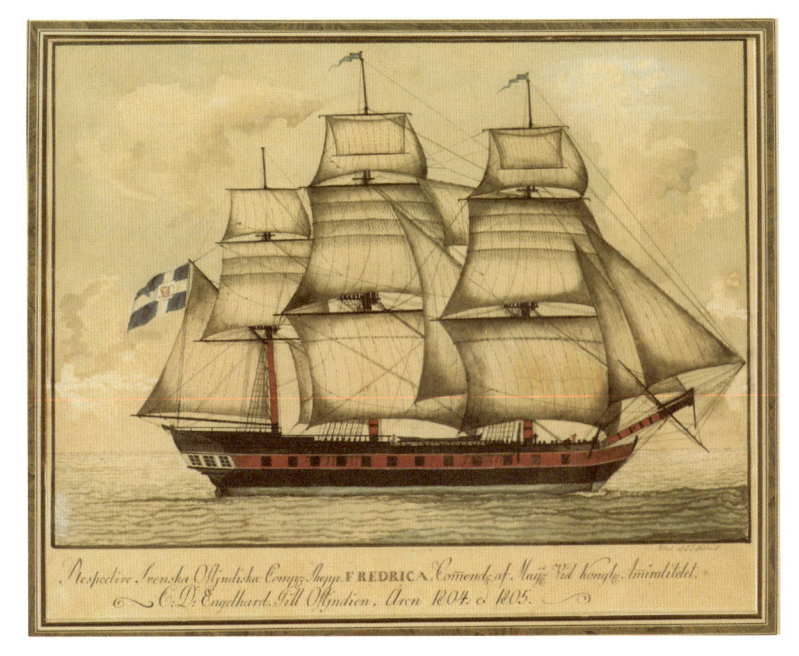

Pic. 2.17: Ship of the *Swedish East India Company* (SOIC).

British, Dutch and French. For their transactions, the SOIC rented a factory in Canton next to the English factory. In paintings of the Canton factories one can see the Swedish flag on the west side of the British one, and on the east side of the US factory, after its establishment in 1784.

The first SOIC ship *Fredericus Rex Sueciae* left Gothenburg on 7 March 1732, arrived in Canton on 19 September, stayed there until 16 January 1733, and turned back to Gothenburg on 7 September 1733. The voyage took 550 days.

Until 1806, the SOIC made a total of 132 voyages, and 129 of them from Gothenburg via Cadiz to Canton and back to Sweden. In Cadiz, Spanish silver dollars were purchased — the only currency Chinese merchants were willing to accept. Most voyages went directly from Cadiz to Canton passing the Cape, crossing the Indian Ocean in the east of Madagascar, and the Sunda Strait between Sumatra and Java. Only three voyages aimed directly at Bengal and not China.

This period can be divided into 3 phases: 61 ships sailed to Asia during the first and second octroi (1731–1766), 39 ships during the third octroi (1766–1786), and 32 during the fourth octroi. The last SOIC ship turned back to Gothenburg in 1806.

Seven SOIC ships got lost in total. The most famous accident happened to the *Götheborg* in 1745 on its third China voyage. The ship sank on its homeward journey at the entrance of the Gothenburg harbor and its cargo was partly excavated later, including several thousand pieces of porcelain and porcelain shards (plate 94). Detailed information on the duration and route can be found in the annex of the analysis of C. Koninckx and in the work of J.F. Nyström.[1] The Swedish SOIC was a latecomer, established 130 years after the Dutch VOC, but nevertheless was very important for the Sino-European porcelain trade.

The other Scandinavian East India company (pic. 2.18) — the Danish *Asiatisk Kompagni* (DAK) — was smaller and was already the third attempt by the Danish government to set up an economically sustainable trading firm. Established in 1732, it focused not only on the Canton trade but also had a foothold on the Indian East Coast — Tranquebar. The DAK carried out 120 voyages to Canton, mostly directly between Copenhagen and China, several also with a stop at their trading post on the Indian Coromandel Coast. The first Danish ship reached Macao and Canton in 1731, and the first DAK ship, the *Slesvig*, reached Canton in 1734. Both Scandinavian companies imported mainly tea and porcelain for domestic use or to smuggle to Great Britain.

Pic. 2.18: Headquarters of the *Danish Asiatisk Kompagni* in Copenhagen, by Petersen (1861–1926).

The history of the Habsburg *Ostend Company* (officially *Compagnie générale établie dans les Pays-Bas Autrichiens pour le Commerce et la Navigation aux Indes*) is much shorter, however economically more successful. The Austrian Netherlands (nowadays Belgium and Luxemburg) became the territory of the Habsburg Monarchy in 1714 following the War of Spanish Succession. With this acquisition, the favorable deep-sea port of Ostend served as a departure point for the vessels of the first Habsburg East India Company in 1722. The headquarter was in Antwerp, the major trading hub of the early spice trade of the Portuguese in the 16th century. Within the relatively short period of existence—ten years, 21 ships were sent out to Canton and India.[2]

The economic success of the *Ostend Company*, however, increased the political pressure by the British, Dutch and French to close it down. In order to secure the

---

[1] Nyström 1883, pp.154–161.
[2] Picard 1966, p.150.

recognition of his daughter Maria Theresia as the ruler of the Habsburg dominions, the Habsburg Emperor ordered the suspension of the *Ostend Company* in 1732. His daughter, the future Holy Roman Empress, having no East India Company, however, became a collector of Chinese and Japanese porcelain. The two — an oval and a round — porcelain "cabinets" or rooms at *Schönbrunn Palace* in Vienna, with 252 pieces, provide evidence of her passion.[①] The *Ostend Company* focused its trading mainly on tea. Data about porcelain imports to Europe are missing.

The same applies to the short living Prussian *Königlich Preußische Asiatische Compagnie in Emden nach Canton und China* (1751–1757) with its headquarter in Emden undertaking only six voyages to Canton. Its business was also destroyed by the outbreak of the Seven Years' War.

Spain acted also under the framework of the *Real Compañia de Filipinas* (RCF) established in 1785 and dissolved in 1814. The RCF had the right to arrange the Philippine-Chinese-Spanish trade. The ships sailed between Spain (Cadiz) and Canton passing the Cape of Good Hope and complemented the old galleon route via the Pacific Ocean, crossing Mexico towards the Atlantic.

Armenian traders used Canton for the Sino-Persian trade too. In 1784 the first US East Indiaman *Empress of China* reached Canton from New York.

The VOC had opened its factory several decades after the British because there was a long dispute between Amsterdam and Batavia about whether a trading post in Canton would damage the position of Batavia as an entrepot of the Chinese junk trade. Junks to Batavia shipped Chinese products so that there was no urgent need to enter into direct trade in Canton. The first VOC ship — the *Coxhorn* — reached Canton in 1729. From then on four to five VOC ships anchored at Whampoa every year — altogether more than 200 ships.

Commodities in the Canton-System

Porcelain was not the most expensive or most sought-after product in the European-Chinese trade relations in Canton. It could be found on most ships either treasured for the profits it could generate, or simply as ballast to form a layer to ensure that the tea and silk cargo would not be affected by seawater. At the beginning of the Canton trade, tea was the most relevant single Chinese commodity for Western

---

① Gawronski 2012, p.90.

companies, but the percentage in terms of cargo value increased over time.

The composition varied also among the various East India companies. As far as statistics are available, tea accounts for 73.5% of the total value of British EIC imports in the years 1765–1769, silk for 20.9%, and others including porcelain for 5.4%.[①] In the case of the Dutch VOC the percentages during that period were rather similar, even though they had imported less in absolute figures. However, over the whole period of the Dutch-Canton trade from 1728 to 1793, the importance of porcelain seems to be higher than in the case of the EIC. The years from 1769 to 1774 were the peak in absolute terms. Each year, the value of Dutch porcelain imports was above 100,000 fl. (or approximately 30,000 taels). This was the purchase price for about one million pieces of porcelain. The EIC in comparison hardly imported more than 500,000 pieces per year, even though they sent many more ships to Canton than the VOC.

In addition, the VOC (pic. 2.19) statistics for porcelain imports are incredibly detailed. This might also reflect that porcelain played a bigger role for the VOC than for the EIC. EIC statistics are rather broad and list the number of chests and the purchase price, rather than the exact numbers of pieces.

Pic. 2.19: The *Noord-Nieuwland* in Table Bay, Anonymous, 1762.

The VOC statistics are somewhat extraordinary also from an art historian's point of view. Not only the exact number of pieces has been recorded, but also details about the

---

① Yang-Chien Tsai 2003, p.82.

form, the use and the decoration. For the year 1770 we can read inter alia the following[1]:

Table 2.2: Imports from Canton 1770 by five Dutch VOC ships *Willem de Vijfde, Princes van Oranje, Bodt, Jonge Hellingman* and *Burgh*

blue and white beer tankards	1,854
beer tankards with enamel colours	1,600
blue and white bottles	6,070
blue and white single bowls	8,260
blue and white single bowls with dragon	2,030
Chinese *Imari* single bowls	4,305
Batavia brown single bowls, blue and white inside	3,760
Batavia brown single bowls, with enamel colours inside	1,575
single bowls with enamel colours	4,285
white single bowls	3,395
half-pint bowls without saucers	42,000
quarter-pint bowls without saucers	21,355
bowls with saucers	15,848
blue and white round butter dishes with lids and stands	997
butter saucers	18,379
blue and white chamber pots	348
chocolate cups with saucer	35,959
coffee cups with saucer and without handles	367,678
blue and white coffee pots	195
Chinese *Imari* coffee pots	199
coffee pots with enamel colours	339
cupboard garnitures	2,516
blue and white cuspidors	387
single dinner plates	62,364
blue and white dinner services	215
round dishes	8,640
fish dishes	240
blue and white milk cups	420
milk jugs	3,151
moorish cups	53,165
punchbowls	7,323
salad bowls	1,709
oval shaving bowls	175
soup plates	12,851
sugar bowls	7,014
teacups and saucers without handles	219,141
tea pots	934
tea and coffee services	821
blue and white tureens	338
	Total items listed: 921,835.

[1] Jörg 1982, pp.226–306.

If one would count cups and saucers separately, the number would be around 1.6 million. To be more exact, one could also calculate each piece of a service or the garniture. This shows the difficulties in getting an estimation of the number of pieces exported.

Koninckx counts each cup and saucer separately and comes to the incredible number of 33.8 million pieces imported by the Swedish SOIC between 1732 and 1766[①], and another 11.3 million for the third octroi until 1786.[②]

In the end, all attempts to get exact figures will be in vain, since the statistics are incomplete or measure different aspects, such as purchase value, selling price, weight, pieces or services, chests, or barrels. As a rule of thumb, one can estimate that 3,000 taels (112 kg of pure silver or £1,000) were about 100,000 pieces and that VOC and EIC East Indiamen ships transported approximately 200,000 pieces per voyage back to Europe. SOIC and Danish ships were bigger than those of the VOC and EIC, and transported more pieces per ship than the other companies.

The purchase lists of the East India companies give us much more information. One gets a good insight into the different types of porcelain exported, their shapes and decorations. While most export ware comprised of mass-produced blue and white tableware, specifically designed pieces for the Western taste — so-called *chine de commande* — could be ordered too. This applied, for example, to the custom-painted armorial designs (plates 83–84) with a family coat of arms, or monogram which became popular specifically in England.[③] Another favored form was the garniture — a set of five vases for display, and tea and dinner services being consistent in shape and decoration. Cups with handles — not common in China — and used for tea, coffee, hot chocolate, and even beer, were produced according to European tastes and drinking habits.

Many different styles of porcelain were exported to Europe, the Spanish Philippines and the Americas: the ivory white and glazed *Blanc-de-Chine*, overglaze enamelware (*Famille verte* and *Famille rose,* armorial porcelain, *Rose Medaillon*); *Nanking, Canton,* and *Fitzhugh* blue and white ware, the brown glazed *Batavia* ware (pic. 2.20), *Chinese Imari* as copies of Japanese export products, unglazed red and brown stoneware from the *Yixing* kilns.

Ninety-nine percent of the items sold in Canton came from Jingdezhen in Jiangxi

---

① Koninckx 1980, p.220.
② Kjellberg 1974, pp.233–234.
③ Ganse 2008, pp.140–145.

Pic. 2.20: Qianlong period *Batavia* ware milk jug with *Famille rose* enamel.

province. Only the white or ivory-colored *Blanc-de-Chine* (plate 219) ware was produced in Dehua in Fujian province and the *Yixing* stoneware in Jiangsu province. The majority of the exports were in the *Nanking* blue and white style. The underglaze blue was applied at the kiln site in Jingdezhen, but the overglaze enameling was often done in Canton. It is because the *chine de commande* enameling was easier to do in Canton workshops according to Western patterns or coat of arms the customers had provided locally.

Millions of pieces had to be transported from Jingdezhen to Canton to reach European and US customers. The journey was mainly by boat on various rivers crossing the province of Jiangxi and Guangdong. "This route began in Lake Poyang and proceeded up the Gan River to Nanchang. Re-loaded onto smaller river boats, the porcelain cargo would then continue upstream to Ganzhou. Continuing on smaller rivers, the cargo boats eventually reached the southern border of Jiangxi province. Here the porcelain had to be carried over the Meiling Pass by manpower, a stretch of some 30 kilometers that reached about 275 meters above sea level. After the Meiling Pass, the goods were again re-loaded onto small boats that navigated the winding narrow upper reaches of the Bei Jiang River before reaching Canton".[1]

Design influences flowed both ways, and sometimes around. The forms of Chinese export ware might have been designed after metal, glass and wood examples, and the decor after drawings the companies brought with them — for instance, many Ming dynasty blue and white ware were imitations of Arabic brass vessels — while the decoration might have been copied from Chinese sources, Japanese sources, Western

---

[1] Sjostrand 2007, p.64.

sources, or a combination. The following part illustrates the main standard types of Chinese export porcelain to Europe and their export period to Europe in brackets.

> ***Kraak* Porcelain (1550–1657)**
>
> Underglaze blue porcelains from Jingdezhen, Zhangzhou, etc., with an outer paneled decoration circle and traditional patterns around a center motif — often auspicious animals or Buddhist symbols.① The porcelain shard is thin and translucent. *Kraak* porcelain was mainly produced in the period of the Ming Emperor Wanli (plates 32–34).
>
> **Transitional Blue and White Porcelain (1620–1670)**
>
> During the transitional period from the Ming to the Qing dynasty, imperial orders in Jingdezhen declined. The producers were seeking new markets by customizing the blue and white porcelain according to the demand of their clients in Europe and Asia. New forms and decors emerged, and the producers became more creative. At the end of this period, the kilns of Jingdezhen became effected by the war and were destroyed.
>
> ***Blanc-de-Chine* (1620–1800)**
>
> Refers to undecorated white or ivory-colored porcelain — often figurines and cups — made in the Chinese kilns of Dehua in Fujian province. Exports to Europe started in the late Ming dynasty (plate 219).
>
> ***Kangxi* Style Blue and White (1683–1760)**
>
> It refers to a high-quality underglaze blue porcelain from Jingdezhen exported mainly to the Netherlands during the reign of the Qing Emperors Kangxi, Yongzheng and early Qianlong with a wide range of images and sceneries (plates 35–51).
>
> **Famille Verte (1685–1730)**
>
> The "green family" (*wucai* in Chinese) is the name for porcelain with bright overglaze enamel colors, mainly green and red, produced in Jingdezhen and exported to Europe during the reign of the Emperors Kangxi and Yongzheng (plates 52–55).②
>
> ***Chinese Imari* (1695–1760)**
>
> This pattern is a combination of a red overglaze enamel color with

---

① See Wu Ruoming, 2014.
② See Jörg Christiaan J. A., 2011: Famille Verte: Chinese porcelain in green enamels.

underglaze blue, often highlighted with gilt. Chinese *Imari* is a copy of Japanese blue-, red- and gold-colored products from Arita (called kinrande) which were shipped from the Japanese harbor city Imari to Nagasaki, and from there to Europe (plates 59–66). Chinese *Imari* has been only produced for export purposes. It did not exist in the domestic market.

Batavia (1695–1790)

It's a decorative style of Chinese export porcelain using a surface covering brown engobe with or without panels in conjunction with underglaze blue or enamels. It has been named after the city of Jakarta, which at that time was Batavia — the Dutch East India Company trading center in Southeast Asia (plates 56–58).[①]

Famille Rose (1720–1800)

The "pink family" (*fencai* in Chinese) is the name for colorful overglaze enamel porcelain including pink and rose colors produced in Jingdezhen. The technique of using opaque and semi-opaque enamels was probably influenced by France. The introduction of white color has allowed gradations of color intensity and shades (pic. 2.21 and plates 70–82).

Armorial Porcelain, *Grisaille* (1720–1820)

It describes porcelain decor produced in China on demand for Europeans, often with their family's coat of arms or flags applied in the center of the object (armorial porcelain). *Grisaille* refers to the painting of European motifs in grey colors. The decoration reflects European taste and usually does not look Chinese. The porcelain is from Jingdezhen, but the painting was done in workshops in Canton (plates 83–85).

Nanking Porcelain (1760–1820)

Refers to various underglaze blue and white porcelains produced in Jingdezhen with specific border decoration and in many cases pavilion, temple, river and tree scenery (pic. 2.22 and plates 86–104). The decoration has been influenced by British Chinoiserie images and vice versa. The quality of the raw material is lower than in the case of the *Kangxi* blue and white. Some of the

---

[①] Not many studies exist about the origins and characteristics of *Batavia* ware: see Li, Baoping, 2012 and Holley, Andrew and Jean Martin: *Illustrated Catalogue of Colonel William Thomlinson's Collection of Chinese 18th Century Export Porcelain. 'Batavian' Style and other Brown Glazed Wares. Hartlepool.*

Pic. 2.21: Qianlong period *Famille rose* plate (c. 1750).

Pic. 2.22: Qianlong period *Nanking* blue and white porcelain platter with pavilion decoration (1785–1800).

Nanking ware has been gilded in the UK (plate 98) or overpainted ("clobbering") with enamels in the Netherlands (plates 67–69).

Fitzhugh Porcelain (1780–1820)

It refers to quality underglaze blue and white porcelain from Jingdezhen consisting of four groups of flowers or plants spaced evenly around a center motif, mainly exported to the US (plate 105).

Canton Porcelain (1785–1853)

It refers to a rather low-quality underglaze blue and white porcelain produced in Jingdezhen and was exported mainly to the US with Chinese river and pavilion scenery similar to *Nanking* porcelain (plates 107–109).

Rose Medallion and *Rose Mandarin* (1860–1911)

Rose Medallion refers to very colorful overglaze enamel porcelains with four alternating panels around a central gold medallion, mainly exported to the US.[1] *Rose Mandarin* is a variety with a Chinese (Chinoiserie) scene of everyday life as the center motif. Some *Mandarin* porcelain goes back to the mid-18th century. Both are called *guangcai* in Chinese since the enameling took place in Canton (plates 110–113).

---

[1] The most detailed study on Chinese export porcelain to the US is: Schiffer, Herbert, Schiffer, Peter and Schiffer, Nancy: *Chinese Export Porcelain*.

第三章 40亿英镑的交易：瓷器贸易经济

贸易规模

从1550年到1800年这两个半世纪的时间里，大约有多少中国瓷器被运往欧洲？从表3.1我们可以看到，答案是约1.86亿件。在1550年之前或19世纪以后，出口欧洲的瓷器数量寥寥无几。14至15世纪通过中东间接出口至欧洲的瓷器屈指可数，以至于我们今天甚至还能一一获知它们的收藏地。比如，一件名为"放山居"的元代青白花瓶，目前收藏在爱尔兰国家博物馆。另一件明初金银镶边的青瓷碗，1433年被一位德国贵族在朝圣途中购买。[①]

1966年，皮卡德等人首次对欧亚瓷器贸易进行汇总，估计欧洲商船承运进口瓷器在1.42亿至1.54亿件之间。[②] 但约尔格的研究（图3.1）表明，皮卡德等人低估了荷兰东印度公司的进口瓷器数量，可能也低估了英国东印度公司的进口数量。此外，他们未曾将其他小型公司和私营贸易商纳入考虑，而且高估了葡萄牙、法国和瑞典的瓷器进口数量。

借助T.沃尔克和约尔格的研究，我们可以获得荷兰东印度公司瓷器贸易的完整统计数据。通过分析荷兰东印度公司在平户、出岛和

---

① 1433—1434年，菲利普·冯·卡岑内尔博根在朝圣途中购买了龙泉青瓷碗。现在，它是卡斯尔艺术博物馆瓷器藏品的一部分，见Schmidt, pp.216-218。
② Picard et al, pp.33-34.

表 3.1 中欧瓷器贸易总览

时期	主要欧洲贸易商	主要贸易地	估计运往欧洲的件数
1550—1650 年	葡萄牙领地	澳门	250 万
1565—1815 年	西班牙马尼拉大帆船商	马尼拉	100 万
1602—1657 年	荷兰东印度公司	台湾、万丹、大泥	350 万
1669—1710 年	英国东印度公司和私营贸易商	厦门、舟山	400 万
1683—1728 年	荷兰东印度公司和私营贸易商	巴达维亚	1 000 万
1699—1805 年	英国东印度公司和私营贸易商	广州	5 000 万
1687—1779 年	法国东印度公司	广州	800 万
1729—1793 年	荷兰东印度公司	广州	4 500 万
1732—1804 年	瑞典东印度公司	广州	4 000 万
1734—1806 年	丹麦亚洲公司	广州	1 200 万
1700—1800 年	其他	广州	1 000 万
			总计：约 1.86 亿件

巴达维亚的商馆的日志，我们可获得 1602—1657 年中荷瓷器贸易的准确数据。在这一阶段，荷兰贸易商主要从停泊在台湾、北大年（属泰国）、万丹（属印度尼西亚），以及后期在巴达维亚和厦门附近的中国商船那里购买瓷器。

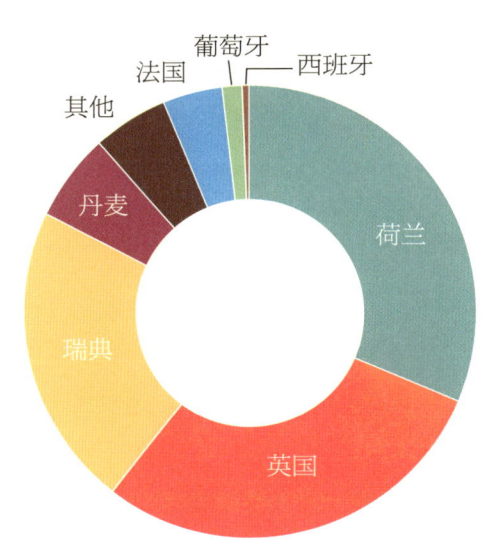

图 3.1 欧洲运输商及各东印度公司在瓷器贸易中所占比重

1683 至 1728 年，中荷瓷器贸易主要依靠停泊在巴达维亚的中国商船和使用荷兰东印度公司商船的荷兰私营贸易商来推动。可惜，此出口阶段没有档案可查。这段时期很大程度上和康熙在位时期（1662—1722年）重合，这是中国出口精美瓷器的生产阶段。如今我们仍然可以在欧洲古董市场以及很多著名收藏馆中欣赏到康熙时期的瓷器，如德累斯顿的奥古斯特二世收藏馆。

存放于海牙的荷兰东印度公司档案完整记录了1730—1789年间荷兰瓷器进口数量。统计数据显示，这期间荷兰东印度公司共购买了4 270万件瓷器，总价值457万荷兰盾。其船只在广东和荷兰之间航行216次，有些是直航，有些途经巴达维亚。共有16艘船失事，其中最著名的是"哥德马尔森号"，1752年在从广州到阿姆斯特丹的归途中沉没。它在1985年被发现，当时有15万多件瓷器，其中许多保存完好。大多数瓷器于1986年在阿姆斯特丹佳士得被拍卖，这也是它们最初的目的地。船上载有203个箱子，里面装有运往欧洲市场的瓷器，以及运往好望角的荷属殖民地的物品（收藏56，66，114）。

遗憾的是，瑞典东印度公司的数据[①]只详细记录了进口货物在哥德堡缴付的关税信息，缺少在广东的购买价格以及货物构成等详细信息，这使得进口数据统计变得更加复杂。英国东印度公司、法国东印度公司（以及后来的法国印度公司）的数据也不完整，但可以比较精确地估计缺失的数据。

其他东印度公司的船载瓷器数据均为据理推测；无论是奥斯坦德公司的运输数量，普鲁士王国亚洲公司驶往广州的船只的运输数量，还是西班牙马尼拉大帆船贸易或者皇家菲律宾公司贸易中的运输量，都仅为推测得出。私营贸易商的运输数据，以及船员公开或私下出售的件数都不得而知（图3.2）。此外，奥斯曼帝国或波斯对西欧的间接贸易数据也缺失。但本文作者认为，通过这一途径间接运输至欧洲的瓷器数量不到1 000万件。

总之，中国出口至欧洲的瓷器超过1.86亿件。约90%的货物被从广州沿着珠江运往南海。

G. 戈登[②]列举了英国东印度公司的大型商船"乔治王子号"1755年在广州向中国商人支付的商品购买价格：10 236件青花瓷盘，共计112英镑。

当时各种货币的汇率大体为：

1两（37.5克银或1.21盎司）=0.33英镑（6s 8d）=3.5荷兰盾（弗罗林）=1.5瑞典达勒（0.826盎司）=1.39八里亚尔

1八里亚尔（亦称西班牙银圆）=25.56克纯银=0.72两=5先令（0.25英镑）

[①] Goddio 1996.

[②] Godden 1979, p.127.

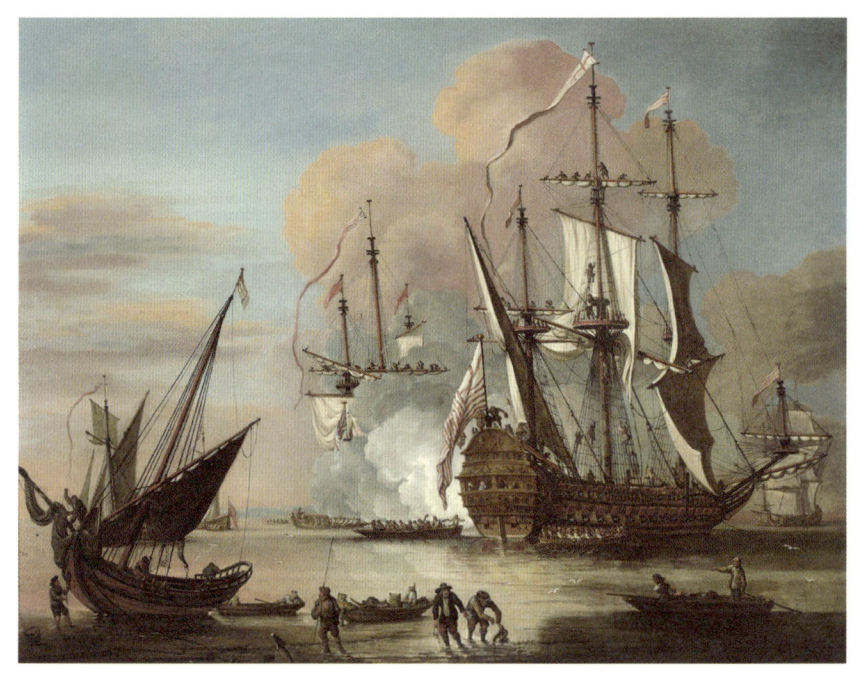

图 3.2　东印度公司船员衣锦还乡，约翰·巴蒂斯特·布塔茨（1680—1743 年）绘

按照这种汇率，则单只盘子的价格（0.11 弗罗林/荷兰盾）与戈尤列举的 1729 至 1765 年间荷兰东印度公司的采购价格相同。[1] 由于瓷器贸易采用白银支付（以中国的白银单位"两"为单位），因此货物价格在很长一段时间内相对稳定。若要计算所有欧洲贸易公司的进口成本，必须查询产品单价并估计平均单价。下面列出了以荷兰盾（或荷兰分）和等值银为单位的其他瓷器商品的采购价格：

- 一个带茶碟的茶杯：8 弗罗林分（约 0.85 克白银）
- 一个剃须盘（收藏 61）：70 弗罗林分（7.5 克白银）
- 一个小青花茶壶（收藏 50）：16 弗罗林分（1.7 克白银）
- 一个釉彩茶壶：30 弗罗林分（3.2 克白银）
- 一个酱汁船（收藏 91）：40 弗罗林分（4.3 克白银）
- 一个直径 23 厘米的粉彩瓷盘（收藏 76）：23 弗罗林分（2.5 克白银）[2]

如上所述，每艘船平均装载瓷器 20 万件，成本估计约为 2 000 英镑，或 21 000 弗罗林，或 8 000 西班牙银圆。1550 至 1800 年，中国出口欧洲的瓷器总价值约为 740 万西班牙银圆，或 185 万英镑，或 185 吨纯银。听起来价值不高，但是，如果按照 2020 年的通货膨胀水平测算，这相当于 2.96 亿英镑。如果将今天人们的收入

[1] Jörg 1982, p.121.

[2] Jörg 1982, pp.121 – 192, purchase prices per item also in Copeland 1980, p.160.

水平考虑进来，相当于 45 亿英镑购买力价值。① 考虑到 2018 年人们会花远超 18 世纪人所支付的 1.7 克白银的价格来购买一只青花茶壶，这种通货膨胀率并不算高。

贸易模式

还有一个问题：欧洲如何支付大约 1.86 亿件瓷器的巨额费用？乍看起来答案非常简单：无外乎使用产自墨西哥和玻利维亚的西班牙银圆。

西班牙银圆（图 3.3）是 16 至 19 世纪的世界货币，也是中国唯一接受的西方货币。在中国使用的银币通常盖有中国戳记。直到 1857 年，西班牙银圆也是美国法定货币。据说，美元符号"$"正是来自西班牙双柱银圆上的海格力斯之柱。

图 3.3　带中国戳记的西班牙银圆，27 克，直径 38 毫米，92% 纯银

西班牙银圆在欧洲铸造，但铸造所用原料来自西属美洲殖民地出产的白银。西班牙于 1535 年建立新西班牙总督领地不久，便在墨西哥的萨卡特卡斯发现了白银。他们的第二个白银开采点是在玻利维亚的波托西，该地在印加帝国时期即已开始白银开采。据估计，16 世纪这两个地区以及墨西哥其他矿场和秘鲁的白银产量为 17 000 吨，17 世纪白银产量增加至 42 000 吨，18 世纪增加至 74 000 吨。② 有关墨西哥和玻利维亚从事银矿开采工作的印第安和非洲奴隶的悲惨处境，学者早已多有描述，此处不赘述。在殖民者开始在秘鲁的万卡维利亚生产提取白银所需的原料汞后，这些人的处境更是雪上加霜。③

---

① Calculation assisted by https://www.measuringworth.com/, accessed on 2 January 2018.
② Frank, p.143.
③ Reinhard, p.340.

开采出来的白银，要么从墨西哥的韦拉克鲁斯和巴拿马的波托贝洛，通过今古巴的哈瓦那，运到西班牙的塞维利亚和加的斯；要么从墨西哥的阿卡普尔科，随西班牙大帆船运到菲律宾的马尼拉。① 大多数欧洲东印度公司会在开启广州之旅前在加的斯购买西班牙银圆，或者在马尼拉用银币购买中国船只运来的丝绸和陶瓷。总体而言，西属美洲白银产量的 25%~30% 最终流向亚洲（主要是中国）。中国吸纳白银数量巨大，而且只接受银币，这令欧洲人不顾一切获取白银。有趣的是，20 世纪末和 21 世纪初，中国与欧洲、中国与美国之间出现了类似的贸易失衡。中国再次吸纳数十亿美元——这种直接从西班牙银圆衍生出来的货币。

欧洲人自然不乐见这种状况。但遗憾的是，大多数用欧洲产品与中国商人以物易物的尝试都以失败告终，中国人唯一大批量接受的只有银币。1793 年，中国乾隆皇帝在召见英国马戛尔尼使团后致信乔治三世，阐明了中国的态度："天朝物产丰盈，无所不有，原不借外夷货物以通有无。特因天朝所产茶叶、瓷器、丝巾为西洋各国必需之物，是以加恩体恤，在澳门开设洋行，俾（使）日用有资，并沾余润。"欧洲人的羊毛织品或金属原料（铜、铅和铁）对中国毫无吸引力，只能用来交换小部分中国商品。

因此，毫不奇怪，18 世纪欧洲和中国之间存在着巨大的贸易逆差。1765 至 1769 年，广州每年出口到欧洲的商品价值平均为 417.7 万两或 157 吨纯银；1785 至 1789 年（包括对美出口），平均为 845.4 万两或 317 吨白银；1820 至 1824 年，每年出口额超过 1467.8 万两或 550 吨白银。

在这种逆差中，瓷器贸易所扮演的角色无足轻重。18 世纪 60 年代至 70 年代，欧洲每年在广州采购 9 000 至 1 万吨茶叶，到 19 世纪初中美贸易开始时，这一数字已增加至 2 万吨。② 19 世纪 20 年代，仅英国东印度公司购买的茶叶，年平均价值便超过 570 万两。换言之，在这 10 年里，英国东印度公司从广州进口的茶叶价值，大体上相当于欧洲 250 年从中国进口的陶瓷价值总和！

对于这种巨额贸易逆差，英国东印度公司所受影响无疑最大。在 18 世纪最后 10 年里，该公司的进口额占西方商人从广州进口商品总额的 75%。他们想方设法采用各种新方案来避免白银流失。最后，他们成功地将鸦片引入一口通商体系。

至少在 1757 年之前，英国东印度公司和其他欧洲国家一样，也是采取白银换中国商品的模式。这种模式由西班牙始创，西班牙或菲律宾商人在马尼拉向中国帆

---

① Reinhard, pp.342–345.

② Yang-Chien Tsai, p.80.

船商支付银币，购买中国商品。丹麦亚洲公司和瑞典东印度公司也采用这种模式，从哥本哈根或哥德堡驶往广州的每艘商船都要经停加的斯，以获取所需西班牙银圆；法国东印度公司同样如此。因为瑞典和法国禁止银币出口，而且中国商人也不接受这些货币。

该时期的统计数据显示，英国东印度公司用银锭购买了 90%~95% 的中国商品，只有 5%~10% 是通过出售金属或羊毛织品等欧洲商品置换。[1] 英国东印度公司试图增加换取茶叶的欧洲产品数量，甚至将提高比例作为与十三行行商开展贸易的条件。但羊毛产品不太适合中国南方的热带气候，此举最终以失败告终。

1753 年英国东印度公司船只将 31 吨白银运至广州（价值 276 333 英镑）。1784 年英国政府颁布《减免法案》，大大降低茶叶进口关税，使得英国茶叶进口急剧飙升，运往广州的白银数量达到顶峰。1789—1790 年交易季，约 20 艘英国东印度公司船运送 80 吨白银抵达黄埔，这是白银出口的顶峰。我们可将其称为"以银换茶"或"以银换瓷器"贸易时期。

但事实上，贸易总体格局已开始发生改变。1757 年以后，英国东印度公司从欧洲出口到广东的白银大幅减少，1772 至 1784 年白银出口大体陷入停滞，1806 年后再次大幅下降。为什么会发生这种情况？要知道，英国东印度公司在此期间进口了数千吨茶叶和几百万件瓷器。这就涉及第二种基于亚洲内部贸易的欧亚贸易模式，或称作"港脚贸易"。

这种贸易模式由葡属印度在 16 世纪创立，主要特点是通过参与亚洲内部贸易，而非通过出口白银，来获得购买所需商品的必要资源。它始于澳门和日本平户之间的丝绸换白银贸易：葡萄牙贸易商在日本出售中国丝绸换取白银，然后用白银购买其他中国商品、东南亚香料或印度棉花。另一个案例是在葡萄牙帝汶岛商馆和澳门之间开展檀香换黄金贸易。

荷兰东印度公司沿用了这种交易方式，甚至继承和发展了中国台湾和日本之间的丝绸贸易。荷属东印度群岛总督简·皮特斯佐恩·科恩对此进行了清晰描述（见第二章信件摘录）："所有贸易无须荷兰投入任何资金，只需船只便可完成。"此举降低了贸易逆差、运输风险以及对欧洲本土的依赖。荷兰东印度公司用日本白银、班达群岛的肉豆蔻、特内特的丁香、苏门答腊的胡椒和帝汶岛的檀香换取欧洲人所需的商品。这一点在荷兰东印度公司的统计数据中得以清晰体现。荷兰东印度公司出口亚洲的白银比例远低于英国东印度公司或其他东亚公司，通过亚洲内部贸易收入

---

[1] Yang-Chien Tsai, pp.118-120.

可完成大部分交易。①

港脚贸易规模的扩大是欧洲商人融入亚洲贸易网络的标志。由于这种模式需要至少在亚洲建立两个强大的据点，只有三个国家及公司实现了这种融合：16世纪的葡萄牙，立足印度果阿，辐射澳门；17世纪的荷兰东印度公司，总部位于巴达维亚，在印度、东南亚、中国台湾、日本出岛拥有领地或商馆；以及18世纪的英国东印度公司。

17世纪，英国东印度公司在印度的三大主要基地为孟买、马德拉斯和加尔各答。1682年，荷兰东印度公司军队占领万丹，英国东印度公司无法继续参与东南亚香料贸易。英国东印度公司只控制了位于苏门答腊岛明古连的一个小据点，在此进行有限的亚洲内部棉花、胡椒贸易。当广州的茶叶和瓷器贸易兴起时，英国东印度公司并没有太多资源可以用于易货交易，而印度生产的棉花也主要出口欧洲市场。因此，英国不得不采用第一种贸易模式，将白银运往亚洲。

然而，随着英国1757年征服印度孟加拉邦，情况发生了变化。英国东印度公司在孟加拉的殖民权力包括对印度公民和企业征税。因此，英国可用其在印度获得的白银购买中国商品。但这并非英国东印度公司政府在印度殖民地获得的唯一好处。正如约翰·达尔文指出，征服亚洲最富裕地区之一，标志着大英帝国统治世界的开始。② 几十年间，棉花的贸易条件发生了改变，英国一跃成为最大的工业化棉纱生产国，在亚洲、欧洲、非洲和美洲之间建立了全球棉花价值链。

随着孟加拉邦被征服以及1765年孟加拉领地的建立，在英国东印度公司的统治下，孟加拉和包括中国在内的其他亚洲地区之间的港脚贸易开始腾飞，英国得以成功复制葡萄牙和荷兰的亚洲内部贸易模式。

最初，英国东印度公司试图像荷兰东印度公司一样垄断印度、印度尼西亚和中国之间的亚洲内部贸易，但未能有效加以控制。他们要求私营贸易商从该公司处购买贸易许可证。随着时间的推移，亚洲内部的港脚贸易变成以私营贸易为主。原棉、棉织品、珍珠、硝石、鱼翅等商品销售成为驻印英国私营贸易商在广州的重要收入来源。从一开始，私营贸易商在与广州十三行商人的贸易中便实现了顺差。他们在广州销售了很多产品，获取的主要是白银。茶叶贸易则完全被英国东印度公司掌控，除了瓷器外，他们对其他中国产品没有很大的需求。1786年，私营贸易商的贸易顺差超过100万两，而英国东印度公司的贸易逆差接近400万两。

随着港脚贸易商继续向中国商人销售商品，中国输入的银锭不断减少。仅仅10

---

① Nierstrasz 2015, pp.39–40.

② Darwin 2007.

年后，1798 至 1799 年，英国对中国贸易自 1699 年"麦克斯菲尔德号"开启广州贸易以来，首次实现贸易顺差。在 18 世纪和 19 世纪之交，中国失去了保持几个世纪的贸易主导地位。"白银吸纳"变为"白银流失"。贸易条件在几年内发生了改变。这其中，一种产自孟加拉的新产品——鸦片——扮演了重要角色，扭转了中英贸易的失衡。

鸦片在中国最早作为药物使用，唐代即已通过阿拉伯商人进口鸦片。1729 年，清廷颁布了一项法令，禁止在中国吸食和买卖鸦片[1]，但未能制止非法鸦片交易。英国东印度公司控制孟加拉邦后，开始将印度鸦片运往中国。1773 年，英国东印度公司在印度对鸦片的购买和销售进行官方垄断，并在加尔各答进行公开拍卖，港脚商人可通过这种方式获得鸦片并在广州销售。

由于与中国进行鸦片交易不合法，英国东印度公司不愿直接参与中国的鸦片运输和销售，因此出现了三角贸易。私营商人在加尔各答购买鸦片，将其走私到中国并获得白银，然后将白银交给广州的英国东印度公司换取汇票。这些汇票可在印度或伦敦兑现。如此，港脚商人无须通过冒险航行将银币从广州运回家乡，而英国东印度公司也无须从欧洲进口白银：这是英国东印度公司在 18 世纪 70 年代结束银锭采购的原因之一。英国东印度公司可以从广州的英国私营贸易商那里获得购买茶叶和瓷器所需的白银。

统计数字表明，随着英国私营贸易商拓展中印港脚贸易，汇票交易也得以发展。1779 到 1785 年，英国东印度公司广州商馆资金的三分之二为汇票形式——该公司用国库券从广州的其他英国私营贸易商手中得白银，[2] 而无须从欧洲进口白银。茶叶贸易格局由"以银换茶"转变为"棉花和鸦片换茶"或"棉花和鸦片换瓷"。

在港脚贸易初期，印度棉花是英国东印度公司出口中国的主要商品。1775 至 1800 年，鸦片仅占出口额的 15%。自 1820 年起，鸦片成为它最重要的出口产品[3]，自此中国贸易逆差变得十分严重，通商贸易演变成"鸦片换茶换银"的方式。不过那时，欧洲与中国开展的欧亚大陆瓷器贸易已经结束——英国东印度公司于 1791 年停止进口瓷器。英国东印度公司的船员仍会私下进行瓷器交易，并且一些港脚商人在中国和印度之间进行规模不大的瓷器贸易。

1833 年，英国东印度公司丧失了亚洲贸易的垄断地位，私营贸易商伺机在广

---

[1] Yang-Chien Tsai, pp.193–194.

[2] Yang-Chien Tsai, p.218.

[3] Yang-Chien Tsai, p.209.

州扩大其贸易活动。中国政府试图在广州扣押鸦片走私贩以阻止白银流失,鸦片战争随之打响。1842年,第一次鸦片战争结束,中英双方签订了不平等条约《南京条约》。随着条约的签订,一口通商制度结束,中国被迫开放另外四个通商口岸进行对外贸易:厦门、福州、宁波、上海。此外,英国对距离广州南部仅100千米的香港岛实行殖民统治,也是西方列强在中国第一次实行殖民统治。同时,中国政府还必须支付2 100万银圆的赔款。[①]

考察一下排名前五的中国瓷器欧洲进口商——荷兰东印度公司、英国东印度公司、瑞典东印度公司、丹麦亚洲公司和法国印度公司,它们进口中国瓷器的数量占欧洲进口总量的90%——我们会发现不同的资金来源。

其中,荷兰东印度公司于17世纪初便开始瓷器贸易,主要通过重要的贸易集散地安平古堡和巴达维亚开展亚洲内部贸易。1680年之前,荷兰东印度公司输出的白银寥寥无几。然而,随着1729年荷兰人开始在广州开展直接贸易,他们不得不从欧洲进口更多白银用以购买瓷器。[②] 与英国东印度公司类似,荷兰东印度公司在18世纪下半叶面向常驻亚洲的外国公民加大了汇票发行力度。

1760年之前,英国东印度公司用白银购买瓷器。之后,他们设法提高了羊毛和金属等欧洲商品的比例。1770年之后,英国私营贸易商的港脚贸易不断扩大,从而可以进行棉花对瓷器以及少量鸦片对瓷器的间接易货交易。由于这种模式起步较晚,因此英国东印度公司只在最后20年的瓷器贸易中采用了这种模式。据估计,只有1 000万件瓷器间接"交换"了欧洲和印度货物,其中只有10%的间接易货交易是通过鸦片贸易实现的。就是说,在整个中欧外销瓷贸易史上,只有大约100万件瓷器是用"黑钱"支付的。

至于瑞典、丹麦和法国的东印度公司,则是简单地将西班牙银圆运到广州来购买瓷器。

因此,正如我们所看到的,瓷器贸易是欧洲和中国之间最后一次平等、公平的交流。瓷器贸易结束后,贸易收支向着有利于欧洲人的方向发展。到18世纪末,由于中国的进口超过了出口,中国陷入贸易逆差,大量白银流向西方。两个主要因素促成了这一历史性的经济变化:英国对印度的征服,以及英国商人出口印度产品,包括合法的棉花和1820年后非法出口的鸦片。后者不仅是对中国人民造成巨大危害的非法有害产品,而且是在1840至1842年的第一次鸦片战争中被粗暴地强加给中

[①] Bai Shouyi 2009, pp.400–404.
[②] Nierstrasz 2015, p.40.

国的。中国花了大约 200 年时间，直到 1995 年才重新实现贸易顺差。

许多作家描述了历史上这种经济优势从东方向西方的结构性转移，典型的如美国经济学家彭慕兰，他将这个过程称为"大分流"，它始于进出口平衡的逆转。但即便如此，中国在当时仍然是世界最大经济体。根据英国经济学家安格斯·麦迪森的测算，要到 1840—1850 年左右，中国才将最大经济体的位置拱手让给西欧。

许多因素促成了这种转变。如上所述，对印度的征服是国际收支发生变化的主要原因。然而，东方的相对衰落和西方的崛起有着多方面的根源。安德烈·贡德·弗兰克列出了至少三个主要因素：其一，美洲，尤其是美洲的黄金和白银的发现；其二，非洲和美洲关于奴隶和农产品的三角贸易以及对人民的剥削；其三，所谓的"站在亚洲的肩膀上"。有了美洲的白银，欧洲就能加入利润丰厚的亚洲内部贸易中。军事力量和工业化进一步加速了这一进程，但并不是主要因素。

客户

我们已经研究了陶瓷产品、贸易路线、承运商和商人、贸易经济，现在来谈谈欧洲、美国或西亚的终端客户。

17 世纪和 18 世纪早期瓷器的欧洲顾客，主要为荷兰的富有家庭以及欧洲各皇室贵族。他们主要收藏康熙青花瓷、日本伊万里瓷、日本柿右卫门烧和中国五彩瓷。这些藏品大多不作为餐具使用，而是作为室内装饰摆在陈列室中。因此，当时购买的瓷器主要为花瓶等收口型瓷器、盘子和碗。

我们从 20 世纪 90 年代越南南部昆岛渔民发现的沉船"头顿号"，可以看出当时欧洲的需求。1690 年"头顿号"在前往巴达维亚的途中沉没（收藏 41）。沉船上发现的 48 000 件物品，大部分为康熙时期景德镇青花瓷，多为带盖或不带盖的小花瓶，仅用于摆设欣赏，并且通常用于摆列成五件式陶瓷饰品。此外，还有一批令人叹为观止的白瓷。

随着 18 世纪瓷器被大宗进口以及随之带来的价格下跌，这种情况发生了变化。陶瓷不仅作为陈列品进行展示，而且成为日常用品。欧洲人有饮茶、咖啡和巧克力的习惯，这就要求烧制出新的瓷器造型。当时货船的货物清单以及被发掘的沉船显示，花瓶不再是流行进口商品，而盘子、茶杯和茶碟等餐具取而代之，逐渐成为主要进口商品。

荷兰人只习惯使用中国青花瓷，英国人也是如此。当日本开始向欧洲出口色彩艳丽的伊万里烧和柿右卫门烧后，人们的品位也发生了变化。法国东印度公司进口的瓷器主要来自康熙之后的时期，其核心客户——法国客户更偏爱色彩艳丽的彩釉瓷器。通常采用西方装饰或"相当西方化"装饰的粉彩瓷器成为出口法国的主要瓷器。

在欧洲，最有名的瓷器收藏家是波兰国王、萨克森选帝侯奥古斯特二世（1670—1733年，图3.4）。他大约收藏了24 000件精美的东亚瓷器，并自称这种喜好为"陶瓷瘾"。这与他在德累斯顿的其他艺术爱好一起，增加了国库负担。他还在德累斯顿的诺伊施塔特区易北河北岸规划建造了一座专门用来展示瓷器的日本宫。他对瓷器的狂热，推动了迈森成为欧洲第一个掌握瓷器制造秘诀的城市。而今，德累斯顿茨温格宫的奥古斯特二世收藏馆可能是世界上最大的中国外销瓷收藏馆，也是迄今为止最大的康熙瓷器收藏馆。

图 3.4 奥古斯特二世

在17和18世纪中国风流行期间，很多欧洲皇室建造了巴洛克式房间作为瓷器陈列室，用于展示中国瓷器或中国风格的欧洲瓷器。其中很多陈列室都湮没在历史的尘沙中，只有少数几处至今仍可供我们瞻仰：葡萄牙的桑托斯皇宫，德国的夏洛特宫（图3.5）、奥拉尼堡宫、阿恩施塔特新宫，奥地利的维也纳美泉宫，以及拉脱维亚的伦代尔宫。其中，年代最久远的当属葡萄牙的桑托斯皇宫，穹顶上装饰有克拉克瓷青花瓷盘。

除了上述历史上的原始收藏外，许多博物馆也收藏了出口西方市场的亚洲外销瓷：中国的广州十三行博物

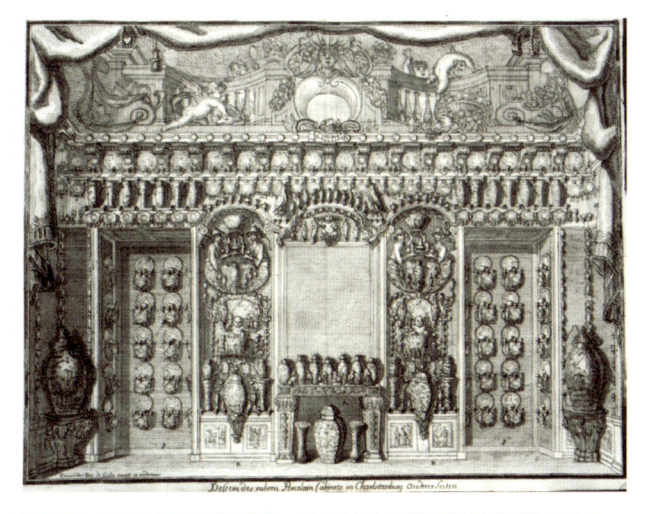

图 3.5 普鲁士国王腓特烈一世在柏林夏洛特宫的瓷器陈列室

馆收藏了大约650件19世纪出口欧美市场的陶瓷。美国的特拉华州温特图尔博物馆收藏了5 000件18世纪末和19世纪出口西方市场的中国陶瓷。荷兰的格罗宁根博物馆和公主瓷器博物馆[①]，英国的牛津阿什莫尔博物馆、伦敦大英博物馆，美国的纽约大都会艺术博物馆、塞勒姆皮博迪·艾塞克斯博物馆，以及瑞典的斯德哥尔摩远东古物博物馆，均是主要的外销瓷收藏馆。

至于亚洲区域，奥斯曼帝国和波斯萨非王朝是外销瓷的重要客户。如果不考虑中国和东南亚博物馆里的沉船物品，伊斯坦布尔的托普卡帕宫博物馆是世界上收藏中国外销瓷最多的地方之一。另一个著名的亚洲收藏家是泰国国王拉玛五世（1853—1910年），收藏了很多光绪年间仿康熙风格瓷器。

由于中国外销瓷多根据西方品位进行定制，今天外销瓷在中国普遍不被欣赏，也不受重视。中国收藏家和历史学家对外销瓷的主流印象还停留在按需生产的瓷器或"中国订单瓷器"上。

没错，西方人对于外销瓷的干预确实存在。早在16世纪，葡萄牙人便开始对中国制瓷工匠施加影响。有时他们会要求采购某种中国市场上不存在的瓷器器型和造型，或者会向制瓷工匠提供家族徽章或耶稣会会徽等主题图样，要求其以白底蓝花的形式将图样绘制在釉面之下。

明末清初（约1620—1670年），荷兰客户要求在中国主题中添加类似郁金香的纹饰。[②] 这一时期荷兰开始了郁金香泡沫。从某种意义上说，荷兰的郁金香狂热在当时已经通过定制的外销瓷影响到中国，中国生产商会根据西方客户需求生产郁金香主题的中国青花瓷。德化瓷窑则开始生产饰有身着传统服饰的荷兰人物或者荷兰家庭的精巧中国白瓷器。

亚洲客户也会对外销瓷提出自己的需求。中国出口日本的，便是定制的"染付"青花瓷。阿拔斯王朝、奥斯曼帝国、波斯或马来亚群岛的客户也要求生产定制瓷器。

不过，人们过高估计了当时瓷器纹饰定制的程度。其实，只有极少数商品纯粹迎合西方口味。纹章瓷（收藏83）以及带有基督教宗教场景、西方风景或巴洛克式边框装饰的中国订单瓷器纯属小众产品，并且主要通过私营贸易商进行贸易。其中，大部分私营贸易商是东印度公司的员工，他们使用分配给个人的贸易配额购买

---

① 荷兰列乌瓦尔登的赫特·普林塞霍夫博物馆也拥有一套大型漳州瓷器画册，由一位荷兰采矿工程师在1868至1918年间在印度尼西亚编纂。
② Volker 1954, p.60.

定制瓷器。通常，他们提供西方素描手稿以及铜版画，要求按照这些图样绘制瓷器纹饰。然而，纯粹的西方风格纹饰并不多见。只是由于很多关于 19 世纪 60 年代和 70 年代外销瓷的著作都是重点关注西方风格纹饰，以至于误导了欧洲人的看法。[1] 而且，欧洲的许多博物馆并未真正收藏典型的外销瓷。分析东印度公司的数据可知，大概只有 1% 至 2% 的瓷器采用指定纹饰。[2]

直至 18 世纪 30 年代雍正皇帝统治时期，中国外销瓷纹饰一直奉行中国设计理念，只有极少数例外，比如明代出口至葡萄牙的青花瓷，出口至荷兰、饰以"荷兰东印度公司"徽章的瓷器。就五彩瓷而言，人们很难分辨出到底是出口到欧洲（如德累斯顿收藏），还是为中国客户生产（如故宫博物院收藏）。在研究这一阶段的瓷器贸易时，我们应该重点关注的是器型和造型，而非纹饰。

事实上，从瓷器外销之初，瓷器造型便反映了其可能的用途。所有外销瓷均是如此。在中国，碗和小盘子是标准餐具。然而，中国元代瓷窑的阿拉伯客户却要求生产大号餐盘，以用于装饰和分享食物。荷兰人也是如此：与中国日用瓷器相比，克拉克青花瓷盘的尺寸较大（直径 20 到 50 厘米），而且扁平的边沿在中国从未出现。不过，这种瓷盘装饰根本不是欧洲风格。

在 1757 至 1800 年一口通商体系兴盛时期，外销瓷的造型完全遵循了西方的饮食习惯：带柄杯、咖啡壶、汤盘、肉盘、酱汁船、船形调味汁壶、盐瓶、盖碗、牛奶罐和糖盒均出现在货物采购清单中（图 3.6）。

这一时期的外销瓷纹饰仍保持中国风格，但会按照西方审美进行改造。令人惊讶的是，景德镇为宫廷烧制的御用瓷器或为中国客户烧制的瓷器也符合西方审美。针对中国国内市场的瓷器和外销的"粉彩"瓷器看起来十分相似。当然，对御用瓷器的要求更严苛，因而质量更好，但其艺术审美或传统并无不同。

另一个例子是中国国内市场常见的瓷器纹饰图案"亭子和河流"（图 3.7）。人们在将这种纹饰应用于外销瓷时，根据欧洲市场审美进行了简化，也可能按照欧洲对"中国风"的想象进行了定制化处理，但整体仍非常接近中国内销瓷器的青花河景图案。这是所有外销瓷的真实故事。

---

[1] 例如 Palmer 1976, p.22："只有器型和纹饰均为西方定制的瓷器，才充分体现了外销瓷的性质"，或者 Beurdeley 1962。

[2] Palmer 1976, p.24.

图3.6　茶会，油画，约瑟夫·范·阿肯（约1704—1749年）绘

欧洲客户习惯了中国装饰，斯塔福德郡和什罗普郡的瓷器工厂对这种纹饰进行仿制，并称之为"柳树"或"双寺"图案。而中国装饰随着时间的推移也发生了变化，明显变得更"西方化"。然而，值得注意的不是中国商品采用了西方风格，或是西方商品采用了中国风格：这是一种跨文化的融合，海上丝绸之路打造了一种新的全球化或欧亚文化。

图3.7　左：英国斯塔福德郡蓝色转印"柳树纹"珍珠色白陶碟（约1800年）；右：中国南京式样青花"柳树纹"瓷碟（约1800年）

中欧瓷器贸易的终结

> 虽然十三行退出了历史舞台，但其诚信务实、敢为人先、开拓进取、兼容并蓄的精神被广州人传承至今。
>
> ——广州十三行博物馆铭牌

19世纪，由于品位的变化、高额的瓷器进口税以及来自欧洲制造商的激烈竞争，中欧瓷器贸易开始走下坡路。

早在明末清初，荷兰的代尔夫特就开始仿制青花陶瓷。1709年，萨克森选侯国的迈森市首次掌握了真正的瓷器制造技术。后来欧洲越来越多的地方也掌握了这种技术。英国软瓷、米色陶器和珍珠色白陶以及其他欧洲陶瓷开始取代中国陶瓷。

到18世纪末，几乎所有的东印度公司都停止了进口瓷器：1790年法国印度公司停止进口，1791年英国东印度公司停止进口，1794年荷兰东印度公司停止进口，1805年瑞典东印度公司停止进口，1806年丹麦亚洲公司停止进口。大多数东印度公司失去了贸易垄断地位并清算停业。从那时起，欧亚贸易以私营贸易为主，主要进行茶叶贸易，几乎不再涉及瓷器贸易。

不过，也有一个例外：从1784年到19世纪末，美国成为青花瓷（广东式样瓷器和菲次休瓷）的重要出口目的地，以及中国的瓷器贸易伙伴。甚至直至清朝灭亡，色彩鲜艳的广彩瓷如玫瑰奖章样式和大奖章样式瓷器仍主要销往美国。据皮卡德等人估计，美国贸易商进口了约3 000万至4 000万件中国陶瓷。不过，对美出口量无法弥补中国对欧出口的下滑。而且，日本开始向美国出口瓷器，与中国展开竞争。

这一时期，外销瓷的质量也开始下降。中国玫瑰奖章样式和大奖章样式瓷器以及日本的伊万里烧、萨摩烧和九谷烧均为批量生产瓷器，这在一定程度上破坏了亚洲外销瓷在专业人员眼中的形象。

1842年，中英第一次鸦片战争结束，一口通商体系随之结束；1856年第二次鸦片战争期间，十三行被纵火烧毁。"就此，外国人在广州生活的第一个时代宣告结束。剩下的商人和领事馆工作人员迁至澳门……"[1] 跨文化交流以一场灾难告终，120年后才实现中西关系正常化。

---

[1] Farris 2016, pp.64–65.

然而，亚洲内部贸易在19世纪仍在继续。在南海发现的几艘沉船就证实了19世纪的贸易：

1817年3月14日，获英国东印度公司贸易许可的帕尔默有限公司商船"黛安娜号"装载24 000件菲次休瓷、南京式样瓷器、广东式样瓷器和青花粗瓷，从广州返回印度马德拉斯，于马六甲海峡中部地区的丹戎比达拉附近沉没。1994年该船被多里安·巴尔马来西亚历史抢救公司发现，打捞出水的瓷器于1995年被阿姆斯特丹佳士得拍卖行拍卖。

1822年，中国大帆船"泰兴号"载着约35万件产自福建德化窑的青花瓷（收藏116），在驶往巴达维亚的途中在苏门答腊岛附近沉没。这是迄今发现的最大的瓷器珍宝之一，1999年在斯图加特被拍卖。

1840年，一艘中国戎克船"迪沙鲁号"[①]在新加坡附近沉没，2001年被发现，由南海海洋考古公司进行打捞。船上装载了大量的青花瓷和棕釉瓷，包括5万个景德镇汤匙（收藏119），以及为居住在英属海峡殖民地的华人生产的峇峇娘惹瓷。"峇峇娘惹瓷"或"海峡中国瓷"（收藏137）是为新加坡和马来西亚市场生产的代表性陶瓷，主要面向海外华人，色彩艳丽，底色为亮粉色、黄色或绿色，通常带有双喜图案。这种瓷器在民国甚至中国被日本侵占时期仍然在出口。

亚洲贸易的另一个例子是中国的班加隆彩瓷（收藏132）。这是景德镇生产的一种五色釉彩装饰瓷器，通常饰以佛教神像，主要器型包括碗、带盖罐和高足碗。它主要于19世纪出口至泰国，后来在泰国本土被仿制。[②]泰国于拉玛一世（1782—1809年）时期开始进口中国班加隆彩瓷，后来以黄金对班加隆瓷器进行外层装饰，打造出色彩艳丽的莱南通彩瓷。

泰国拉玛五世朱拉隆功（1868—1910年）时期，开始进口康熙时期风格的精致中国青花瓷。[③]这种瓷器如今被称为仿康熙瓷器，展示了其与200年前瓷器造型和纹饰的关联（收藏127-130）。清朝晚期的光绪时期（1875—1908年）主要生产和外销这种瓷器。

20世纪，中国经历了内战、被占领、革命以及被孤立，艺术创新和生产能力遭到严重破坏，出口陷于停顿。而在曾经仿制亚洲陶瓷、模仿亚洲工艺的欧洲，则涌现出了多个瓷器制造和创新艺术中心。在德国的萨克森、巴伐利亚和图林根，奥地

---

① The Desaru ship.
② Robinson 1982 and Rooney 2017.
③ Chandhavij 2015.

利的维也纳和波希米亚，法国的利摩日和塞夫勒，英国中部和丹麦的哥本哈根，新设计、新形式和新纹饰层出不穷。韦奇伍德工厂、斯波德工厂、德国唯宝工厂等瓷器厂量产的米色陶器和珍珠色白陶，使陶瓷变成大众消费得起的产品。受中国白瓷影响的陶瓷小像生产成为欧洲制造商的重要艺术领域。虽然欧洲陶瓷至今仍在使用一些亚洲装饰图案（如柿右卫门烧和伊万里烧设计、之前提到的蓝色洋葱以及柳树图案），但中国对欧洲新陶瓷的影响越来越小。

就产量而言，景德镇如今仍然是中国乃至全世界最重要的陶瓷中心。但今天批量生产的大部分产品要么是仿制明清瓷器用于装饰，要么是价格便宜的餐具。但是这座城市有潜力基于其厚重的瓷器历史和制瓷工艺，再次振兴中国的陶瓷作坊文化。中国陶艺文化依然欣欣向荣。希望有朝一日，中国制瓷艺术能够重振巅峰时期的荣光。

陶瓷生产和使用的历史就是一部贸易史，它体现了全球化的早期形式（表3.2）。许多商品在东亚、南亚、中亚、中东和欧洲之间流通进出口：纺织品、金属、纸张、玉石、香料、茶叶、木材、动物，甚至奴隶和毒品。然而，只有陶瓷凭借手工制作工艺彰显原产地文化，并与目的国文化相互融合。因此，陶瓷传达了品位和艺术，促进了人与人、国与国之间的交流。

表3.2 主要陶瓷外销时期

时间	原产地	主要目的地	主要产品
700—1500年	中国	中东、越南、暹罗（泰国）、马来群岛、日本	青瓷、长沙瓷、青白瓷
1300—1500年	中东、西班牙	意大利、法国、神圣罗马帝国	白锡釉陶
1330—1550年	中国	马穆鲁克苏丹国、波斯、奥斯曼帝国	景德镇青花瓷
"明朝空白期"：1368年至1567年			
1370—1560年	泰国	马来群岛	青瓷、釉下黑彩炻瓷
1370—1650年	缅甸	马来群岛	马尔塔班酱釉陶罐
1400—1680年	越南	马来群岛、暹罗、奥斯曼帝国	青花炻瓷
1500—1670年	中国	马来群岛、暹罗、越南、日本、波斯、葡萄牙、荷兰、西属墨西哥	漳州窑青花瓷和克拉克瓷
1659—1720年	日本	荷兰、英国、萨克森、奥地利、波斯	青花瓷、伊万里烧和柿右卫门烧

续表

时间	原产地	主要目的地	主要产品
1678—1810 年	中国	荷兰、英国、瑞典、丹麦、法国、德意志神圣罗马帝国	康熙青花瓷、五彩瓷、粉彩瓷、纹章瓷、中国伊万里瓷、中国白、南京式样和广东式样瓷器、巴达维亚瓷、宜兴紫砂
1678—1850 年	中国	马来群岛、暹罗	质量较差的景德镇和德化青花瓷
1784—1911 年	中国	美国	广东式样青花瓷和菲次休青花瓷、玫瑰奖章样式和大奖章样式瓷器、纹章瓷
19 世纪—1911 年	中国	暹罗	班加隆彩瓷、光绪年间仿康熙青花瓷
19 世纪—1911 年	中国	越南	顺化青釉瓷
19 世纪—1930 年	中国	新加坡、马来西亚	峇峇娘惹粉彩、娘惹青花瓷
1873—1940 年	日本	英国、美国	伊万里烧、九谷烧和萨摩烧

Chapter 3

The Four Billion Pound Deal: The Economics of the Porcelain Trade

The Extent of Trade

How many porcelains were shipped to Europe from 1550 to 1800? The table below gives an overview of the estimated number of Chinese porcelains shipped to Europe within two and half centuries. In total, about 186 million pieces have been exported. Not much was exported to Europe before or after. The items that reached Europe indirectly through the Middle East in the 14th and 15th centuries are so few, that we even know where they are today. One of them is the so-called *Fonthill* Vase—a *Qingbai* vase of the Yuan dynasty — which is now located in the *National Museum of Ireland*. The other is an early Ming celadon bowl — mounted in silver and gold, bought during a pilgrimage in 1433 by a German aristocrat.[1]

Picard et al, who first tried to summarize the Eurasian porcelain trade in 1966, estimated export of between 142 and 154 million pieces for the European carriers[2], but the research of C.J.A.Jörg showed that the authors underestimated the imports of the VOC and probably the imports of the EIC. In addition, other smaller companies and private traders were

---

[1] Philipp von Katzenelnbogen bought the Longquan celadon bowl during his pilgrimage in 1433/34. It is now part of the porcelain collection of the Staatliche Kunstsammlungen Kassel: see Schmidt, pp.216–218.

[2] Picard et al, pp.33–34.

Table 3.1: Summary of the European-Chinese Porcelain Trade

Period	Main European Trader and Carrier	Main Trading Places	Estimated Number of Pieces Shipped to Europe
1550—1650	Portuguese Estado	Macao	2.5 million
1565–1815	Spanish Manila galleon	Manila	1 million
1602—1657	Dutch VOC	Taiwan, Patani, Banten	3.5 million
1669—1710	British EIC and private traders	Xiamen, Zhoushan	4 million
1683—1728	Dutch VOC and private traders	Batavia	10 million
1699—1805	British EIC and private traders	Canton	50 million
1687—1779	French Compagnie des Indes	Canton	8 million
1729—1793	Dutch VOC	Canton	45 million
1732—1804	Swedish SOIC	Canton	40 million
1734—1806	Danish DAK	Canton	12 million
1700—1800	Others	Canton	10 million
			Total: 186 million

not taken into consideration, and the imports of the Portuguese, French and Swedish had been overestimated.

By far the best porcelain trade statistics are available for the Dutch VOC — the biggest carrier of porcelain to Europe (pic. 3.1) — thanks to the research of T. Volker and C.J.A.Jörg. For the first Dutch-Chinese trade period from 1602 to 1657, the exact figures are known through the analysis of the daily reports from the VOC factories in Hirado,

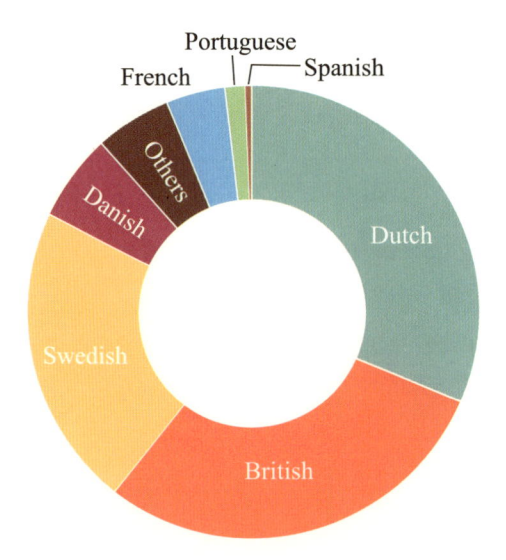

Pic. 3.1: Shares of the European carriers and East India companies in the porcelain trade.

Dejima (Japan) and Batavia. Most of the ceramics during this period did the Dutch purchase from Chinese junks anchoring at the island of Taiwan, in Patani nearby the Isthmus of Kra, in Banten, and in Batavia on Java and nearby Xiamen after 1620.

From 1683 to 1728, the Dutch porcelain trade was facilitated mainly by Chinese junks coming to Batavia and private traders using VOC ships. Unfortunately, this period is not documented. This is quite unfortunate since this period covers by and large the reign of the Chinese Emperor Kangxi (1661–1722) when the finest Chinese export porcelain was produced. Many pieces have been imported as we can still see in the number of *Kangxi* porcelain on the contemporary antique markets in Europe, and in the number of *Kangxi* porcelain in famous collections such as the collection of August the Strong in Dresden.

The VOC archives in the Hague keep detailed records for the 50 years of 1739–1789. Statistics show that 42.7 million pieces were purchased between 1730–1789 for a total value of 4.57 million Dutch guilders (fl.) and shipped in 216 journeys between Canton and the Netherlands — some directly, some via Batavia. Sixteen ships got lost — the Geldermalsen which sunk in 1752 on her homeward voyage from Canton to Amsterdam being the most famous one. The discovery of the so-called "Nanking cargo" was the first spectacular porcelain found in 1985 with more than 150,000 pieces — many of them in very good conditions. Most of the chinaware has been auctioned at Christie's 1986 in Amsterdam — the place where the cargo has been meant to be delivered originally. The Geldermalsen had 203 chests with porcelain on board for the European market and items for the Dutch colony at the Cape of Good Hope (plates 56, 66, 114).

Data for the Swedish SOIC[①] is unfortunately only detailed with regard to the duty paid on the imports in Gothenburg, but it omits the purchase prices in Canton and information on the exact composition of the cargo. This makes it more complicated to calculate the possible numbers of pieces. Data for the EIC, the French *Compagnie des Indes Orientales* and *Compagnie des Indes* respectively are also incomplete, but missing figures can be estimated relatively closely.

The porcelain cargos of other European carriers, such as the Portuguese *Estado da India* and the Danish DAK, are an educated guess; the shipments of the Habsburg Ostend Company, the Prussian *Königlich Preußische Asiatische Compagnie in Emden nach Canton und China* (1751–1757), the Spanish galleon trade from Manila via Mexico to Spain (most of the imports were not transshipped to Spain but stayed in

---

① Goddio 1996.

Mexico) or the *Real Compañía de Filipinas*, are estimated. Data of the shipments by private traders, and the numbers of pieces carried officially or smuggled by crew members are not available. Also, the secondary trade data from the Ottoman Empire or Persia toward Western Europe is missing. However, I assume that through these carriers less than 10 million pieces reached Europe.

In summary, more than 186 million pieces were exported from China to Europe — and about 90% of the ware left China from Canton through the Pearl River towards the South China Sea.

Pic. 3.2: An East Indiaman returning home, by Johann Baptiste Bouttats (1680–1743).

G. Godden[1] lists the purchase prices the supercargo of the English East Indiaman *Prince George* paid in 1755 to a Chinese merchant in Canton: £112 for 10,236 blue and white plates.

The standard conversion rate of European and Chinese currencies in the era of the porcelain trade was approximate as follows:

1 Chinese tael 两 (37.5 g of silver or 1.21 oz) = £0.33 British Pound (6s 8d) = 3.5 fl. Dutch guilder = 1.5 Swedish Riksdaler specie = 1.39 Real de a ocho;

1 Real de a ocho ("piece of eight" or Spanish silver dollar with approx. 25 g fine silver) = 0.72 tael = 5 shilling (£0.25 British Pound).

---

[1] Godden 1979, p.127.

The price for a single plate (0.11 fl. Dutch guilder) is the same C.J.A.Jörg has given for the purchases of the Dutch VOC for the period from 1729 to 1765[①], if we use the standard conversion rate. Since porcelain has been paid in silver currency (and measured in the Chinese silver unit tael) the prices were relatively stable for a long period of time. If we want to calculate the costs of all imports of the various European trading companies, we have to look at the prices of the individual piece and estimate an average price per piece. In the following list, the purchase prices of other items in Dutch guilder (or cents) and in the silver equivalent are listed:

- one teacup with saucer: 8 cents fl. (approximately 0.85 g silver)
- one shaving bowl (plate 61): 70 cents fl. (7.5 g silver)
- one small blue and white teapot (plate 50): 16 cents fl. (1.7 g silver)
- one enameled teapot: 30 cents fl. (3.2 g silver)
- one sauce boat (plate 91): 40 cents fl. (4.3 g silver)
- one 23 cm diameter enameled dinner plate (plate 76): 23 cents fl. (2.5 g silver)[②]

As calculated above, the average porcelain cargo per ship amounted to 200,000 items. The estimated cost of 200,000 pieces is about £2,000 or 21,000 fl. or 8,000 Spanish silver dollars. The whole porcelain export from China to Europe from 1550–1800 cost approximately 7.4 million Spanish silver dollars or £1.85 million or 185 ton of pure silver. Less than £2 million does not sound much, but in inflated prices of 2020 this amounts to £296 million, and the income value (reflecting the purchasing power) in 2020 would be approximately £4.5 billion.[③] The effect of inflation is not surprising if we take into consideration that in 2020 one would pay much more than the 1.7 grams of silver for a blue and white teapot paid in the 18th century.

The Patterns of Trade

One question remains: what could Europe offer to settle the huge bill for approximately 186 million pieces of porcelain? The answer, at first sight, is quite simple: nothing more than Spanish silver coins from Mexico and Bolivia.

The Spanish silver dollar (pic. 3.3) was, from the 16th to the 19th century, the world currency and the only accepted western currency in China. It was also legal tender in the US until 1857. Silver dollar coins used in China have often been stamped

---

① Jörg 1982, p.121.
② Jörg 1982, pp.121–192, purchase prices per item also in Copeland 1980, p.160.
③ Calculation assisted by https://www.measuringworth.com/, accessed on 3 July 2022.

Pic. 3.3: Global legal tender: Silver from Latin America, minted in Europe and paid in Asia. Spanish silver dollar with Chinese counter chops, diameter 38 mm, 27 g of 92% fine silver.

with Chinese chop marks. It is said, that the column surrounded by a ribbon of the Spanish coat of arms is the origin of the USD "$" sign.

The Spanish silver dollar was minted with silver from the Spanish colonies in North and South America. Soon after the Spanish conquest of the Americas and the establishment of the Viceroyalty of New Spain in 1535, silver was discovered in Zacatecas, Mexico. Potosi in nowadays Bolivia was the second place where silver had already been exploited during the Incan Empire. It is estimated that the silver production in these two areas together with some other mines in Mexico and Peru was 17,000 tons in the 16th century; the production rose to 42,000 tons in the 17th century and 74,000 tons in the 18th century.[1] Much has been written about the miserable conditions for the Indian and African slaves working as silver miners in Mexico and Bolivia. The production of mercury in Huancavelica necessary for extracting silver from ore might have been the only thing worse.[2]

The silver went either from Veracruz and Portobello (Panama) via Havana to Seville and Cadiz, or from Acapulco with the Spanish galleon trade to Manila.[3] Most East India companies then purchased the Spanish silver dollars in Cadiz on their way to Canton, or silver dollars were used in Manila to pay for silk and porcelain arriving with Chinese junks. About 25–30% of the American silver production ended up in Asia — mostly in China to finance the huge European trade deficit. China attracted the silver like a magnet, and the Europeans were desperate because nothing else was accepted by the Celestial Empire. Interestingly enough, a similar trade imbalance emerged at the turn of the 21st century

---

[1] Frank, p.143.

[2] Reinhard, p.340.

[3] Reinhard, pp.342–345.

between China and Europe, and between China and the US. Again, China attracted billions of US dollars — a currency that has directly derived from the Spanish silver dollar.

The Europeans were worried about such a trade imbalance. Nonetheless, most of the attempts to pay Chinese merchants with European products failed. The letter of the Chinese Emperor Qianlong sent to King George III after the Macartney Embassy in 1793 summarized the Chinese view on that:

"Hitherto, all European nations, including your own country's barbarian merchants, have carried on their trade with our Celestial Empire at Canton. Such has been the procedure for many years, although our Celestial Empire possesses all things in prolific abundance and lacks no product within its own borders. There is therefore no need to import the manufactures of outside barbarians in exchange for our own produce. But as the tea, silk and porcelain which the Celestial Empire produces, are absolute necessities to European nations and to yourselves, we have permitted, as a signal mark of favour, that foreign hongs [merchant firms] should be established at Canton, so that your wants might be supplied and your country thus participate in our beneficence."

The fact is, European products, such as woolens or raw metal (copper, lead and iron), were not attractive and could only be bartered for a small percentage of Chinese goods.

Fact is also, as we have seen above, that there was a huge trade deficit between Europe and China in the 18th century. It is estimated that approximately 25–30% of all American silver exploited within 250 years ended up in China to finance the huge merchandise imports by the European East India companies.

Porcelain, as we will see, contributed only a very small part to this deficit, but the pattern is the same. Europeans purchased annually 9,000–10,000 tons of tea in Canton during the 1760s and 1770s, and this increased to 20,000 tons in the first decade of the 19th century when the US started to trade with China.[①] The average yearly value of tea purchased in the 1820s by the EIC alone exceeded 213 tons of silver. That means, that by in large the tea imports by the EIC from Canton for only one year in the decade of the 1820s are valued at as much as the whole European porcelain imports from China for 250 years!

The EIC was the most important single company and contributed in the last decade of the 18th century to approximately 75% of all exports from Canton by Western merchants. Being such a crucial customer, Britain and EIC tried various ways

---

① Yang-Chien Tsai, p.80.

to circumvent the silver drain by introducing new schemes. Finally, they succeeded by pumping drugs into the Canton system.

This silver-based trade has also been the main trading pattern for the EIC at least until 1757. This pattern has been the one of Spain via their colonies in America and the Philippines. Spanish or Philippine traders paid the Chinese junks shipping silk and porcelain to Manila in silver coins. This was also the pattern for the two Scandinavian East India companies. Each voyage to Canton either from Copenhagen or from Gothenburg stopped in Cadiz to get the necessary silver coins. The same way applied to the French *Compagnie des Indes*. The export of the Swedish *Silver Riksdaler specie* and the French silver currency was forbidden by law and was not accepted by Chinese merchants.

The statistics show that the EIC paid for 90−95% of the Chinese goods with silver bullion and paid for only 5−10% by selling European goods such as metals or woolens.[1] The EIC tried to increase the volume of European products in return for tea and even wanted to make higher proportions a condition for business with *Hong* merchants. But wool products were not very suitable in the tropical climate of South China.

In 1753 for example, EIC ships brought about 31 tons of silver to Canton (worth £276,333). The peak of the physical transport of silver to Canton took place in the years after the *British Commutation Act* passed in 1784, which drastically reduced the British import duty on tea, and lead therefore to a sharp expansion of tea imports. The 1789−1790 season required a shipment of 80 tons of silver transported by approximately 20 EIC ships landing at Whampoa Island. One could call this the "silver for tea" trade period, but of course, also the "silver for porcelain" period.

However, even though 1789 was the peak for silver exports by the EIC, the overall pattern had already started to change. The EIC silver exports from Europe to Canton after 1757 reduced drastically and came to a standstill in the years from 1772 to 1784, and again after 1806. How could this happen in a time when still thousands of tons of tea were imported by the EIC? Answering this question leads us to the second Eurasian trading pattern, which is based on intra-Asian trade or so-called "country trade".

The Portuguese *Estado da India* invented this pattern in the 16th century and the Dutch perfected the idea. Getting the necessary resources for buying desired goods not by using silver exports but by getting involved in intra-Asian trade is the main feature. It started with the silk for silver trade between Macao and Hirado when Portuguese traders sold Chinese silk in Japan to get silver, which then could be used to buy other Chinese goods, Southeast Asian spices, or Indian cotton. Another example was the

---

[1] Yang-Chien Tsai, pp.118−120.

sandalwood for gold trade between the Portuguese trading posts Timor and Macao.

The VOC imitated this approach and even inherited the silk for silver trade organizing it between Taiwan and Japan. Jan Pieterszoon Coen, the Governor-General of the Dutch Indies described it very well (see letter quoted in Chapter 2): *"And all of it can be done without any money from the Netherlands and with ships alone"*. It reduced trade deficits, transport risks, and the dependence on the European home base. They used Japanese silver, nutmeg from Banda, clove from Ternate, pepper from Sumatra, and sandalwood from Timor to buy products in demand in Europe. This is perfectly reflected in the statistics of the VOC. The proportion of silver exports from Europe to Asia was much lower than in the case of the EIC or the other East Asian companies. Much could be financed from intra-Asian revenues.[①]

The extent of country trade is a good indicator of the incorporation of Europeans into the Asian networks. Only three countries reached this kind of integration which requires at least two strong footholds in Asia: Portugal in the 16th century with its base in Goa and the satellite in Macao; and the VOC in the 17th century with its Asian headquarters in Batavia, several other possessions and factories in Southeast Asia—on Taiwan, Dejima Island in Japan and trading posts in India.

The EIC was, during the 17th century, mainly concentrated in India with three presidencies in Bombay, Madras and Calcutta. The incorporation of the EIC into the Southeast Asian spice trade ended in 1682 when Banten was captured by the VOC troops. The EIC could only control a small trading post in Bencoolen, Sumatra, for a limited intra-Asian cotton-pepper trade. When the Canton tea and porcelain trade started the EIC did not have much to offer. Indian cotton was produced for the European market. Therefore, England had to follow the traditional trading pattern by shipping silver to Asia.

However, the situation changed with the conquest of Bengal in 1757 after the battle of Plessey. The colonial power of the EIC in Bengal included the right of taxation of Indian citizens and businesses. The silver generated in India could then be used to finance Chinese commodities. However, this was not the only advantage of the EIC government in Calcutta. As John Darwin points out, this conquest of one of the richest regions in Asia marked the beginning of a British Empire ruling the world.[②] The terms of trade for cotton had been changed and England became, over the decades, the biggest industrialized cotton yarn producer, organizing the worldwide cotton value chain between Asia, Europe, Africa and America.

---

① Nierstrasz 2015, pp.39–40.
② Darwin 2007.

With the conquest of Bengal and the establishment of the Bengal presidency in 1765, under the rule of the EIC, the country trade between Bengal and other Asian regions including China took off, and the British were able to copy the Portuguese and Dutch intra-Asian trade pattern.

Initially, the EIC tried to monopolize, similar to the VOC, the intra-Asian trade between India, Indonesia and China, but they could not control it effectively. Instead, they at least required private merchants to have a license for trade. Over the years the intra-Asian country trade became a mainly private business. The sale of raw cotton, cotton goods, pearls, saltpeter, shark fins, and many other items became an important source of income for India-based British private traders in Canton. From the beginning, the trade balance of the private merchants with the Chinese *Hongs* in Canton was positive. They sold many things in Canton but received mainly silver. The tea business was exclusively in the hands of the EIC and other Chinese items except porcelain were not really in demand. In 1786 the positive trade balance of the private traders exceeded one million taels whereas the EIC had a negative balance of almost four million taels.

With the proceeds of the sales further silver bullion export could be reduced. Only ten years later in the 1798–1799 season, the British trade balance with China became positive for the first time since the *Macclesfield* started the Canton trade in 1699. At the turning point from the 18th century to the 19th century, China lost the trade dominance it had maintained for centuries. The silver magnet turned into a silver pump in the other direction. The terms of trade had been changed within a few years. And a new product from Bengal became fashionable in China, which had the power to reverse the trade imbalance between England and China: opium.

The use of opium as medicine had a long tradition in China and was imported first from Arab merchants during the Tang dynasty. In 1729 an imperial decree prohibited the smoking and domestic trading of opium in China[①], but the Chinese government was not able to stop the illegal trade. When the EIC took over control of Bengal, the British started shipping Indian opium to China. In 1773 the EIC established a government monopoly over opium purchase and sales in India and organized public auctions in Calcutta where country traders got their opium for the Canton trade.

Since the opium trade with China was illegal, the EIC did not want to get involved directly in the transport and sale to and in China. A triangular business was established. Private traders bought opium in Calcutta, smuggled it into China, and received silver on-site, which then was handed over to the EIC in Canton for which the traders got bills of

---

① Yang-Chien Tsai, pp.193–194.

exchange. The bills could be cashed out either in India or in London. The country traders had no trouble any more shipping silver coins from Canton on a risky trip back home, and the EIC had no need anymore to ship silver from Europe: one of the reasons the silver bullion purchase of the EIC came to an end in the 1770s. The EIC was able to get the necessary silver from the private British merchants in Canton for purchasing Chinese tea and porcelain.

The statistics show the expansion of the bills of exchange together with the expansion of the Indian-Chinese country trade carried out by British merchants. From 1779 to 1785 two thirds of the funds of the EIC Canton treasury consisted of bills of exchange — silver purchased in Canton from private British traders in return for treasury receipts.① No silver had to be imported from Europe during these years. The trade pattern for tea had changed from the "silver for tea" into the "cotton and opium for tea" or the "cotton and opium for porcelain" scheme.

At the beginning of the country trade, Indian cotton was the major export article to China. Opium made up only about 15% between 1775 and 1800. Starting from 1820 opium became the most important export product② and the trade balance became highly negative for China. From then trade turned into the "opium for tea and silver" scheme. However, at that time the Eurasian porcelain trade with China had already ended. The EIC stopped the import of porcelain in 1791. Private trade on EIC ships continued and some country traders also facilitated a reduced porcelain trade between China and India.

The EIC lost its Asian trade monopoly in 1833 and private merchants were able to expand their trading activities in Canton. When the Chinese government tried to stop the silver drain by detaining the British opium smugglers in Canton, the opium war was the response. The first opium war ended in 1842 with the unequal *Treaty of Nanjing*. With the treaty, the Canton system ended, and four additional treaty ports had to be opened for trade with foreigners: Xiamen, Fuzhou, Ningbo, and Shanghai; and Hong Kong Island — just 100 km to the south of Canton—became a Crown colony, the first colonial possession of a Western power in China. In addition, 21 million silver dollars compensation had to be paid by the Chinese government.③

In summary, if one tries to figure out how the huge porcelain export was financed, different sources can be identified. We consider only the top five European importers of porcelain, the Dutch VOC, the British EIC, the Swedish SOIC, the Danish DAK, and the French CDI, who together carried more than 90% of all Chinese porcelain to Europe.

---

① Yang-Chien Tsai, p.218.
② Yang-Chien Tsai, p.209.
③ Bai Shouyi 2009, pp.400–404.

The VOC — similar to the Portuguese — started its porcelain trade, right from the beginning, in the early 17th century as an intra-Asian trade with Fort Zeelandia and Batavia as the main hubs. Not much silver was exported by the VOC until 1680. However, when the Dutch started direct trade in Canton in 1729, the mass imports of porcelain also had to be purchased by increasing silver exports from Europe.[1] Similar to the EIC, in the second half of the 18th century, they increased the emission of bills of exchange to foreign citizens in Asia.

In contrast, the British EIC spent silver to buy porcelains till 1760. Then they were able to increase the acceptance of European merchandise such as woolens and metals. After 1770 the expanding country trade of British private merchants allowed an indirect barter business of cotton and a small amount of opium for porcelain. Since this pattern started rather late — it applied for only the last two decades of the EIC porcelain trade — one can assume that probably only 10 million pieces have been indirectly "bartered" for European and Indian goods and only 10% of these have been indirectly bartered by opium. Only one million pieces of porcelain may have been purchased by drug money—silver gained by British traders selling opium illegally and then exchanged against EIC bills.

As for the Swedish, Danish and French companies, they simply shipped Spanish silver coins to Canton for porcelain trade.

As we have seen, the porcelain trade has been the last period of equal and fair exchange between Europe and China. When the porcelain trade came to an end, the trade balance also changed in favor of the Europeans. By the end of the 18th century, China lost its positive export balance by buying more than it exported. This led to a drain of silver towards the West. Two major factors have contributed to this historical economic change: the British conquest of India and the export of Indian products by British traders legally (cotton) and illegally (opium). The latter has not only been an illegal and harmful product with devastating effects on the Chinese people, but it has also been violently forced on China during the first opium war from 1839 to 1842. It took China approximately 200 years until 1995 to realize again constant trade surpluses.

Many authors have described the tectonic shift of economic power from the East to the West — "the great divergence", as Kenneth Pomeranz called it. It started with the changes in the export-import balance. However, China was still the biggest economy in the world, even when the trade surpluses against Western Europe turned into trade deficits. According to the calculations of the British economist Angus Maddison, it lost its

---

[1] Nierstrasz 2015, p.40.

position as the biggest economy against Western Europe around 1840–1850.

Many factors have contributed to this shift. The conquest of India as pointed out above has been the main reason for the changes in the balance of payments. However, the relative decline of the East and the rise of the West had their roots in various factors. Andre Gunder Frank lists at least three main factors: first the discovery of America including the silver and gold of the Americas, second the triangular slave and agricultural commodity trade and exploitation of people in Africa and America, and third the so-called "climbing up on Asian shoulders".[①] With the silver of America, Europe became incorporated into the rich Asian trade as we have described above. Military power and industrialization have further accelerated the process but have not been the major factors.

The Customers

We have studied the ceramic products, the trading routes, the carriers, the merchants, and the economics of trade, but have hardly cast an eye on the ultimate customers in Europe, the US, or West Asia.

In the 17th century and the early 18th century, European customers were wealthy families from the Netherlands and aristocrats from all European courts. In many aristocratic collections of the early 18th century, one would find mainly *Kangxi* blue and white porcelain, Japanese *Imari*, Japanese *Kakiemon*, and Chinese *Famille verte* porcelain. Most of these types have not been used as tableware but displayed in the interior and in special cabinets. Therefore, vases, plates, and big bowls dominate the collections.

The cargo of the *Vung Tau* shipwreck is a good example of what was demanded by Europeans during that time (plate 41). The ship sank on its way to Batavia in 1690. Most of the 48,000 recovered items are small vases with or without covers, for display only and often arranged as garnitures.

This changed in the 18th century when millions of porcelains were imported and the prices dropped. Porcelain was not only displayed but became rather a commodity for daily use. The tea, coffee and chocolate drinking habits made new forms necessary. The trade lists and pieces discovered on the shipwrecks illustrate that plates, cups and dishes replaced vases as major imports.

---

① Frank 1998, pp.277–283.

The Dutch had been used to blue and white only; the same applied to the British. When Japan started exporting the more colorful *Imari* and *Kakiemon* porcelain to Europe, tastes were changing. French customers — being the focus of the French *Compagnie des Indes* who imported most of their porcelain only after the Kangxi period had a preference for colorful enameled ware. *Famille rose* porcelain often with western decor or with a quite westernized decoration dominated the export to France.

In Europe, by far the most addicted collector was the Elector of Saxony and King of Poland, August the Strong (1670–1733) (pic. 3.4). His collection consisted of approximately 24,000 pieces of porcelain. He himself called his addiction the *maladie de porcelaine* which, together with other artistic plans he realized in Dresden, was a burden for the state treasury. Many courts around Europe were touched by China and contributed to a new Chinoiserie fashion wave by building East Asian cabinets, Chinese pavilions, or Japanese lacquer rooms. However, August the Strong was unique in planning a whole Porcelain Palace (*Japanisches Palais*) in Dresden Neustadt,

Pic. 3.4: August the Strong, King of Poland and Elector of Saxony (1670–1733).

facing the river Elbe. His passion for porcelain also led to the discovery of the secrets of porcelain making in Europe. The collection of August the Strong now in the Dresden *Zwinger* is probably the biggest Chinese export porcelain collection in the world and by far the biggest collection of Kangxi period porcelains.

Many European courts designed baroque rooms ("porcelain cabinets") during the Chinoiserie fashion period of the 17th and 18th centuries, dedicated to displaying Chinese or European porcelain in the Chinese style. Many have gone, but few are still visible such as the *Santos Palace* in Lisbon, *Charlottenburg* (pic. 3.5) and *Oranienburg Palace* in Berlin,

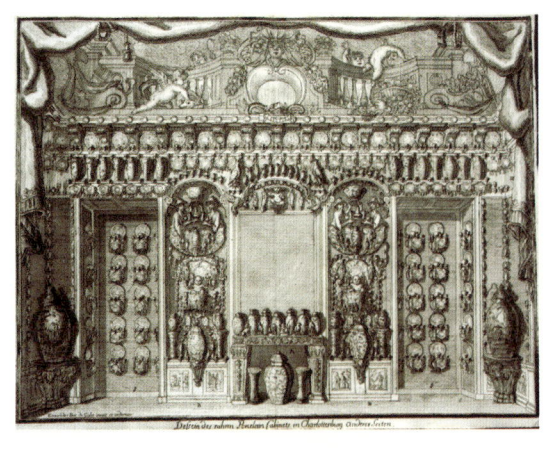

Pic. 3.5: Porcelain Cabinet of the Prussian King Frederick I in the Charlottenburg Palace in Berlin.

the *Neues Palais* in Arnstadt, the already mentioned *Schönbrunn Palace* in Vienna, and *Rundale Palace* in Latvia. The earliest example is the *Santos Palace* in Lisbon with a roof decorated with *Kraak* blue and white dishes.

Apart from these original collections, many museums own Asian export porcelains for Western markets: The *Guangzhou Thirteen Hongs Museum* hosts approximately 650 pieces of 19th-century export ceramics for the European and US market. The *Winterthur Museum* in Delaware has a collection of 5,000 Chinese Western market export porcelains focusing on the late 18th and 19th centuries. Other important export porcelain collections can be found in the *Groninger Museum* and the *Princessehof Museum* in the Netherlands[①], the *Ashmolean Museum* in Oxford, the *British Museum* in London, the *Metropolitan Museum of Art* in New York, the *Peabody Essex Museum* in Salem, and the *Östasiatica Museum* in Stockholm.

In Asia, the Ottoman Empire and Safavid Persia were the most important customer in the intra-Asian trade. The *Topkapi Palace Museum* in Istanbul hosts the biggest collection of Chinese export porcelains worldwide if we do not take into consideration the shipwreck founds stored in Chinese and Southeast Asian museums. Another famous Asian collector of Chinese porcelain in the Kangxi style (*Kangxi revival*) was the Thai King Rama V.

These days, Chinese export porcelain is not highly valued and lacks appreciation in China mainly for the notion that it has been customized to the Western taste. The porcelain on demand or *chine de commande* still dominates the perception of many Chinese collectors and historians on Chinese export porcelain.

Indeed, Western customers shared great intervention in the design of export porcelain. Already the Portuguese started to influence Chinese potters in the 16th century by asking for specific forms and shapes which did not exist in China and providing samples of the coat of arms or religious motifs such as the Jesuit "IHS" monogram to be painted in blue under the glaze.

In the transitional period from the Ming to the Qing dynasty (c. 1620–1670), Dutch clients asked for example for adding tulip-like un-Chinese ornament to the Chinese decoration.[②] This was the time when in Amsterdam a tulip bulb price bubble just started. In a sense, the Dutch *Tulip Mania* even reached China in those days creating the so-called "transitional ware". At the same time, the kilns of Dehua started producing small porcelain "*Blanc-de-Chine*" figurines of Dutch people and Dutch

---

① The Museum Het Princessehof in Leeuwarden in the Netherlands owns also a big Zhangzhou porcelain collection compiled by a Dutch mining engineer between 1868 and 1918 in Indonesia.
② Volker 1954, p.60.

families in their traditional costumes.

Asian customers also have unique requirements. During the transitional period, Chinese producers learned to tap again the Japanese market with customized blue and white porcelain in the *sometsuke* style. Customization also took place for Muslim clients in the Abbasid Caliphate, the Ottoman Empire and Persia, or for Southeast Asian clients in the Malayan Archipelago.

However, the degree of customization of the decor is by far overstated. In fact, only a very small percentage of items reflect purely Western taste. Armorial porcelain (plate 83) and *chine-de-command* with Christian religious scenes, Western landscape, or Baroque rim decoration are an exception. Their import to Europe has been mainly facilitated through private traders — mostly staff of the East India companies using their allotment of private trading items. Western sketches and copper engravings have in some cases been provided to the producer in order to be copied on porcelain. However, the pure Western decor is rather unusual. In Europe, the perception has been misled because many publications on export porcelain in the 1960s and 1970s have been mainly devoted to Western style decoration.[1] Also, many museum collections in Europe do not really have a representative collection of export porcelain. If we analyse the figures provided by the East India companies, we see that probably only one or two percent has been porcelain on demand in terms of decoration.[2]

The decoration of Chinese export porcelain follows Chinese design principles until the reign of Emperor Yongzheng in the 1730s — few exceptions as mentioned were some blue and white Ming porcelains for the Portuguese and Jesuits or items decorated with the "VOC" emblem or transitional porcelain for the Dutch. Whether *Famille verte* items were exported to Europe (as shown in the collection of Dresden) or produced for Chinese customers (as in the Imperial Palace collection) can hardly be distinguished. If we talk about customization in this first half of the porcelain trade, then we have to focus rather on the forms and shapes than on the decoration.

Indeed, probably right from the beginning, porcelain shapes have reflected the potential use. This is true for all export porcelain. In China bowls and small plates are the standard tableware. Muslim customers of Chinese Yuan dynasty potters however asked for huge dishes — for decoration and for sharing food. The same applied to the Dutch. The blue and white *Kraak* porcelain dishes are big (20–50 cm diameter)

---

[1] For example Palmer 1976, p.22: "It is only in the porcelains designed for the West in both form and decoration that the nature of the export trade can be fully understood." Or Beurdeley 1962.

[2] Palmer 1976, p.24.

Pic. 3.6: Tea Party, by Joseph van Aken (c. 1704–1749).

in comparison to what has been used in China. Also, flattened rims were unknown in China. However, decoration is not at all European.

During the main Canton system period of 1757 to 1800, the shapes of the exported products followed definitely the Western eating and drinking habits: cups with handles, coffee pots, soup plates, meat platters, sauce boats, salt cellars, tureens, milk jars, and sugar boxes have been on the purchase list of the supercargoes (pic. 3.6).

Also the decoration — still Chinese — became friendlier for Western eyes. But surprisingly, the same applied to the imperial ware made in Jingdezhen for the court or for Chinese clients. The *Famille rose* decorated items ("*fencai*" in Chinese) produced for the inner Chinese market look quite similar to those exported abroad. Of course, the quality differs, which is not an expression of a differing artistic view or tradition, but of a highly demanding imperial client.

Another example is the "pavilion and river" and "willow" decoration (pic. 3.7). River scene decoration is a very common pattern in China also for the local market. Still, it has been simplified for the European market and probably also customized according to European Chinoiserie images. However, the export items are very close to the blue and white river scene decorated pieces for the Chinese market. This is the true story of all export porcelain.

European customers got used to Chinese decor, but Chinese decor changed over time and became apparently more "Western", too. However, the notable thing is not that Chinese things adopted the Western style and Western things adopted Chinese style: what took place was a cross-cultural amalgamation, and a new global or Eurasian culture has been created by the Maritime Silk Road.

Pic. 3.7: Left: English pearlware saucer with blue "Willow" pattern (c. 1800), Right: Chinese *Nanking* blue and white porcelain saucer with "Willow" decoration (c. 1800).

The End of the Chinese-European Porcelain Trade

"Although having stepped down from the stage of history, the Thirteen Hongs' spirit of honesty and pragmatism, opening up and tolerance, as well as daring, has been handed over to the Guangzhou people."

(Plate in the Guangzhou *Thirteen Hongs Museum*)

In the 19th century, the Chinese-European porcelain trade declined due to changing tastes, high import taxes on porcelain, and fierce competition by European manufacturers.

The production of blue and white copies had started in Delft and the knowledge to produce true porcelain had been acquired first in *Meissen*, Saxony in 1709 and later in more and more European regions. The British soft-paste porcelain, creamware and pearlware (both white earthenware), and European porcelain started to substitute ceramic imports from China.

By the end of the 18th century, almost all East India companies stopped the import of porcelain: The CDI in 1790, the EIC in 1791, the VOC in 1794, the SOIC in 1805, and the DAK in 1806. Most of the East India companies lost their trading monopolies and were liquidated. From then, the Eurasian trade became an open endeavor for private traders who primarily traded in tea and hardly in porcelain.

There was only one exception. The US became an important destination and trading partner from 1784 until the end of the 19th century, for blue and white ceramics (*Canton porcelain* and *Fitzhugh porcelain*), and even until the end of the Chinese empire for some very colorful *Guangcai* porcelain called *Rose Medallion* and *Rose Mandarin*. Picard et al estimate an import of Chinese ceramics by US traders of about 30−40 million pieces. In terms of volume, it could not compensate for the European export market. In addition, Japan started to compete with China on porcelain exports to the US.

The quality of the exported porcelain declined as well. The Chinese *Rose Medallion* and *Rose Mandarin* porcelain, and the Japanese late *Imari*, *Satsuma* and *Kutani* ware are mainly mass-produced items damaging the image of Asian export porcelain in the view of experts, to a certain extent.

The Canton-system ended in 1842 with the first Opium War between the UK and China, and the thirteen factories were set on fire during the second Opium War in 1856. "*So ended the first era of foreign life in Guangzhou (Canton). The remaining merchants and consular staff removed to Macao…*".[1] Intercultural interaction ended in a disaster and it took more than 120 years to normalize the relationship between China and the West.

The intra-Asian trade however continued during the 19th century. Several shipwrecks found in the South China Sea give evidence of the 19th-century trade.

The *Diana* was owned by *Palmer and Co.*, a powerful Calcutta-based British merchant, and was licensed by the English East India Company for the "country trade" to sail from Calcutta or Madras to Canton, carrying cotton and opium. The ship would then return to India from China, laden with silks, tea, preserved fruits, and thousands of pieces of fine and coarse blue and white porcelain (plate 115). It sunk in the Strait of Malacca in 1817. The captain and two of the Indian crew lost their lives, the others managed to survive. The wreck was identified and recovered in 1994 and pieces were auctioned in Amsterdam in 1995.

The Chinese *Tek Sing* junk sunk in 1822 nearby Sumatra on its way to Batavia. It is the story of an incredible shipping disaster with more than 1600 dead people. With around 350,000 pieces of porcelain, it was one of the biggest porcelain treasures that have ever been recovered. The treasure has been auctioned in Stuttgart in 1999 (plate 116).

The *Desaru*, a Chinese junk[2] sunk in 1840 off Singapore with a huge shipment of blue and white, and brown glazed porcelains including 50,000 spoons (plate 119) and *Nonya* porcelain for the Chinese living in the Straits Settlements.

Fine blue and white *Bleu de Hue* porcelain was exported to Vietnam. The so-called *Peranakan* or *Straits* porcelain (plate 137) is a famous example of Chinese porcelain produced for markets in Singapore and Malaysia mainly to target the Chinese overseas

---

[1] Farris 2016, pp.64−65.

[2] The Desaru ship.

population. *Straits* porcelain is very colorful enamelware with a bright pink, yellow or green base. It has still been exported during the period of the Republic of China (1912–1949), even during the Japanese occupation of China.

Another example is the Chinese *Bencharong* ware (a five-colored enamel overglaze decorated ware) exported to Thailand mainly in the 19th century and later imitated in Thailand itself (plate 132).[①] The first imports of Chinese *Bencharong* porcelain fell during the period of the Thai king Rama I (1782–1809). Later gold was added to create the very colorful *Lai Nam Thong* ware.

During the reign of the Thai king Chulalongkorn or Rama V (1868–1910), Thailand started the import of fine Chinese blue and white porcelain in the former Kangxi period style.[②] Today this porcelain is called "*Kangxi Revival*", indicating the reference it made to the forms and decorations of the porcelain made 200 years before (plates 127–130). It was mainly produced and exported during the Guangxu period (1875–1908) of the late Qing dynasty.

In the 20th century, due to civil wars, occupation, revolutions and isolation, China lost much of its artistic innovation and production capacity. Exports came to a standstill. In Europe — once copying Asian ceramics and techniques — innovative artistic centers of porcelain production emerged. In Germany (Saxony, Bavaria, and Thuringia), the Austrian Empire (Vienna and Bohemia), France (Limoges and Sevres), the English Midlands and Denmark (Copenhagen), new designs, forms and decorations were innovated. The mass production of creamware and pearlware (e.g. by *Wedgewood*, *Spode*, and *Villeroy & Boch*) made ceramics affordable to everybody (plates 189–190). The production of porcelain figurines — influenced by the *Blanc-de-Chine* items — became an important field for the art departments of European manufacturers. But Chinese influence on new European ceramics became less and less, even though some Asian decor patterns are still produced today (such as *Kakiemon* and *Imari* designs, the *Meissen* "Dragon" decor, the already mentioned "Blue Onion" and the "Willow" pattern).

Jingdezhen is still the most important ceramic center in China, and probably in the world, in terms of output. However, most of the mass-produced products of today are either replicas of Ming and Qing porcelain for decorative purposes or rather cheap tableware. But the city has the potential to rejuvenate based on its expertise and skills.

The history of the production and use of ceramics is a history of trade — an early form of globalization (see table 3.2). Many commodities have been exported and imported

---

① Robinson 1982 and Rooney 2017.
② Chandhavij 2015.

between East Asia, South Asia, Central Asia, the Middle East, and Europe: textiles, metals, paper, jade, spices, tea, wood, animals, and even slaves and drugs. However, only ceramics were able by the hand-made nature to represent the culture of the place of its origin and to integrate the culture of the place of destination. Therefore, ceramics were able to become the ambassador of taste and art, and to facilitate the exchange between people and countries.

Table 3.2: Main Eurasian Ceramic Export Periods

Time	Origin	Main Destinations	Main Products
700–1500	China	Middle East, Vietnam, Siam, Malay Archipelago, Japan	Celadon stoneware, *Changsha* ware, *Qingbai* porcelain
1300–1500	Middle East, Spain	Italy, France, Holy Roman Empire	Faience
1330–1550	China	Mamluk Sultanate, Persia, Ottoman Empire	Jingdezhen Blue and white porcelain
Ming gap: 1368–1567			
1370–1560	Thailand	Malay Archipelago	Celadon, underglaze black stoneware
1370–1650	Burma	Malay Archipelago	*Martaban* storage jars
1400–1680	Vietnam	Malay Archipelago, Siam, Ottoman Empire	Blue and white stoneware
1550–1670	China	Malay Archipelago, Siam, Vietnam, Japan, Portugal, Netherlands, Spanish Mexico	Blue and white Zhangzhou porcelain, *Kraak* and transitional porcelain
1659–1720	Japan	Netherlands, Great Britain, Saxony, Austria, Persia	Blue and white, *Imari* and *Kakiemon* porcelain
1678–1810	China	Netherlands, Great Britain, Sweden, Denmark, France, Holy Roman Empire	*Kangxi* blue and white, *Famille verte*, *Famille rose*, armorial, *Chinese Imari*, *Blanc-de-Chine*, *Nanking* and *Canton* procelain, *Batavia* porcelain, *Yixing* stoneware
1678–1850	China	Malay Archipelago, Siam	Lower quality Jingdezhen and *Dehua* blue and white porcelain
1784–1911	China	USA	*Canton* and *Fitzhugh* blue and white, *Rose Mandarin and Medallion*, armorial porcelain
19th century–1911	China	Siam	*Bencharong* enamel porcelain, Blue and white *Kangxi Revival*
19th century–1911	China	Vietnam	*Bleu de Hue* porcelain
19th century–1930	China	Singapore, Malaysia	*Peranakan* enamel porcelain, *Nonya* blue and white porcelain
1873–1940	Japan	UK, USA	*Imari* and *Kutani* porcelain, *Satsuma* earthenware

第四章 欧亚文化熔炉——贸易背后的故事

> 日本人复制了中国商品,中国人反过来复制了日本商品,欧洲人复制了全部上述商品。然后中国人又复制了欧洲商品。①

我们已经了解了沿着海上丝绸之路建立的欧亚陶瓷市场。然而,这只是欧亚陶瓷故事的第一篇章。东亚陶瓷的欧洲和中东客户不仅进口了数以亿计的陶瓷,而且开始仿制,发明新工艺,进一步发展陶瓷生产。从长远来看,这对欧亚文化融合的影响比单纯的贸易影响更大。欧洲人从进口的亚洲陶瓷汲取审美灵感,拓宽对装饰艺术的理解,然后将亚洲的装饰元素、色彩和造型运用到自己的产品中。这反映了亚洲文化的传播,反映了不断变化的关系和身份认同。

海上丝绸之路沿线的伊斯兰陶瓷

图 4.1 以及表 4.1 总结了青花瓷的不同发展路线及在欧亚大陆的传播方式。前面我们已经阐述了青花瓷在中国和东亚其他国家的发展,我们将在本节分析它在伊斯兰世界和欧洲的发展。

---

① Ganse 2008, p.65.

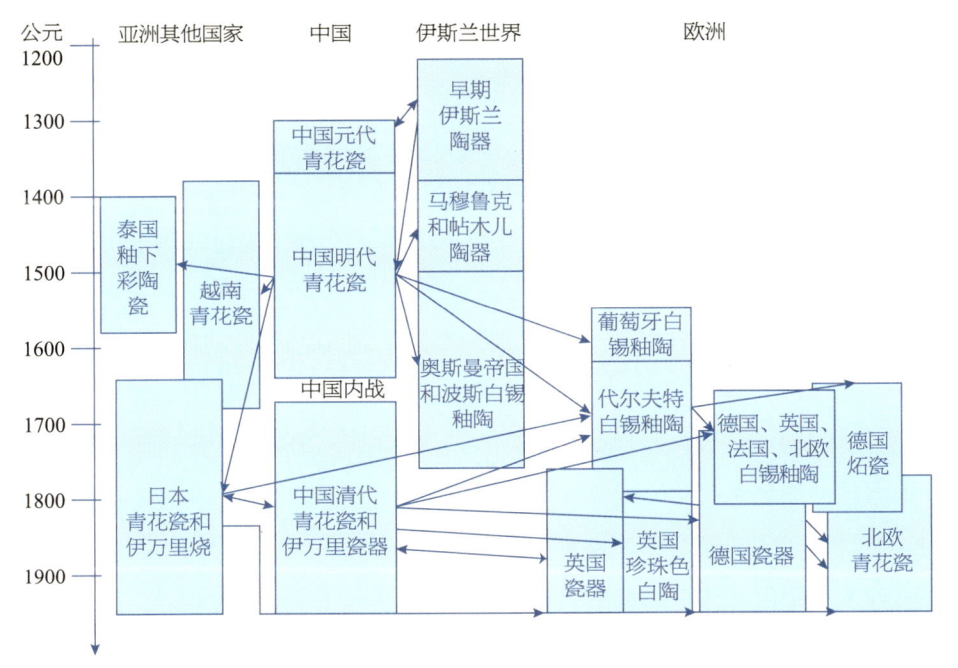

图 4.1 青花瓷生产中心的联系

受伊斯兰教影响的地理区域错综复杂、分布广泛，在历史上横跨西班牙、北非、中东、巴尔干半岛、中亚、南亚和马来群岛等。在发现了古瓷窑的伊朗、伊拉克、叙利亚、土耳其、埃及等国家，许多文学作品反映出伊斯兰国家制瓷艺术的共同特征：在建筑中使用釉面砖、虹彩工艺、釉下纹饰以及三彩装饰。这些瓷窑烧制出的伊斯兰陶瓷，如今收藏于世界各地著名的博物馆。我在这里介绍这些发现，是为了探讨一个问题：伊斯兰世界、中国、东南亚和欧洲的工艺、设计和品位在多大程度上相互影响，相互交流？

正如前文所述，从中国唐代开始，中东就成为中国陶瓷出口的主要目的地，也很早就走上了瓷器生产的道路。

9 到 14 世纪，伊朗卡尚和尼沙普尔是伊斯兰地区产量最高的制瓷中心。卡尚发明釉下彩绘技术，比中国江西还早 100 到 120 年。它生产的蓝色釉和绿松石釉单色釉陶瓷也是精美绝伦，充满异域神秘感。这里还是熔块胎陶的发明地。熔块胎陶是一种人造硅制膏，由石英砂、少量细碎玻璃和一些黏土混合而成，加热时，玻璃熔块熔化并将其他部分黏合在一起。熔块胎陶并非陶瓷，但具有陶瓷的某些特征。这种人造凝胶可被加工成薄壁，这是用粗陶或陶土无法实现的。

尼沙普尔的瓷窑在 10 世纪生产在透明釉下施以绿色、黄色和棕色彩绘的赤陶，不禁让人联想到唐三彩。然而，由于唐代陶器主要用作丧葬品，在伊朗也未发现相关出口商品，目前尚不清楚唐三彩装饰交流是如何发生的。

另外，在今天的叙利亚拉卡市，发现了13世纪早期生产的绿松石釉下黑色装饰的陶瓷。拉卡在阿拔斯王朝哈伦·拉希德哈里发在位时期，曾作为第二个首都。

13世纪，蒙古人建立了一个跨越欧亚的庞大帝国，在其内部实现开放政策。中国元朝青花瓷的诞生便得益于此。青花瓷的出现，可能就源自同属这个帝国的中东对釉下蓝彩陶瓷的需求。1320年，江西瓷窑开始从伊朗进口制青花瓷所需的钴蓝色料。

青花瓷最初主要为外销至伊斯兰地区而生产，这一点可以从以下事实得到证明：在15世纪上半叶明朝宫廷将其纳入御用商品之前，青花瓷在中国国内并没有被重视，大多数中国顾客仍然偏爱单色釉青瓷。而且，在明朝初期，许多中国的青花瓷实际上是仿制阿拉伯或帖木儿帝国的黄铜器皿或花瓶。北京故宫博物院前陶瓷组组长冯先铭对马穆鲁克苏丹国黄铜制品与早期的明青花进行了广泛比较，发现这两个地区的文化互动非常明显。[1]

在14世纪末，青花瓷已经开启了走向世界的文化之旅。统治埃及和叙利亚的马穆鲁克苏丹国（1250—1517年）进口中国青花瓷，促使当地制瓷工匠仿制青花瓷。除了成千上万的来自中国的陶瓷碎片，在开罗[2]和叙利亚也发掘出了马穆鲁克青花熔块胎陶和白锡釉陶。这些文物目前主要珍藏在科威特的阿沙巴收藏馆或塔里克·拉贾巴博物馆。遗憾的是，只有少数藏品保存至今。[3]其中一个出土于叙利亚的青花瓷盘非常罕见，它可能出自大马士革的瓷窑，产自14世纪末或15世纪初，属于中国境外首批中国青花瓷仿制品。[4]

14世纪建立的帖木儿帝国（1370—1507年，包括如今的伊朗、伊拉克、阿富汗、土库曼斯坦和乌兹别克斯坦），首都撒马尔罕和尼沙普尔的制瓷工匠从明初进口的中国商品汲取灵感，烧制出青花瓷。现收藏于塔里克·拉贾巴博物馆的一件15世纪晚期的青花罐带有花卉纹饰，就是波斯仿制青花瓷的早期佳作。[5]

波斯萨非王朝（1501—1722年）建立后，制瓷工匠在更大程度上汲取中国瓷器灵感，进行陶瓷生产。所谓的库巴奇陶瓷（见图4.2）可能就产自波斯大布里士。我们可以从这种瓷器的细节，窥见中国陶瓷以及奥斯曼帝国伊兹尼克陶瓷影响的痕

---

[1] Feng Xianming in: Orientations, 2004, pp.172–186.
[2] Carswell 2000, pp.65–66.
[3] Watson 2004, pp.419–423.
[4] Fehérvári 1998, p.54.
[5] Fehérvári 1998, p.68.

迹。与荷兰的代尔夫特陶器相似，这种瓷器的白色不是来自瓷胎，而是来自深色瓷片上的白色不透明釉彩。它并非瓷器，而是熔块胎陶。①

17 世纪，波斯青花瓷品质达到很高的程度，甚至荷兰东印度公司也开始将其进口至荷兰。著名的荷兰郁金香花瓶便原产于波斯。直至 18 世纪，波斯一直在生产青花锡釉陶瓷，但由于材料易碎、容易开裂或破损，保存下来的陶瓷寥寥无几。伦敦维多利亚和阿尔伯特博物馆是最大的萨非青花瓷收藏馆。②

图 4.2　波斯库巴奇陶瓷，17 世纪

要想完整概述伊斯兰世界陶瓷艺术的主要特征，不可不提及将釉面砖作为建筑的主要装饰元素。我们在西班牙的阿尔罕布拉宫、土耳其的托普卡帕宫、阿富汗的赫拉特星期五清真寺、伊朗的伊斯法罕清真寺以及乌兹别克斯坦的雷吉斯坦广场，均能发现这种瓷砖。在这方面，波斯再次扮演了重要角色。清真寺都有一个主要入口，且装饰传统上以蓝色瓷砖为主，这两个特征均起源于蒙古帝国时期的波斯，并影响了中亚、阿富汗、巴基斯坦和印度的清真寺设计。我们在拉卡和卡尚陶瓷上看到的绿松石釉，同样见诸 14 世纪兴建的伊斯法罕清真寺、苏丹尼耶的蒙古统治者完者都的陵墓以及亚兹德的星期五清真寺。蒙古人在伊斯兰艺术经波斯传至印度的过程中发挥了至关重要的作用。印度莫卧儿王朝（1526—1857 年）的"莫卧儿"（Mughal）便是由"蒙古"（Mongol）一词衍生而来，凸显了这种关系。莫卧儿王朝和帖木儿帝国的建筑深受波斯风格元素的影响，创造了从阿塞拜疆到中国西部，从乌兹别克斯坦到印度的统一建筑设计风格。

伊斯兰陶瓷发展的另一个关键时期，是奥斯曼帝国安纳托利亚西部的伊兹尼克陶瓷制造时期。如上文所述，奥斯曼帝国是中国瓷器出口的主要目的地。从 15 世纪后期开始，伊兹尼克的陶瓷工匠们开始在熔块胎陶上施以透明釉，并使用钴蓝色料进行釉下彩绘。工匠们在熔块胎陶胎体上施以釉底料，在少数情况下施以锡釉，从而形成彩绘所需的白色涂层，仿制中国明代青花瓷，生产青花熔块胎陶。③ 所谓的"金角湾"陶器便是青花瓷的衍生品，在 15 世纪 30 到 50 年代风靡一时。这种瓷器

---

① Langer 2006, pp.26–32 and Watson 2004, pp.449–481.
② Langer 2006.
③ Carswell 1998.

图 4.3　伊兹尼克陶瓷，罗地安风格，约 1550—1600 年

的装饰包括一系列细小的带有小叶子的同心螺旋图案。伊兹尼克于 16 到 18 世纪生产的大马士革陶器（带有绿色和紫色）和罗地安陶器（包括红色，见图 4.3），色彩更加艳丽。

20 世纪，土耳其屈塔希亚的陶瓷制造业复兴，仿制伊兹尼克风格陶瓷，供国内使用以及作为旅游销售产品。从某种意义上说，现代土耳其算是最后加入近 500 年欧亚瓷器贸易的选手之一。

总而言之，从埃及至阿富汗的广大地区在推广欧亚青花装饰方面发挥了关键作用，先是统治埃及和叙利亚的马穆鲁克苏丹国，继之而起的是统治波斯和中亚的帖木儿帝国。而到 16 和 17 世纪，奥斯曼帝国和波斯萨非王朝的青花瓷生产达到顶峰。同期，这种装饰也传播至葡萄牙和荷兰（表 4.1）。

表 4.1　青花瓷在世界范围内流行的里程碑

时间	事件
13 世纪	波斯采用了釉下钴蓝装饰
1320 年	中国景德镇开始烧制釉下蓝彩瓷器
1330 年	中国开始向阿拉伯国家出口青花瓷
约 1380—1400 年	越南和叙利亚生产中国风格青花瓷，这是首次在中国之外生产青花瓷
1499 年	中国青花瓷首次到达欧洲（里斯本）
1500—1750 年	奥斯曼帝国和波斯萨非王朝大量生产中国风格青花瓷
1550—1800 年	中国青花瓷大量出口欧洲
约 1580 年	欧洲（里斯本）开始生产中国风格青花瓷
约 1620 年	日本有田市成为中国境外首个生产出半透明釉下蓝瓷的地方
1660 年	日本青花瓷开始出口到欧洲
1660—1750 年	荷兰代尔夫特大量生产白锡釉陶
1717 年	欧洲（迈森）首次生产出半透明釉下蓝瓷
1760 年	英国伍斯特采用铜板转印技术生产釉下蓝瓷
18—20 世纪	德国、英国和北欧大量生产中国风格青花瓷以及青花珍珠色白陶

中国对欧洲陶瓷制造业的影响

从前面章节我们可以了解到，葡萄牙人开启了从中国进口陶瓷入欧洲的先河，但大规模进口中国陶瓷是在17世纪由荷兰东印度公司开启的，克拉克青花瓷进口一直持续至明末。明清交替期，日本陶瓷部分取代了中国外销瓷，直至1683年清朝重新打开对欧大规模出口的大门。

欧洲对东亚陶瓷的需求不断增加，并在18世纪下半叶达到顶峰。当时，欧洲上层蔓延着一股中国潮流，富裕的荷兰企业主和许多国家的统治者开始收藏中国陶瓷，在宫殿里建造中国厅，用进口中国瓷器来饮茶、进餐，或者摆放在家里进行欣赏。

和中国的亚洲邻国一样，这个巨大的陶瓷市场也促使欧洲进行实验尝试，力图发现陶瓷生产的秘诀。不过，他们真正发现瓷器制造的秘诀，已经是在首批瓷器登陆欧洲之后200年了。在此之前，欧洲人模仿的重点是中国陶瓷的外观，尝试在炻瓷、赤陶、白陶、骨灰瓷以及玻璃制品等器皿上模仿中国风格瓷器的外观。例如，德国韦斯特瓦尔德的霍何-格伦茨豪森等村庄的高白瓷主要为青白色，这毋庸置疑是受到亚洲瓷器风格的影响（收藏165）。

一个特别的例子是灵感来自中国陶瓷的白锡釉陶工艺在欧洲的出现。这是一种白釉棕色陶器，其白釉是对瓷器的模仿，白釉上容易用蓝色或其他任何颜色进行着色装饰。约1580年它在葡萄牙里斯本生产，之后在荷兰，短短几十年遍及欧洲。事实上，该工艺也来源于亚洲。第一批锡釉陶通过西班牙马洛卡岛到达意大利，因而最初被称为马约利卡陶器。16世纪，白锡釉陶产业在意大利的法恩扎和德鲁塔等城市蓬勃发展。在佛罗伦萨，德拉·罗比亚家族创作了白锡釉雕塑。至今，这些雕塑、锡釉产品以及钴料彩绘装饰，仍是亚洲世界在欧洲留下痕迹的证明。

17和18世纪，葡萄牙里斯本、荷兰代尔夫特以及德国哈瑙、法兰克福（收藏167）、纽伦堡或拜罗伊特（收藏173）等城市生产的白锡釉陶，大多是模仿中国青花瓷或具有中国元素的产品。英国利物浦和伦敦（收藏172）、法国鲁昂（收藏175）和纳维尔（收藏176）、丹麦的哥本哈根和瑞典的斯德哥尔摩也生产青花白锡釉陶。法国穆斯特成为非青白锡釉陶以及中国风设计的中心（想象的中国场景和风景）。但是，白锡釉陶和其他陶器均是低温焙烧产品，易开裂、易碎、厚重、不透明且透水。因此，这些陶瓷主要用于装饰，而不能作为日常餐具使用。

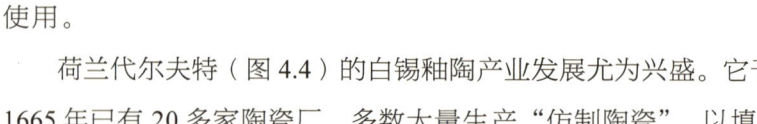

荷兰代尔夫特（图4.4）的白锡釉陶产业发展尤为兴盛。它于1625年兴起，到1665年已有20多家陶瓷厂，多数大量生产"仿制陶瓷"，以填补中国明清交替时期留下的交易空白。制瓷工匠们模仿中国的青花瓷，如17世纪下半叶仿制克拉克瓷（收藏166）。陶瓷厂产品开发的重点是纹绘，画师们精心纹饰的图案常常是独一无二的佳作。

除了中国瓷器仿制品，代尔夫特还出产了很多介于中国设计和纯欧洲设计之间的产品：从克拉克瓷仿制品到伪中国款陶瓷，从中国风景的自由诠释到宗教场景和荷兰风景。后来，粉彩瓷、日本的伊万里烧和柿右卫门烧也被代尔夫特工厂仿制（收藏199）。

图4.4　代尔夫特风景，油画，约翰内斯·维米尔（1632—1675年）绘

由于陶器容易破碎或受损，代尔夫特生产的数百万件陶器大部分都未得以幸存。1683年以后，由于能再度从中国进口瓷器，加之德国以及后来法国、英国生产出真正的瓷器所带来的巨大竞争，代尔夫特陶瓷制造业逐渐衰落。19世纪初，代尔夫特乃至整个欧洲的白锡釉陶瓷制造业销声匿迹，并被许多国家至今仍在生

产的陶瓷和珍珠色白陶所取代。只有一家代尔夫特公司——代尔夫特皇家陶瓷厂幸存下来，它至今仍在生产装饰用的青花珍珠色白陶。20世纪前30年，维也纳制造商戈德沙伊德开始生产艺术装饰风格雕像，这使得白锡釉陶工艺在奥地利重新繁荣起来。

欧洲人真正掌握高温烧制陶瓷的配方和工艺是在18世纪初。1708年，萨克森选侯国的迈森首次成功仿制了中国宜兴紫砂，次年首次生产出青花瓷。这种技术与中国一千多年来的技术路线不同。中国出口了数亿件瓷器到欧洲，中国的制瓷技术传播到日本、朝鲜、泰国和越南，却一直对欧洲保密。正如序言所说，欧洲瓷器的诞生，归功于两个人的不懈努力和多次实验：约翰·弗里德里希·伯特格尔和埃伦弗里德·瓦尔特·冯·奇恩豪斯。

亚洲对欧洲陶瓷设计的影响显而易见。迈森陶瓷厂的早期产品均是直接仿制奥古斯特二世收藏的中国和日本陶瓷。1717年，迈森陶瓷厂首次生产出青花瓷。此后，它还先后仿制过中国白、青花瓷、巴达维亚瓷、粉彩瓷、五彩瓷，以及日本的伊万里烧和柿右卫门烧。没有哪家欧洲瓷器制造商像迈森陶瓷厂这般，生产出如此多样的中国风和日本风陶瓷。

迈森陶瓷厂想要对瓷胎配方保密，却无法避免其他国家厂商挖墙脚。1718年，该配方传至奥地利维也纳，维也纳陶瓷制造随之发展起来。几十年后，该配方被德国赫斯特获得。1768年，瓷器配方传到英国普利茅斯，1781年斯塔福德郡的新霍尔陶瓷厂也获得该技术。①

也是在18世纪，英国洛斯托夫特、伍斯特（收藏178-180）、利物浦、伦敦、斯塔福德郡，以及法国圣克鲁和尚蒂利开始生产软瓷，它们同样受到中国青花瓷、五彩和粉彩瓷或日本伊万里烧和柿右卫门烧的影响。这些陶瓷制品均未能达到瓷器标准。

总的来说，欧洲陶瓷制造主要在两个方面深受亚洲影响。一是技术采用，例如采用锡釉工艺制作白锡釉陶，采用瓷砖装饰墙壁和房屋，这些装饰特征至今仍能在西班牙和葡萄牙见到。特别是在使用彩绘瓷砖装饰教堂、外墙和房屋内部的葡萄牙，阿拉伯风格的影响不容忽视。荷兰的青花瓷砖也借鉴了这种融合中国元素的伊斯兰传统风格（图4.5）。二是艺术风格借鉴，包括借鉴中国设计、色彩和象征图案。

---

① Godden 2004, p.381.

图 4.5　荷兰白锡釉陶瓷砖（1620—1650 年），饰以士兵图案和万字纹

　　18 世纪，瓷器和软瓷取代了锡釉陶，但仿制中国和日本设计的历史仍然持续。中国青花瓷被迈森、维也纳、劳恩斯坦、伍斯特、考利、皇家哥本哈根等陶瓷厂仿制并重新诠释。迈森陶瓷厂最著名的"蓝色洋葱"纹饰灵感就来自康熙时期的中国瓷盘，当时欧洲人将中国瓷盘上的瓜果纹饰误认作洋葱。1739 年起，这种瓷盘开始投入生产。"洋葱图案"（图 4.6）和"蜡菊"（收藏 185），直至 20 世纪中期仍属于德国和北欧典型的中国风青花装饰，并且是最常见的咖啡器皿或餐具的纹饰风格之一。

图 4.6　德国迈森马尔科利尼担任德国迈森陶瓷厂技术主管时期（1774—1814 年）生产的蓝色洋葱瓷盘

地图 4.1 显示了 17 至 19 世纪期间生产中国和日本风格产品的欧洲陶瓷中心。主要的白锡釉陶生产中心包括荷兰的代尔夫特、法国的鲁昂和德国的哈瑙；主要的软瓷生产中心包括法国的尚蒂利，英国的伍斯特、洛斯托夫特和斯塔福德郡；主要的瓷器生产中心，18 世纪上半叶为德国的迈森和奥地利的维也纳，下半叶则有德国的图林根和巴伐利亚东北部的许多制造商，之后是英国斯塔福德郡的新霍尔陶瓷厂。与法国白锡釉陶不同，法国陶瓷受到东亚装饰影响不大。

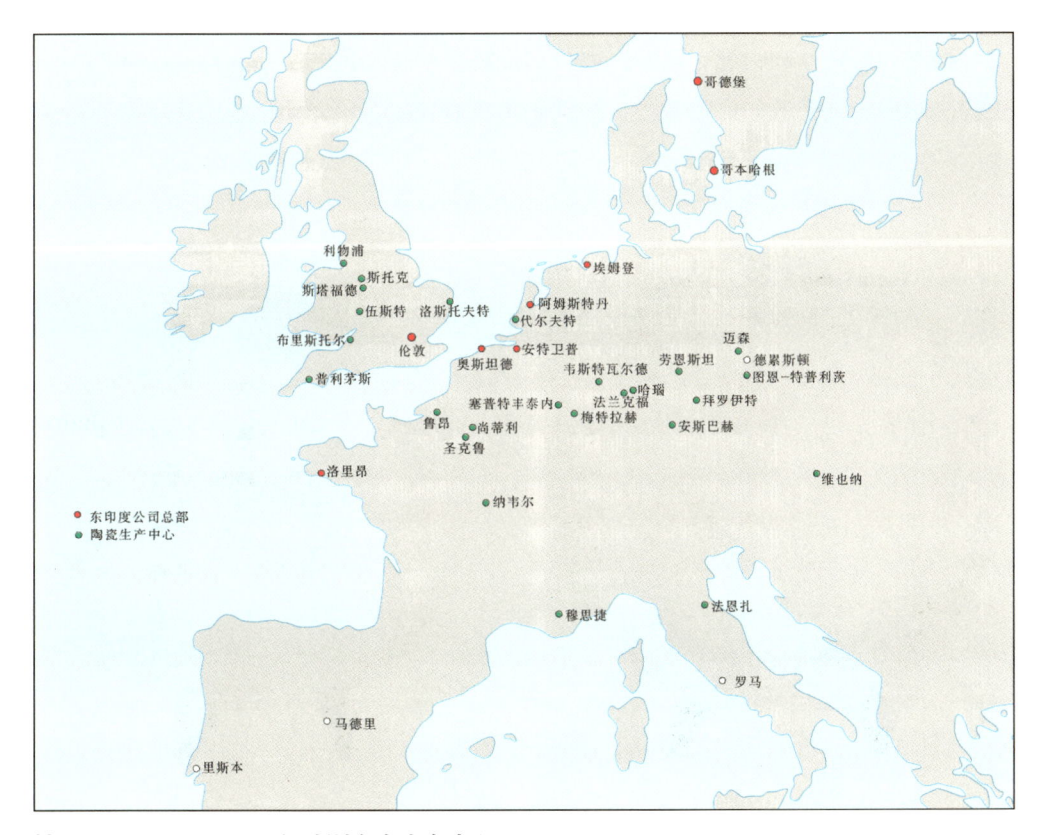

地图 4.1　17—19 世纪欧洲陶瓷生产中心

地图 4.1 还显示了各家东印度公司的主要进口港和总部。进口中国陶瓷数量最多的国家和地区，尤其是英国和荷兰，也成为中国风格陶瓷的主要生产中心，这绝非巧合。特别是英国，根据戈登估计，超过 50% 的陶瓷都受到了东方影响。[1] 英国不但仿制中国陶瓷的种类最多，还制造了不少伪中国款陶瓷。

18 世纪，随着英国成为中国陶瓷的主要外销地，许多英国陶瓷制造商开始仿制

---

[1]　Godden 1979, p.339.

中国的青花装饰，最初的目的可能是替换运输过程中破损的中国商品。随着欧洲人发现了制瓷所需原材料，以及逐渐掌握软瓷和瓷器的生产技术，中国瓷器进口量在18世纪末出现下滑。

英国的中国陶瓷爱好者迈尔斯·马森，原本是英国东印度公司的批发客户，进行了大量中国陶瓷贸易。[①] 1791年英国东印度公司停止了中国陶瓷的官方进口，政府也采取高关税政策来保护本国陶瓷产业，他便在利物浦和斯塔福德郡建立起了陶瓷厂。

当时，伦敦、利物浦、洛斯托夫特和英格兰中部地区的制造商都是优秀的中国瓷器仿制者。今天我们一眼看去，很难将中国青花瓷、粉彩瓷和英国青花瓷、粉彩瓷（图4.7）区分开来。

图4.7 左：英国斯塔福德郡斯波德陶瓷厂彩釉陶盘，采用转印技术绘制釉下粉彩式样纹饰，口沿饰有釉上彩纹饰（1805—1815年）；右：清乾隆中国粉彩瓷盘（约1760年）

1750年，英国斯塔福德郡的制瓷工匠发明了施以透亮釉彩的白色陶器。之后，韦奇伍德陶瓷厂的创始人乔赛亚·韦奇伍德通过添加钴料，让釉彩更加璀璨夺目，使得陶器看起来更像瓷器。他称之为"珍珠色白陶"。1760年，伍斯特发明了釉下蓝转印技术[②]（收藏179），但起初用于瓷器制造，难以应用到陶器上。1784年，乔

---

① Haggar 1977, pp.53–56.
② Godden 2004, p.156.

赛亚·斯波德采用蓝色转印技术替代手绘来制造珍珠色白陶。此后，英国瓷器和陶器上的中国纹饰几乎都是通过釉下转印技术纹绘的，而德国或丹麦瓷器上的蓝色纹饰则为手绘。

斯波德及斯塔福德郡的其他制瓷工匠主要通过对中国纹饰进行复制或者从中国纹饰中汲取灵感，设计出下列图案：柳树样式、双寺样式（图4.8）、长桥样式、水牛样式和菲茨休样式。尤其是前两者，非但在19世纪的英国名噪一时，至今在英国仍被应用，且基本保持原貌。

图 4.8　左：中国南京式样"双寺"青花汤盘，口沿饰以菱纹锦和鱼子纹（1780—1800年）；右：英国马森陶瓷厂蓝色转印"双寺"软瓷盘（1800—1816年）

尽管18世纪下半叶的中国外销瓷上也有类似图案，但我们难以确认，究竟是中国人根据欧洲人的意愿再造了一些梦幻景观，还是欧洲人模仿了从广州运来的商品。这似乎是中亚联合打造共同设计的趣谈，最终却不知道谁才是真正的鼻祖。

表4.2展示了17和18世纪生产亚洲风格或者中国风青花瓷的欧洲著名陶瓷制造商。

一代又一代欧洲人的成长都伴有青花瓷杯、瓷碟和瓷盘的身影，这是欧亚文化认同最具影响力的艺术表现之一。这种文化认同源自13世纪的波斯，大约1320年在中国南方开始成型，于14世纪覆盖中东，并在16世纪到达欧洲。

表 4.2　早期欧洲青花瓷制造商

国家和地区	开始	主要生产地点	陶瓷类型
葡萄牙	约 1600 年	里斯本	白锡釉陶
荷兰	1625 年	哈勒姆、代尔夫特	白锡釉陶
神圣罗马帝国	约 1600 年	韦斯特瓦尔德	炻瓷
	1661 年	哈瑙	白锡釉陶
	1666 年	法兰克福	白锡釉陶
	1709 年	安斯巴赫	白锡釉陶
	1712 年	纽伦堡	白锡釉陶
	1714 年	拜罗伊特	白锡釉陶
	1717 年	迈森	瓷器
	1747 年	维也纳	瓷器
	1770 年	塞特方坦斯（唯宝陶瓷厂）	奶油白陶瓷
	1783 年	劳恩斯坦	瓷器
	1794 年	泰陶	瓷器
英国	1630 年	伦敦、布里斯托尔、利物浦	白锡釉陶
	1749 年	伦敦（弓陶瓷厂，切尔西陶瓷厂）	软质瓷
	1750 年	伍斯特	软质瓷
	1754 年	利物浦	软质瓷
	1757 年	洛斯托夫特	软质瓷
	1775 年	什罗普郡（考利陶瓷厂）	软质瓷
	1768 年	普利茅斯	瓷器
	1781 年	斯塔福德郡（新霍尔陶瓷厂）	瓷器
	1790 年	斯托克，斯塔福德郡（斯波德陶瓷厂，马森陶瓷厂）	珍珠色白陶
北欧	1723 年	哥本哈根，斯德哥尔摩	白锡釉陶
	1775 年	哥本哈根	瓷器
法国	约 1650 年	鲁昂，纳韦尔	白锡釉陶
	1673 年	鲁昂	软质瓷
	1693 年	圣克鲁	软质瓷
	1750 年	尚蒂利	软质瓷

模仿与创新

中国青花瓷是对欧洲影响最大的亚洲风格,为欧洲陶瓷制造商提供了很多灵感,青花装饰被其广泛用于炻瓷、白锡釉陶、软瓷、奶油白陶瓷以及瓷器。

起源于日本、中国后来仿制的伊万里烧装饰对欧洲的影响仅次于青花瓷(见表4.3)。18和19世纪,德国、英国和法国陶瓷厂仿制伊万里烧,英国几家瓷器制造商甚至专注于生产伊万里风格陶瓷。19世纪60年代,日本有田伊万里烧复兴,并且大量出口欧洲和美国。日本的陶瓷生产商以专业的方式融入国际贸易,主要聚焦美国和欧洲市场,出口标准化的伊万里瓷盘和花瓶(收藏142)。深川家族1875年创建的香兰社是日本最著名的生产商之一。[①] 一直到20世纪,英国马森、斯波德、皇家皇冠德比(图4.9和收藏204-208)或者斯波德陶瓷厂生产的伊万里风格陶瓷都备受推崇。

图4.9 英国马森陶瓷厂生产的伊万里风格"日本篱笆"样式软瓷盘(约1820年)

柿右卫门样式瓷器也被仿制,例如德国迈森陶瓷厂(收藏220)、法国尚蒂利陶瓷厂以及英国的切尔西陶瓷厂和伍斯特陶瓷厂。

日本的萨摩烧也出口海外。萨摩烧是在乳色陶器上饰以彩色和金色的釉上彩装饰,釉面透明并有龟裂(收藏147-148)。[②] 它源自九州岛南部,明治时期成为畅销欧洲和美国的出口产品,日本各地瓷窑均有生产。直至1940年,石川县(九谷烧)、名古屋(诺太克烧)一直在生产和出口西方风格和西方化的日本产品。[③] 萨摩烧的

[①] Schiffer 1986, pp.61–108.
[②] Lawrence 2011.
[③] Jahn 2004.

设计影响了波希米亚新艺术陶瓷生产商，如位于图恩－特普利茨的施特尔马赫陶瓷厂和安蓬陶瓷厂（收藏 222）。

表 4.3　欧洲陶瓷生产的主要灵感来源

风格	荷兰	神圣罗马帝国	英国	法国	北欧
中国克拉克瓷	有重要影响	有影响			
中国康熙青花瓷	有主导影响	有重要影响	有重要影响	有影响	有主导影响
中国南京式样瓷器	有重要影响	有影响	有主导影响		有影响
中国五彩瓷	有影响	有重要影响			
中国粉彩瓷	有影响	有重要影响	有重要影响	有重要影响	有影响
中国白		有影响	有影响	有影响	
中国或日本伊万里烧	有影响	有重要影响	有主导影响		
日本柿右卫门烧	有影响	有重要影响	有影响	有影响	有重要影响

日本陶瓷纹饰对欧洲陶瓷的影响仅次于青花纹饰的亚洲设计。而且日本对印象派绘画、欧洲新艺术家具、玻璃、银铜作品、建筑和其他应用艺术等欧洲艺术的影响无可比拟。日本的设计风格和文化传播至欧洲和美国，掀起了一股日本艺术新风尚，并影响了欧洲新艺术运动或青春风格。[①] 法德艺术品贸易商萨米埃尔·西格海姆·宾曾游历日本，并通过横滨一家公司将日本艺术品出口至欧洲。他于 1888 年开始出版《日本艺术》杂志，并在巴黎开设了一家名为"新艺术之家"的著名画廊，新艺术运动由此得名。[②] 尤其是北欧的宾和格伦达尔、皇家哥本哈根和罗斯特朗陶瓷厂，荷兰的罗曾堡，德国的罗森塔尔等陶瓷厂都深受日本影响，它们设计生产出的雅致花瓶，模仿日本柿右卫门或日本青花瓷风格（例如锅岛烧）。陶瓷在东方设计理念传播至其他地方的过程中扮演了重要角色。

H. 戴维斯将受中国图案和设计影响的欧洲陶瓷分为三类[③]，他仅将第三类视为真正的中国风陶瓷。第一类是中国产品的精准"复制品"；第二类是"复制品的复制品"，即经过修改或添加的设计；第三类是对中国相关主题进行富有想象力的加工，从而产生真正的中国风设计。但我认为真实情况更为复杂，因为我们不应该忽略中国陶瓷设计也受到了其他生产商和消费者的影响。在此举几个例子。

---

① Irvine 2014.
② Wolf 2015, p.108.
③ Davis 1991, p.43.

许多早期的迈森陶瓷应属于第一类。迈森陶瓷厂几近完美地仿制了日本的柿右卫门烧和伊万里烧，中国的中国白、粉彩和巴达维亚瓷器。这是精致的复制品（收藏186），或者至少尝试精确复制其设计，即使他们并非总能复制出陶瓷材料。

埃德姆·桑松等法国陶瓷厂的主要灵感来源于粉彩，其生产的瓷器几乎是对粉彩的完全复制，也应该纳入第一类。

英国斯塔福德郡的"柳树和双寺"瓷器也可归入此类（图4.8）。

英国斯波德陶瓷厂后期的"柳树图案"（收藏189）等其他设计图案、迈森陶瓷厂的蓝色洋葱（收藏182）和哥本哈根的蜡菊则可归入第二类。但是，如果我们记得"柳树和双寺"设计可能是英国人的发明，而中国制瓷工匠只是根据客户要求生产，那就很难进行归类。在这种情况下，它们在英国被归入第三类。

中国的粉彩、玫瑰奖章样式和大奖章样式瓷器深受欧洲想象力的影响，并形成了中国设计风格。迈森陶瓷厂在霍洛特（图4.10）和冯·勒文芬克主持时期生产的中国风陶瓷，以及斯塔福德郡（新霍尔和希尔迪奇＆索恩陶瓷厂）或法国陶瓷小镇生产的中国风陶瓷明显属于第三类，但也可能属于第一类，因为中国内销瓷器中也有这些中式风格的场景（比较收藏82和215）。

图4.10 约翰·格雷戈留斯·霍洛特（1696—1775年）设计的迈森中国风带盖罐

中国伊万里瓷及其英国版让这个故事更加令人费解。伊万里瓷（釉下蓝和釉上红，有时带釉上金）原产于日本，在欧洲成为受追捧的进口商品。中国制瓷工匠沿袭其设计,最初是用两种颜色装饰,后来进一步尝试采用纹饰装饰。18世纪,荷兰和英国的许多生产商也模仿这种设计,并在中国进口的釉下蓝瓷器上加施红彩或镀金,从而将标准的蓝色图案转换为伊万里图案。这种釉上加彩工艺是独具创造力的欧亚联合生产方式(收藏68),通过在陶瓷上镶嵌银或黄铜(收藏69)[1],赋予陶瓷西洋化色彩。其间,可能也有一些彩绘陶瓷被寄回中国,作为样品进行生产。许多英国陶瓷厂都生产过伊万里瓷,因此我们无法确定谁复制了哪部分。我们可以看到,在跨文化效应中,"复制"一词可能具有误导性。青花瓷的发展展示了跨文化影响何等复杂。事实上,没有复制,各个要素都为全球应用艺术的发展做出了贡献。

至于中国青瓷,虽然是明朝之前亚洲内部贸易的主要外销瓷装饰风格,却几乎从未外销到欧洲。当明末开始中欧贸易时,这种风格在中国已不再受推崇;而当清朝重新发现并模仿昔日的造型和上釉工艺时,中国已经失去了欧洲市场。然而,在20世纪上半叶,许多欧洲陶瓷艺术家从古老的中国青瓷中获得灵感。在法国和比利时的装饰艺术陶瓷中[2],我们可以找到宋代陶瓷的纹片釉,也可以看到现代包豪斯陶艺家用青瓷釉进行实验。丹麦和其他北欧国家陶瓷工作室的艺术家经常在陶器上施以绿色和青绿色釉彩。这种中国传统陶瓷艺术甚至成为欧洲文化遗产的一部分。

---

[1] Cultural Affairs Bureau of the Macao S.A.R. Government, 2013, pp.92–97, 141–147.
[2] Hardy 2009.

Chapter 4

The Eurasian Cultural Melting Pot — the Story after the Trade

The Japanese had copied the Chinese, who in turn copied the Japanese, all of which were copied by the Europeans. And then the Chinese copied the Europeans, who copied each other. [1]

The creation of a Eurasian ceramic market along the Maritime Silk Road has now been described. However, this is only the first part of the Eurasian ceramics story. The customers of East Asian ceramics — in Europe and the Middle East — have not just imported hundreds of millions of pieces of porcelain. They also started themselves to replicate, to invent, and to further develop the production of ceramics. In the long run, this had even more culturally unifying effects on Europe and Asia than mere trade. The import of Asian ceramics influenced and broadened European senses and their feeling for decor. However, applying Asian decor elements, colors, and shapes to their own products, has been much more: a reflection of Asia and an expression of a changing relationship and identity.

Islamic Ceramics along the Maritime Silk Road

Pic. 4.1 and table 4.1 are a summary of the various routes the blue and white decor took and how it spread out within Eurasia. In the chapters

---

[1] Ganse 2008, p.65.

above we have described the story of blue and white porcelain in China and other East Asian countries; in this chapter, we want to look at the reflections East Asian ceramics had in the Islamic world and in Europe.

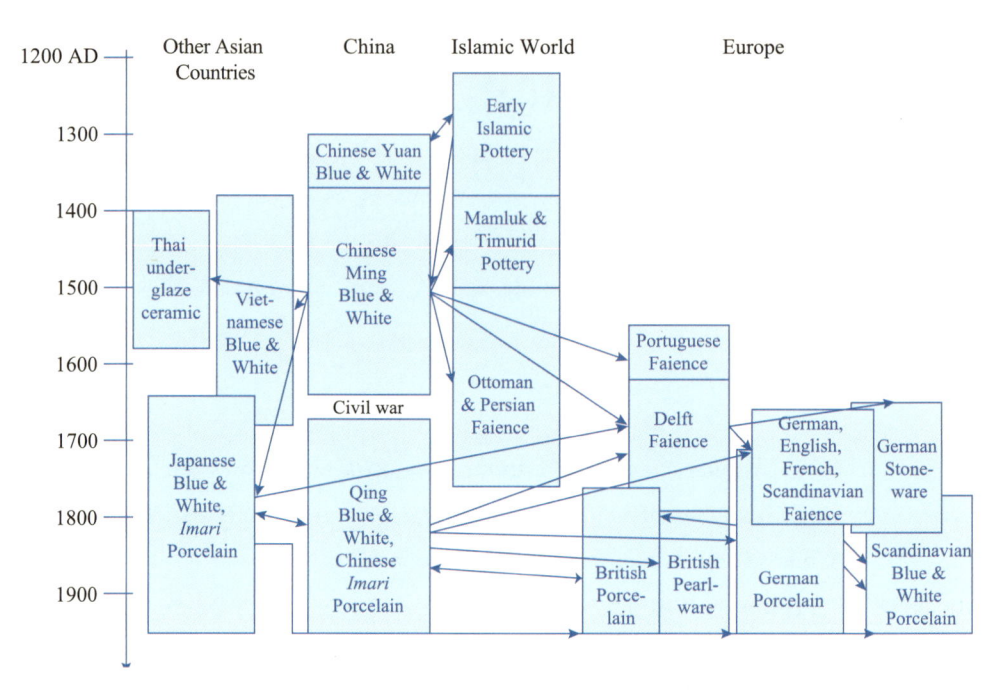

Pic 4.1: The linkages of the blue and white ceramic production centers.

The geographic area influenced by Islam is too heterogeneous and too wide — historically stretching from Spain, North Africa and the Middle East to Turkey, the Balkans, Central Asia, South Asia and the Malay Archipelago — to be reasonably summarized under just a religious category. However, more and more literature can be found where common features of the pottery art of several Islamic countries are presented: the use of glazed tiles in architecture, the luster painting, the underglaze painting technique, and the three-color splash decor. At the center of the research are countries, such as Iran, Iraq, Syria, Turkey, and Egypt where kilns have been found and specimens are part of famous collections all over the world. Relevant in the context of this introduction is of course the question, to what extent the Islamic World, China, Southeast Asia, and Europe have interacted and exchanged techniques, designs and tastes.

As already pointed out, the Middle East started to be the main destination for the export of Chinese ceramics during the Chinese Tang dynasty and began to produce its own ceramics early.

Kashan and Nishapur in Persia were the most productive ceramic centers in the Islamic lands from the 9th to 14th centuries. Underglaze painting techniques were used by Persian potters in the city of Kashan probably 100-120 years earlier than in China. Kashan is not only famous for its underglaze paintings but also for producing beautiful and mysterious blue and turquoise monochromes, and it is known for inventing fritware — a technical innovation of an artificial siliceous paste. Fritware is a composite material made from quartz sand mixed with small amounts of finely ground glass and some clay. When fired, the glass frit melts and binds the other components together. Fritware is not porcelain, but it shares some of its features. The artificial paste can be thrown to produce a very thin wall, which normally, cannot be achieved with stoneware or terracotta.

The kilns of Nishapur in Iran produced in the 10th century terracotta painted in green, yellow, and brown under a transparent glaze which reminds very much of the three-color ceramics of the Tang dynasty. However, since the Tang pottery was mainly used as funeral decoration and no export pieces have been found in Iran, it is still unclear how the exchange of the three-splash color decoration took place.

In addition, black decorated pieces under a turquoise glaze of the early 13th century were also found in the city of Raqqa in Syria — the former capital of the Abbasid Caliph Harun Al-Rashid.

In the 14th century, the Mongolian Yuan dynasty in China created an immense empire not only facilitating the trade between China and Islamic countries through its open-door policy within its reign, but also the production of blue and white porcelain. It is likely it was the demand for underglaze blue ceramics from the Middle East that prompted the beginning of a ceramic style in China, which later became the synonym for Chinese porcelain. And the cobalt-based blue color used in the kilns of Jiangxi province from the year 1320 on was imported from Iran.

That blue and white porcelain was initially mainly produced for the trade with Muslim customers, can also be evidenced by the fact that domestically it did not play an important role until the first quarter of the 15th century when the Ming court acknowledged it as imperial ware. Most Chinese customers in the 14th century still preferred the monochrome celadons. And still under the early Ming Emperors many Chinese blue and white pieces are actually copies of Arabic or Timurid vessels or vases made of brass. The former head of the ceramics department of the *Beijing Palace Museum* made extensive comparisons of Mamluk brass products with early blue and white Ming porcelains. The cultural interaction of both regions is more than obvious.[1]

In the late 14th century, blue and white had already started its cultural journey

---

[1] Feng Xianming in: Orientations, 2004, pp.172-186.

toward the world. The import of Chinese blue and white porcelain during the Mamluk Sultanate of Egypt (1250-1517) influenced local potters to imitate blue and white ceramics. Next to hundreds of thousands of sherds of Chinese origin, Mamluk blue and white fritware and faience have been excavated in Cairo[1] and in Syria. Many of these pieces are now part of the *al-Sabah Collection* or the *Tareq Rajab Museum* in Kuwait. Unfortunately, only a very few complete items exist.[2] One rare example is a blue and white dish, excavated in Mamluk Syria and probably produced from a kiln in Damascus. The dish is from the late 14th or early 15th century, which makes it one of the first imitations of Chinese blue and white porcelain outside China.[3]

At the time when Egypt and Syria were ruled by the Mamluks, the region of nowadays Iran, Iraq, Afghanistan, Turkmenistan, and Uzbekistan was conquered by Tamerlane (also called Timur), a nomad of Turkish origin. He came into power in 1370 and the Timurid Empire he created, within three decades, lasted more or less until 1500.[4] Potters of the Timurid capital Samarqand and later also in Nishapur produced blue and white ceramics inspired by Chinese imports of the early Ming dynasty. One blue and white jar with the floral decoration of the late 15th century, now in the *Tareq Rajab Museum*, is an extraordinary example of these very early blue and white imitations of the Timurid period of Persia.[5]

After the establishment of the Safavid dynasty in Persia (1501-1722), this ceramic tradition continued on a much larger scale. The so-called *Kubachi* ware (pic. 4.2), probably produced in the Persian Tabriz shows not only Chinese influences but also influences from the Ottoman *Iznik* ceramics. Similar to the Dutch Delftware, the white does not come from the ceramic paste but is a white opaque glaze on a dark shard. Instead of porcelain, Iranian potters have used fritware.[6]

Pic. 4.2: Persian *Kubachi* ware, 17th century.

In the 17th century, the blue and white products of Persia reached such a quality

---

[1] Carswell 2000, pp.65-66.
[2] Watson 2004, pp.419-423.
[3] Fehérvári 1998, p.54.
[4] Barnes 1998, pp.94-95.
[5] Fehérvári 1998, p.68.
[6] Langer 2006, pp.26-32 and Watson 2004, pp.449-481.

that the Dutch VOC started to ship them to the Netherlands. The famous Dutch Tulip vase is originally from Persia. The blue and white faience of Persia was produced until the 18th century, but most got lost as the material was quite fragile and got easily chipped or broken. The Victoria & Albert Museum in London has one of the biggest collections of Safavid oriental blue and white ceramics.[①]

A short overview of the main features of ceramic art in the Islamic world would not be complete without mentioning the use of glazed tiles as the main decorative element of architecture. One finds it in the Alhambra in Spain, in the *Topkapi* Palace in Istanbul, in the Friday Mosque of Herat in Afghanistan and Isfahan in Iran, and at the Registan Square in Samarqand. Again, Persia plays an important role since the main architectural design of mosques with a dominant *ivan* (portal) and the custom of decorating them with mainly blue-colored tiles originated in Persia during the Mongolian empire and influenced the design of mosques in Central Asia, Afghanistan, Pakistan, and India. The same turquoise glaze we find on the ceramics from Raqqa and Kashan, we can find on the tiles decorating the entrances of the mosques from Isfahan, at the mausoleum of the Mongolian ruler Oldjaitu in Sultaniyeh, and at the Friday Mosque in Yazd, all built in the 14th century. The Mongolians played an essential role in bringing Islamic art via Persia to India. The term Mughal Empire (1526–1857) which derives from the word Mongol makes this relationship obvious. The architecture of the Mogul emperors in India and the Timurids in Central Asia is heavily influenced by stylistic elements of Persia, creating a continuum of architectural design features from Azerbaijan to West China, from Uzbekistan to India.

Another crucial period for the development of Islamic ceramic was the Ottoman Empire and the pottery of Iznik in western Anatolia. It has been already mentioned that the Ottoman Empire has been a major destination for Chinese porcelain exports. From the late 15th century, potters in Iznik and later also in Kütahya began producing wares that were decorated in cobalt blue on white fritware under a clear glaze. In the 13th century, the town of Kashan in Iran was already an important center for the production of fritware. The fritware body in Iznik was covered by a white engobe and in a few cases also by a tin-glaze in order to achieve the white cover necessary for applying the paint. From the 15th century on, blue and white fritware was produced with many references to the Chinese blue and white ware of the Ming dynasty.[②] The so-called *Golden Horn* ware was a variation of blue and white ceramics and was popular from the 1530s to 1550s. This type of decoration consists of a series of thin concentric spirals adorned with small

---

① Langer 2006.

② Carswell 1998.

Pic. 4.3: Iznik ceramic, *Rhodian* style (c. 1550–1600).

leaves. The more colorful products from Iznik called *Damascus* ware (with green and purple) and *Rhodian* ware (including red) were produced between the 16th and 18th centuries (pic. 4.3).

In the 20th century, the pottery industry experienced a revival in Kütahya reproducing Iznik-style products both for domestic use and for tourists. In a sense, modern Turkey has been one of the latest countries to join the almost 500 year history of the Eurasian porcelain trade.

In summary, the region stretching from Egypt to Afghanistan played a crucial role in the promulgation of a Eurasian blue and white decor. First examples were made in the Mamluk Sultanate in Egypt and Syria, later also in the Timurid Empire in Persia and Central Asia. The height of the production of blue and white ceramics has been reached in the Ottoman Empire and Safavid Persia in the 16th and 17th centuries. At the same time, the decor had arrived also in Portugal and in the Netherlands (see table 4.1).

Table 4.1: Major Milestone in the World-Wide Promulgation of Blue and White Ceramics

13th century	Introduction of cobalt underglaze blue decoration in Persia
1320	Emergence of underglaze blue porcelain in Jingdezhen during the Mongolian Yuan dynasty
1330	Start of the export of Chinese blue and white porcelain to Muslim countries
c. 1380—1400	First China-inspired blue and white ceramics produced outside China in Vietnam and Mamluk Syria
1499	First Chinese blue and white porcelain reached Europe (Lisbon)
c. 1580	First China-inspired blue and white ceramics (faience) produced in Europe (Lisbon)
1500—1750	Production of China-inspired blue and white ceramics in the Ottoman Iznik and in Safavid Persia
1550—1800	Mass export of Chinese blue and white porcelain to Europe
1660	Beginning of the Japanese export of blue and white porcelain to Europe
1660—1750	Mass production of blue and white faience in Delft
1717	First translucent underglaze blue porcelain produced in Europe (Meissen)
1760	Introduction of underglaze blue transfer printing in Worcester, UK
18th–20th century	Mass production of China-inspired blue and white porcelain and pearlware in Germany, UK, and Scandinavia

Europe under Chinese Influence

The import of Chinese porcelain was first arranged by the Portuguese, but—as we have seen—it was the Dutch VOC that started importing on a larger scale in the 17th century. The blue and white *Kraak* ware was exported until the end of the Ming Dynasty and the transition period to the new Qing dynasty. Then, Japanese porcelain partly replaced Chinese exports for about 25 years, until around 1683 when the new Qing Emperor Kangxi restarted mass exportation to Europe.

The European demand for East Asian porcelain increased over time and reached its peak in the second half of the 18th century. A China fashion broke out, and wealthy Dutch entrepreneurs and rulers from many countries started their collections, created China rooms inside palaces, used them as tea and dinner services, or displayed imported Chinese pieces at home.

Similar to the Asian neighboring countries of China, this big market also prompted experiments in Europe to find out the secret of porcelain production. However, it took around two hundred years after the first Chinese porcelain arrived in Europe before the formula for porcelain was discovered in Meissen in 1709. Before, European manufacturers tried to imitate the appearance of Chinese porcelain. Not knowing the secrets of the porcelain paste, European producers tried at least to get the same look applied to various ceramic types such as stoneware, terracotta, white earthenware, and other formulas including bone ash or glass. Stoneware from the German Westerwald (villages such as Höhr-Grenzhausen) is mainly blue and white, and cannot deny Asian influences (plate 165).

A special case is the emergence of a China-inspired faience industry in Europe — first in Lisbon approximately in 1580, then in the Netherlands, and within a few decades all over Europe. Faience is a white-glazed brown earthenware, imitating the white color of porcelain, and easy to be decorated in blue or in any other color. The faience technique was actually an import from Asia too. The first tin-glazed ceramics reached Italy via the Islamic Iberian Peninsula and were first called *Majolica* — named after the Spanish island Mallorca from where exports to Italy were handled. In Italy, faience production flourished during the 16th century in the cities of Faenza (from which the name faience was derived) and Deruta. In Florence, the Della Robbia family modeled faience sculptures, which are still the evidence of the Asian heritages in Europe, including tin-glazed products and cobalt color decoration.

The faiences of Lisbon in Portugal and Delft in the Netherlands of the 17th and

18th century, and also from various German cities such as Hanau, Frankfurt (plate 167), Nuremberg, or Bayreuth (plate 173) are, in many cases, imitations of Chinese blue and white ceramics or China-inspired products (see map 4.1). Blue and white faience has been produced also in Liverpool and London (called "Delft" by the English, plate 172) in Rouen (plate 175) and Nevers (plate 176) in France, and in Copenhagen and Stockholm in Scandinavia. Moustiers in France became a center for non-blue colored faience and for Chinoiserie design: imaginations of Chinese scenes and landscapes. Faiences, however, are low-fired products, get easily chipped or broken, are heavily pottered, are not translucent, and are pervious to water. Therefore, one could use them mainly for decorative purposes but not as tableware.

One of the most prosperous faience factories was the Dutch faience of Delft. The Dutch faience industry started in Delft around 1625 (Pic. 4.4). By 1665 there were already more than twenty faience potteries in Delft, most of which produced "imitation porcelain" en masse in order to fill the Ming-Qing transition gap left by the Chinese. The Dutch potters imitated Chinese blue and white porcelain, such as *Kraak* ware (plate 166) during the second half of the 17th century. In the Delft faience industry, the focus of product development was painting. The best painter in the factory almost always decorated exceptional pieces with immense care.

In addition to the copies of Chinese originals, we can find everything between Chinese design and pure European design: From *Kraak* copies to pseudo-Chinese characters, or from free interpretations of Chinese landscapes to religious scenes and Dutch scenery. Later also *Famille rose*, Japanese *Imari*, and *Kakiemon* were copied by Delft factories (plate 199).

Much of the millions of pieces produced in Delft disappeared or were thrown away because earthenware is easy to break or damage. The Delft industry gradually declined during the 18th century due to Chinese imports being available again, the competition created by real porcelain made in Germany, and later also by manufacturers in France and England. The Delft and with it the whole European faience industry disappeared in the early years of the 19th century and were replaced by porcelain and pearlware now produced in many countries. Only one Delft company survived — the *Koninklijke Porceleyne Fles* (*Royal Delft*), which still produces blue and white pearlware for decorative purposes. A revival of the faience technique took place in Austria in the first three decades of the 20th century when the Vienna manufacturer *Goldscheider* produced Art Deco figurines.

It was not until the early 18th century that the Europeans mastered the real formula

Pic. 4.4: View of Delft by Johannes Vermeer (1632–1675).

and craft of the high-temperature fired ceramics. In 1708, the first copy of the Chinese brown *Yixing* stoneware was successfully produced in Meissen. The discovery of porcelain in Europe was an effort independent of the technological knowledge China had accumulated for more than 1500 years in porcelain production. Even though millions of pieces were exported to Europe, the porcelain-making technology has been kept a secret. China has provided the know-how to the emergence of porcelain production in Japan, Korea, Thailand, and Vietnam, but this know-how never reached West Asia or Europe. As Julia Weber pointed out in the foreword, it needed the efforts and experiments of mainly two persons — Böttger and von Tschirnhaus — to reinvent porcelain in Europe.

The Asian influence on this early European porcelain design is more than obvious. The early *Meissen* pieces are direct copies of the huge collection of Chinese and Japanese originals of August the Strong, the Elector of Saxony and King of Poland. The first cobalt underglaze blue porcelain was produced in Meissen in 1717. One can find imitations of *Blanc-de-Chine*, blue and white, *Batavia ware*, *Famille rose*, *Famille verte*, *Imari*, and *Kakiemon*. No other European producer shows such a big variety of design influences from China and Japan.

The *Meissen* manufacturer intended to keep the formula for the porcelain paste a secret but was not able to avoid that other German manufacturers were able to attract some of their workers. In 1718 the formula reached Vienna, where the Vienna porcelain manufacture was established and some decades later the secret became known in Höchst near Frankfurt. In England, the composition of the porcelain paste was discovered in Plymouth in 1768, and the patent was later transferred to the *New Hall* manufacturer in Staffordshire in 1781.[①]

Also in the 18th century, the soft-paste porcelain from Lowestoft, Worcester, Liverpool, London, Staffordshire (plates 178–180) in England, and Saint-Cloud and Chantilly in France started to be in production. It is also very much influenced by Chinese blue and white, *Famille verte* and *Famille rose*, or Japanese *Imari* and *Kakiemon*. None of these ceramic products were able to reach the characteristics of porcelain.

In summary, European pottery has been influenced by Asian ceramics in two ways. First, technically, European Potters adopted the white tin glaze for producing faience and also used tilework to decorate walls and houses, as we can still see in Spain and Portugal. Especially in Portugal, where tiles (*azulejos*) decorate churches, outside walls and the interior of houses, the Arabic influence cannot be ignored. Also, the Dutch blue and white tiles refer to this Islamic tradition mixed with Chinese elements (pic. 4.5). Second, artistically, they adopted Chinese and Japanese designs, colors, and symbols.

Porcelain and soft-paste porcelain replaced the tin-glazed terracotta in the course

Pic. 4.5: Dutch faience tile with a soldier and "Wanli corner" pattern (1620–1650).

[①] Godden 2004, p.381.

of the 18th century, but the history of copying Chinese and Japanese designs continued. Chinese blue and white porcelain was copied and newly interpreted by European factories—*Meissen, Vienna, Rauenstein, Worcester, Caughley, Royal Copenhagen*, etc. The so-called "Zwiebelmuster" ("Blue Onion", pic. 4.6) and "Strohblume" ("Blue fluted" in English, "Musselmalet" in Danish, plate 185) were typical China-inspired blue and white decorations, and one of the most common coffee or dining service styles in Germany and Scandinavia until the mid-20th century.

Pic. 4.6: German "Blue Onion" decor ("Zwiebelmuster") porcelain dish from the *Meissen* manufacture, Marcolini period (1774–1814).

Map 4.1 shows the locations of the main European ceramic centers producing China-inspired and Japan-inspired products from the 17th century to the 19th century. This includes the main faience production centers, Delft in the Netherlands, Rouen in France, and Hanau in Germany; the centers of soft-paste porcelain such as Chantilly in France, and Worcester, Lowestoft and Staffordshire in England. Meissen and Vienna were the two main porcelain production centers in the first half of the 18th century, followed by many manufacturers in Thuringia and northeastern Bavaria in the second half of the century, and then by *New Hall* in Staffordshire. Other than French faience, French porcelain has not been so influenced by East Asian decoration.

Map 4.1 also shows the main import harbors and headquarters of the East Asian companies. It is by no means a coincidence that the countries and regions, which have imported most of the Chinese porcelain — especially Great Britain and the Netherlands — became also the major production centers of China-inspired ceramics. Godden estimates that over 50% of British ceramics show an oriental

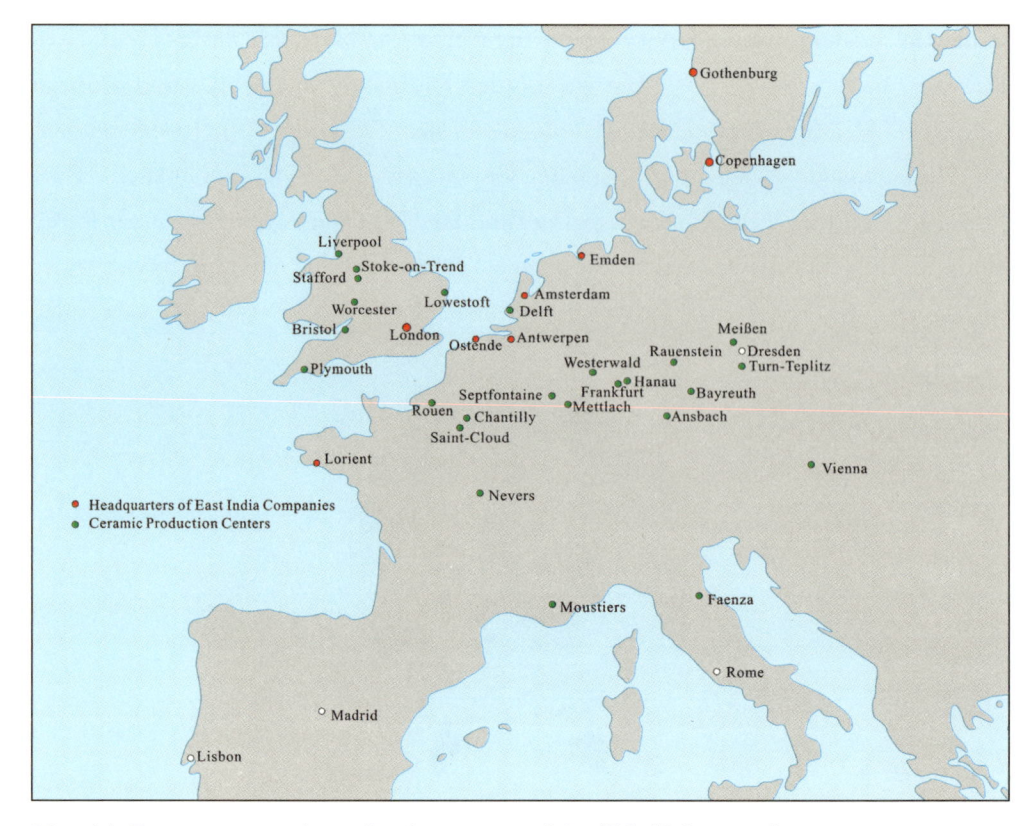

Map 4.1: European ceramic production centers of the 17th-19th centuries.

influence.[①] The biggest variety of imitations and pseudo-Chinese ceramics can be found in the UK.

Already a major destination for Chinese porcelain in the 18th century, many British soft-paste porcelain manufacturers started to imitate Chinese blue and white decor. To replace broken items from China may have been the initial reason. Millions of pieces were shipped from Canton to the ports of Great Britain by the EIC. However, with the discovery of the necessary raw material and the techniques of producing soft-paste porcelain and porcelain, the import of Chinese porcelain declined at the end of the 18th century. The EIC ceased to order Chinese porcelain in 1791.[②] Only private trade continued. This was a protective measure for the local British ceramic industry, which was able to substitute imported goods, step by step.

Miles Mason who established factories in Liverpool and Staffordshire was an important "china-man" — merchant of Chinese porcelain and wholesale client of the

---

① Godden 1979, p.339.

② Godden 2004, p.36.

British EIC — before starting his ceramic production.[1] He established the first factory in 1796 after the EIC ceased the official import of Chinese ceramics in 1791 as a consequence of the high duties imposed by the British Government.

Producers from London, Liverpool, Lowestoft, and the Midlands of England were excellent imitators and it is today sometimes difficult at first sight to distinguish Chinese blue and white porcelain or *Famille rose* porcelain from the British counterpart (pic. 4.7).

Pic. 4.7: Left: English glazed earthenware plate with a Chinese *Famille rose* transfer print and enamel decoration from Staffordshire, Spode *Company* (1805–1815). Right: Chinese porcelain Qianlong period *Famille rose* plate (c. 1760).

In 1750 English potters from Staffordshire invented white earthenware with a brilliant lead glaze. Josiah Wedgewood perfected this type of ceramic by adding cobalt, making the glaze shinier and more porcelain-like. He called this product pearlware. The transfer printing technology in blue under the glaze has been invented for porcelain at Worcester in 1760[2], but was initially difficult to use on earthenware. Josiah Spode introduced in 1784 blue transfer printing for white earthenware (pearlware) products instead of hand painting. The Chinese decoration on English porcelain and earthenware is almost exclusively transfer printed underglaze in contrast to German or Danish porcelain where the blue decoration is hand painted.

---

[1] Haggar 1977, pp.53–56.
[2] Godden 2004, p.156.

Spode and the other Staffordshire potteries have developed and used mainly the following patterns copied and further developed from Chinese originals: the "Willow" pattern, the "Two Temple" pattern (pic. 4.8), the "Long Bridge" pattern, the "Buffalo" pattern and the "Fitzhugh" pattern. Especially the former two patterns became very famous in the UK in the 19th century, and both are still in production in England until today without major changes.

Pic. 4.8: Left: Chinese *Nanking* blue and white soup plate with the "Two Temple" design (1780–1800); right: English soft-porcelain plate with the blue "Two Temple" transfer print pattern from *Miles Mason* (1800–1816).

Similar patterns can be found in Chinese export ceramics of the second half of the 18th century but it is somehow unclear whether the Chinese reproduced some dream landscapes according to European wishes or European producers imitated what had been shipped from Canton. This is a somewhat funny story of generating joint Eurasian designs where, in the end, nobody knows who the actual originator was.

Table 4.2 shows the most famous European producers of blue and white ceramic with Asian influences or in the chinoiserie style during the 17th and 18th centuries.

Table 4.2: Early European Producers of Blue and White Ceramics

Country	Start	Main Production Location (*Company Name*)	Type of Ceramic
Portugal	c. 1600	Lisbon	Faience
Netherlands	1625	Haarlem, Delft	Faience
Holy Roman Empire	c. 1600	Westerwald	Stoneware
	1661	Hanau	Faience
	1666	Frankfurt	Faience
	1709	Ansbach	Faience
	1712	Nürnberg	Faience
	1714	Bayreuth	Faience
	1717	Meissen	Porcelain
	1747	Vienna	Porcelain
	1770	Septfontaines (*Villeroy & Boch*)	Creamware
	1783	Rauenstein	Porcelain
	1794	Tettau	Porcelain
Great Britain	1630	London, Bristol, Liverpool	Faience
	1749	London (*Bow, Chelsea*)	Soft-paste porcelain
	1750	Worcester	Soft-paste porcelain
	1754	Liverpool	Soft-paste porcelain
	1757	Lowestoft	Soft-paste porcelain
	1775	Shropshire (*Caughley*)	Soft-paste porcelain
	1768	Plymouth	Porcelain
	1781	Staffordshire (*New Hall*)	Porcelain
	1790	Stoke–on–Trent, Staffordshire (*Spode, Mason*)	Pearlware
Scandinavia	1723	Copenhagen, Stockholm	Faience
	1775	Copenhagen	Porcelain
France	c. 1650	Rouen, Nevers	Faience
	1673	Rouen	Soft-paste porcelain
	1693	Saint–Cloud	Soft-paste porcelain
	1750	Chantilly	Soft-paste porcelain

Generations of Europeans grew up with cups, saucers and plates decorated in blue and white, which has been one of the most influential artistic expressions of a Eurasian cultural identity. An identity, which originated in 1200 in Persia, shaped up around 1320 in South China and made its way first to the Middle East in the 14th century and then to Europe in the 16th century.

Imitation and Innovation

Chinese blue and white porcelain has inspired many European producers (see table 4.2). The decor has been applied on stoneware, faience, soft-paste porcelain, creamware and porcelain.

In addition to the Europe-wide promulgation of blue and white porcelain, the Japanese and *Chinese Imari* and the *Kakiemon* decoration became the second most influential Asian style in European ceramics (see table 4.3). Japanese *Imari* from Arita experienced a rebirth in the 1860s and was shipped to Europe and the US in big volumes. Japanese porcelain producers were integrated into the international trade in a professional manner targeting mainly the US and European markets with standardized *Imari* plates and vases (plate 142). The *Koransha Company* established in 1875 by the Fukagawa family is one of the most famous Japanese *Imari* producers[1] still operating today. German, British and French porcelain factories imitated *Imari* already during the 18th and 19th centuries, and in the UK, *Imari* -style products, for example, by *Spode, Royal Crown Derby*, or *Miles Mason* (pic. 4.9 and plates 204–208) were very popular until the 20th century.

Pic. 4.9: English soft-paste porcelain *Imari* plate with the "Japan Fence" pattern from the *Miles Mason* factory in Staffordshire (c. 1820).

Also, *Kakiemon* porcelain has been copied in Europe, for example, by the *Meissen* factory in Saxony (plate 220), by *Chantilly* in France, and by *Chelsea* and *Worcester* in the UK.

Japanese *Satsuma* ware — multi-colored and gold enamel decoration on ivory-colored earthenware with transparent and crackled glaze — was another example of oversea popularity (plates 147–148).[2] The design of *Satsuma* ware has also influenced

---

[1] Schiffer 1986, pp.61–108.
[2] Lawrence 2011.

Bohemian Art Nouveau ceramic producers such as *Stellmacher* and the *Amphora Company* in Turn-Teplitz (plate 222). New or reactivated kilns from the Ishikawa prefecture (*Kutani* ware) or Nagoya (*Noritake*) have produced and exported Western style and westernized Japanese products until 1940.[1]

Japanese porcelain decor became the second most influential Asian design on European ceramics after the blue and white decor. However, Japan's influence on European art — Impressionist painting, European Art Nouveau furniture, glass, silver and copper works, architecture, and other applied arts — cannot be overstated. Japanese design and culture spread out to Europe and the US, and a new fashion — *Japonism* — influenced the European Art Nouveau or *Jugendstil*.[2] Samuel Siegfried Bing, a French-German art dealer, traveled to Japan and facilitated the export of Japanese art through a company in Yokohama, helped introduce Japanese design to Europe. He started publishing in 1888 the journal *Le Japon Artistique* and opened in Paris a famous gallery "Maison de L'art Nouveau", which gave this new art movement its name.[3] Especially Scandinavian porcelain factories such as *Bing and Gröndahl*, *Royal Copenhagen* and *Rörstrand*, but also the Dutch *Rozenburg* and the German *Rosenthal* were under Japanese influence and designed elegant vases with flower or floral decoration in the Japanese *Kakiemon* style and in the style of domestic blue and white products (such as the so-called *Nabeshima* ware). Again, ceramics played their role in transmitting oriental design to other places.

H. Davis distinguishes three design categories of European porcelain influenced by Chinese patterns and designs.[4] And he qualifies only the third category as true Chinoiserie. In category 1 fall "exact copies" of Chinese items, in category 2 fall "copies of copies" — modified or amended designs, and in category 3 fall true Chinoiserie designs based on the imaginative use of Chinese motifs. Generally, one could categorize European porcelain in that way. However, I still believe that it is more complex than that because one should not underestimate the fact that Chinese porcelain design was also influenced both by other producers and by customers. Let me give some examples:

Many of the early *Meissen* porcelains would fall into category 1. *Meissen* produced almost perfect copies of Japanese *Kakiemon* and *Imari*, Chinese *Blanc-de-Chine*, *Famille rose* and *Batavia* ware. They were exact copies (plate 186), or at least

---

[1] Jahn 2004.
[2] see Irvine 2014.
[3] Wolf 2015, p.108.
[4] Davis 1991, p.43.

the manufacturer tried to copy exactly the design, even if they were not always able to copy the ceramic material. The French porcelain producer *Edmé Samson* was very much inspired by *Famille rose* porcelain and produced almost exact copies.

One could also put the "Willow" and "Two Temple" pieces from Staffordshire into this category (see Chinese and English plates in pic. 4.8).

Others like the later "Willow" plate from *Spode* (plate 189) would be an example for Category 2, similar to *Meissen*'s "Blue Onion" (plate 182) and the Copenhagen "Musselmalet". However, we start having difficulties in categorizing if we bear in mind that the "Willow" and "Two Temple" design is probably English invention, and Chinese potters produced them according to the requirements of their customers. This would put them then into Category 3.

Also, the *Famille rose*, *Rose Mandarin* and *Rose Medallion* porcelains of China have been very much influenced by European imagination but have also shaped Chinese design. The Höroldt and von Löwenfinck Chinoiserie porcelains of *Meissen* (pic. 4.10), the Chinoiserie ceramics from Staffordshire (*New Hall*, *Hilditch*) or the French Moustiers could be obvious examples of Category 3, but probably also of Category 1 since many of the Chinoiserie scenes can also be found on Chinese originals (comparing plate 82 and plate 215).

The case of Chinese *Imari* and its interpretation in England makes the story even more puzzling. *Imari* porcelain (underglaze blue and overglaze red plus sometimes gold) was originally from Japan and became the desired export product to Europe. Chinese potters took over this design initially in the two-color version and further experimented with the decor. In Europe, the design has been used by many producers, and red color or gilding was added to Chinese imports of underglaze blue pieces to convert standard blue patterns into the *Imari* pattern. This kind of clobbering is a creative way of Eurasian joint production done in the 18th century both in the Netherlands and in England (plate 68). Westernization also took place by mounting porcelain (plate 69) with

Pic. 4.10: *Meissen* covered vase and Chinoiserie decor by Johann Gregorius Höroldt (1696–1775).

silver or brass.[1] Probably also clobber ware then was sent back to China as reference pieces for the producers. Many English factories, such as *Miles Mason* or *Royal Crown Derby* have produced *Imari* ware, and in view of this, it is impossible to decide who copied what. Thus, we can see that the term "copy" might be misleading when cross-cultural effects take place. The development of the blue and white ceramic shows how complicated cross-cultural effects can be. In the end, no one copies, but all contribute to the emergence of a global piece of applied art (see table 4.3).

Table 4.3: Main sources of inspiration for European ceramic producers

Style	Netherlands	Holy Roman Empire	Great Britain	France	Scandinavia
Chinese *Kraak*	××	×			
Chinese Kangxi blue and white	×××	××	××	×	×××
Chinese *Nanking*	××	×	×××		×
Chinese *Famille verte*	×	××		×	
Chinese *Famille rose*	×	××	××	××	×
Chinese *Blanc-de-Chine*		×	×	×	
Chinese or Japanese *Imari*	×	×	×××		
Japanese *Kakiemon*	×	××	×	×	××

×: influence on producers, ××: important influence, ×××: dominant influence.

The monochrome green glazed celadons of China — the dominant decoration style of Chinese export ceramics until the Ming dynasty have never been exported to Europe. When the Chinese-European trade started during the late Ming dynasty they had already lost much of their appreciation in China, and when the Qing emperors rediscovered them and imitated the old shapes and glazes, China had already lost its European market. However, in the first half of the 20th century, many European ceramic artists felt inspired by the old Chinese celadons. In the Art Deco ceramics of France and Belgium,[2] we can find the green craquelure glaze of Song dynasty ceramics, and the modern Bauhaus potters experimented with the colored celadon glazes. Studio ceramic artists in Denmark and other Scandinavian countries were applying green and bluish green glazes on their pottery. Even this traditional ceramic art of China became a heritage to Europe.

---

[1] Cultural Affairs Bureau of the Macao S.A.R. Government, 2013, pp.92–97, pp.141–147.
[2] See Hardy 2009.

第二部分 收藏

笔者的收藏主要包括两种陶瓷：①来自中国、日本、东南亚的外销陶瓷制品；②受亚洲影响的欧洲陶瓷。

第二部分的章节按照以下顺序排列：中国外销瓷，亚洲其他国家外销瓷（包括日本、越南、泰国），以及受亚洲外销瓷影响的欧洲陶瓷。223张图片均为笔者拍摄，且展示的均为笔者个人收藏。对部分瓷器，笔者还标注了记录类似或相同瓷器的出版文献，以供读者参考。

出于两个显而易见的原因，个人收藏中缺少国际上广泛研究的中国官窑瓷器或朝鲜瓷器：首先，大多数这类陶瓷保存在世界上最著名的陶瓷收藏馆，如故宫博物院和台北故宫博物院、很多中国省级博物馆、大维德基金会、伦敦维多利亚和阿尔伯特博物馆，或伊斯坦布尔的托普卡帕宫博物馆。其次，近年来中国艺术品价格飙升，那些未被博物馆收藏的稀有艺术品价格变得让人难以承受。另外，个人收藏中也缺少伊斯兰陶瓷，因为这种陶瓷非常罕见，且鲜有出口欧洲。

目前，关于民窑瓷器以及中国向亚洲邻国及欧洲外销瓷器的出版物数量仍然非常有限。通常不被欧洲宫廷收藏的中国出口餐具，以及通常用于贸易目的的泰国和越南餐具尚未得到透彻研究。研究中国对欧陶瓷出口的早期文献，主要聚焦在中国订单瓷器和纹章瓷。如果考虑到按需生产的装饰性瓷器在外销瓷中只扮演一个无足轻重的角色——在约1.86亿件外销瓷中，只有不到5%采用铜版画或欧洲徽章等欧洲图案进行装饰——这点着实令人惊讶。本人试图收藏更具代表性的外销瓷，并择其要者进行重点分析。此书力求在一定程度上填补上述空白，从而传达一种观点：陶瓷首先是日常用品。这一点往往容易被人遗忘，因为大部分博物馆的藏品是宫廷御用品或装饰品，而且只可"远观"而不可"亵玩焉"。

陶瓷易碎，年代越久，受损或破碎的可能性就越大。有的人希望拥有、触摸承载和见证数百年历史的物件，感受历史的年代感，对这样的人来说，陶瓷无疑具有很大吸引力。但是，除了博物馆里的幸运的历史藏品外，很多亚洲陶瓷经历几个世纪的战争、自然灾害、人口迁徙、城市和帝国的兴衰后未能幸存。那么一个细腻纤薄的餐具，是如何在数世纪的破坏、重建和现代化过程中得以幸存呢？

答案就藏在那些引人入胜的海洋考古学故事中：无论是寻宝者的故事和冒险经历，还是探险家所面临的危险，都是那么惊心动魄。在过去40年里，我们已经发现了约200艘沉船，150余万件亚洲沉船陶瓷。[①] 大多数陶瓷制品是针对亚洲内部市场。

---

① Wu 2016, p.1.

澳大利亚人米歇尔·哈彻[①]发掘了著名的中国"泰兴号"沉船，包括约35万件中国陶瓷，1999年在斯图加特拍卖；以及荷兰东印度公司的"哥德马尔森号"沉船，包括15余万件陶瓷，在阿姆斯特丹佳士得拍卖会出售。后者在被打捞出水前，在苏门答腊岛附近的海床上沉睡了大约250年。其他著名的沉船包括主要装载着越南陶瓷的"会安号"、已经被打捞上来的"南海1号"，以及清初沉没的、装载着出口欧洲陶瓷的"金瓯号"等。中国国家文物局水下文化遗产保护中心、越南打捞公司等官方机构，以及专门从事水下考古的海事勘探公司[②]、南海海洋考古公司[③]等私营公司，在南海发现了数十艘沉船。海洋考古学家米歇尔·弗莱克、弗兰克·戈迪奥和斯滕·肖斯特兰德为破解沉船之谜做出了巨大贡献。

海洋考古学这个主题涉及的范围非常广泛，非本书所能全面概括。有关亚洲沉船的更全面的列表，可参见亚洲沉船项目[④]和联合国教科文组织丝绸之路项目[⑤]等数据库。

[①] Edwards 2001.
[②] 海事勘探公司所有者为米歇尔·弗莱克，协助发掘了黑石号、头顿号和平顺号沉船。
[③] http://www.mingwrecks.com/.
[④] http://www.shipwreckasia.org, Kimura 2010, Wu 2016 or Brown 2009.
[⑤] https://en.unesco.org/silkroad/silk-road-themes/underwater-heritage.

Part II

The Collection

The author's collection focuses mainly on two types of ceramics:

i) the trade ware or export porcelain from China, Japan, and Southeast Asia

ii) the Asia influenced ceramics of Europe

The sections of part II follow the sequence of the book: Chinese export ceramics, export ceramics of other Asian countries (including Japanese, Vietnamese and Thai), and European ceramics influenced by imports from Asia. All following photographs were made by the author. Descriptions below the photographs are references made to similar items documented in other publications.

The widely studied imperial ware of China (called *guanyao*) or Korea is missing in this collection for obvious reasons. First, most originals are safely located in the most famous ceramic collections, for instance, in the *Palace Museums* of Beijing and Taipei, in numerous Chinese provincial museums, in the *Percival David Foundation* and the *Victoria & Albert Museum* in London, or in the *Topkapi Museum* in Istanbul. Second, the Chinese art price boom in recent years made the rare pieces, which are not part of museum collections unaffordable. Also, early Islamic ceramics are unfortunately missing, since they are quite rare and have hardly been exported to Europe.

Publications on ceramics of daily use for common people (called *minyao* in China) and on the Chinese export ceramics to Europe and Asian neighbors are still quite limited in number. This applies to Chinese export tableware which is normally not part of European court collections, but also to Thai and Vietnamese ware which was mainly produced for trading purposes. Older publications on Chinese export porcelain to Europe focus mainly on *armorial* porcelain. This is quite astonishing bearing in mind, that porcelain decoration on demand has played a minor role. Less than five percent of the approximately 186 million pieces have been decorated with European motives such as copper engravings or European coats of arms. Most of the cargo has been blue and white and *Famille rose* with Chinese designs or at least in a "kind-of China" style. The collection and the analysis have tried to be more representative. The documentation shall help to partly fill these gaps and shall also highlight that ceramics are in the first place products for daily use. The fact might get lost because most of the current museum collections display pieces that have been made for courts or for decoration only, and which are not allowed to be touched anyway.

Ceramics are not only fragile but also easy to break, and the likelihood that they get damaged or broken grows the older they are. Ceramics fascinate everyone who is attracted by the idea of owning and touching something which is hundreds of years old and has experienced generations of human beings and the history of past centuries. But still, apart from the old collections we find these days in museums, not many Asian ceramics have survived the centuries of war, natural disasters, migration, and the rise and fall of cities and empires characterizing this region. How could a fine and thin dish have survived all these centuries of destruction, rebuilding and modernization?

This brings us to the fascinating story of maritime archaeology—because of not only the treasure hunters' stories and adventures, but also the hazards the explorers have faced. Approximately 1.5 million pieces of Asian shipwreck ceramics together with about 200 ships have been discovered over the last four decades.[1] Most ceramics were products for the Asian markets.

Famous hoards have been found by the Australian Michael Hatcher[2] who discovered, for example, the Chinese junk *Tek Sing* with around 350,000 pieces of porcelain auctioned in 1999 in Stuttgart, and the Dutch VOC ship *Geldermalsen* with over 150,000 pieces of porcelain sold in auction by *Christie's* in Amsterdam. The latter hoard slept on the seabed off Sumatra for about 250 years before it was lifted and sold in Europe with an auction number and record. Other famous shipwrecks are the *Hoi An* carrying mainly Vietnamese ceramics, the *Nanhai No. 1,* which have been lifted and the *Ca Mau* which sank with early Qing dynasty porcelain produced for European markets. Public institutions such as the *National Conservation Center for Underwater Cultural Heritage* in Beijing or the *Vietnam Salvage Corporation*, but also private companies such as *Maritime Explorations*[3] and *Nanhai Marine Archaeology*[4] specialized in underwater archaeology have found and excavated dozens of shipwrecks in the South China Sea. The maritime archaeologists Michael Flecker, Franck Goddio and Sten Sjostrand have contributed a lot to deciphering the secrets of shipwrecks.

The topic of maritime archaeology is too broad to be covered in this research.

---

[1] Wu 2016, p.1.

[2] Edwards 2001.

[3] The company Maritime explorations owned by Michael Flecker assisted in the excavation of the *Belitung*, *Vung Tau* and *Binh Thuan* wreck.

[4] Nanhai Marine Archaeology: http://www.mingwrecks.com/.

Extensive lists of Asian shipwrecks can be found in databases e.g. of the *Shipwreck ASIA* project[①] or the *UNESCO Silk Roads* project[②].

[①] http://www.shipwreckasia.org, Kimura 2010, Wu 2016 or Brown 2009.
[②] https://en.unesco.org/silkroad/silk-road-themes/underwater-heritage.

第五章 中国陶瓷
Chapter 5 Chinese Ceramics

出口到亚洲其他国家的中国外销瓷
Chinese Export Ceramics to Asian Countries

1　中国外销至印度尼西亚的宋代"哲帕拉号"沉船青白花瓶（约 1130 年）。瓶体附着沉积物。直径 14 厘米，高 23.5 厘米。参考：Koh Antique。

1　Song dynasty pale green (*Qingbai*) glazed vase from the *Jepara* shipwreck with encrustations (c. 1130) — Chinese export ware to Indonesia. Diameter 14, height 23.5 cm. Ref.: Koh Antique.

183

2 元代龙泉窑双鱼小青瓷盘。直径 12 厘米，高 4 厘米。参考：Stevenson 1997，第 138、265 页。

2 Yuan dynasty small celadon dish with an incised double-fish motive from the Longquan kiln. Diameter 12 cm, height 4 cm. Ref.: Stevenson 1997, pp.138, 265.

3 元代或明初沉船青花小执壶。直径 7 厘米，高 12 厘米，参考：Crick 2010，第 236-237 页。

3 Yuan or early Ming dynasty small blue and white shipwreck ewer. Diameter 7 cm, height 12 cm. Ref.: Crick 2010, pp.236-237.

4 元代或明初浙江龙泉窑双系青瓷罐。出口印度尼西亚的外销瓷，直径 9 厘米，高 8 厘米。参考：Fung Ping Shan，插图 71；Crick 2010，第 118-119 页。

4 Yuan or early Ming dynasty celadon jar for the Indonesian market (called "buli buli" in Java) from the Longquan kiln in Zhejiang province. Diameter 9 cm, height 8 cm. Ref.: Fung Ping Shan, plate 71 and Crick 2010, pp.118-119.

5 元代或明代青白釉执壶，复原碎片。 直径 14 厘米，高 15 厘米。参考：Crick 2010，第 205 页，插图 116。

5 Restored fragments of a Yuan or Ming dynasty pale green (*Qingbai*) glazed ewer. Diameter 14 cm, height 15 cm. Ref.: Crick 2010, p.205, plate 116.

6 明代青瓷碗。 直径 16 厘米，高 6 厘米。

6 Ming dynasty celadon bowl. Diameter 16 cm, height 6 cm.

7 明代沉船单色釉碗。 两只，口沿豁口，附着沉积物。一只直径 15 厘米，高 6 厘米；一只直径 16 厘米，高 7.5 厘米。

7 Two Ming dynasty monochrome shipwreck bowls with chips and encrustations. Diameter 15 cm, height 6 cm; diameter 16 cm, height 7.5 cm.

8 外销至日本的明代天目（建窑）碗。直径 11 厘米，高 5 厘米。参考：南京市博物馆、宁波博物馆、上海中国航海博物馆，2017，第 204 页。

8 Ming dynasty *Temmoku* (*Jian Yao*) bowl for the Japanese market. Diameter 11 cm, height 5 cm. Ref.: Nanjing City Museum 2017, p.204.

9 明晚期沉船青花盖罐。釉面经海水侵蚀，为销往印度尼西亚的产品。直径 8.5 厘米，高 8 厘米。

9 Late Ming dynasty blue and white shipwreck covered box with eroded glaze, exported to Indonesia. Diameter 8.5 cm, height 8 cm.

10 明万历景德镇青花瓷碗。直径 12 厘米，高 6 厘米。

10 Late Ming dynasty (Wanli period) blue and white bowl from Jingdezhen. Diameter 12 cm, height 6 cm.

11 明万历景德镇青花瓷碗。 直径 15 厘米，高 7.5 厘米。参考：Staatliche Schlösser，第 42 页，插图 25；故宫博物院、上海博物馆，2015，第 78-79 页。

11 Late Ming dynasty (Wanli period) blue and white bowl from Jingdezhen. Diameter 15 cm, height 7.5 cm. Ref.: Staatliche Schlösser, p.42, plate 25 and the Palace Museum 2015, pp.78-79.

12 明代小盘。 直径 10 厘米，高 2.5 厘米。参考：Kerr 2011，第 116 页。

12 Ming dynasty small dish. Diameter 10 cm, height 2.5 cm. Ref.: Kerr 2011, p.116.

13 明代沉船青花碗。 直径 11 厘米，高 6 厘米。

13 Ming dynasty blue and white shipwreck bowl. Diameter 11 cm, height 6 cm.

14 明代沉船青花小碟。直径 10.5 厘米，高 3.5 厘米。参考：Crick 2010，第 264-265 页。

14 Ming dynasty small blue and white shipwreck dish. Diameter 10.5 cm, height 3.5 cm. Ref.: Crick 2010, pp.264-265.

15 明代沉船青花小碟。直径 11 厘米，高 2.5 厘米。参考：Chen 2012，第 125 页。

15 Ming dynasty blue and white small shipwreck dish. Diameter 11 cm, height 2.5 cm. Ref.: Chen 2012, p.125.

16 明代沉船酱釉罐。中国出口印度尼西亚。直径 11 厘米，高 7 厘米。参考：Brown 2009，第 119 页，插图 36.13。

16 Ming dynasty brown glazed shipwreck jar. Chinese export ware to Indonesia. Diameter 11 cm, height 7 cm. Ref.: Brown 2009, p.119, plate 36.13.

漳州窑瓷器
Zhangzhou or *Swatow* Ware

17 明代漳州窑青花盘。直径 28 厘米，高 6 厘米。参考：Crick 2010，第 395 页，插图 273。

17 Ming dynasty blue and white *Swatow* plate. Diameter 28 cm, height 6 cm. Ref.: Crick 2010, p.395, plate 273.

18 明晚期"平顺号"沉船漳州窑双凤盘（约 1600 年）。直径 27 厘米，高 4.5 厘米，贴有 2004 年澳大利亚墨尔本佳士得拍卖会标签。参考：Christie's 2004，第 38 页。

18 Late Ming dynasty *Binh Thuan* shipwreck *Swatow* plate with two confronting standing phoenixes (c. 1600). Diameter 27 cm, height 4.5 cm with the stickers from the *Christie's* auction 2004 in Melbourne, Australia. Ref.: Christie's 2004, p.38.

19 明晚期"平顺号"沉船漳州窑菊花碗（约1600年）。 直径10.5厘米，高5.5厘米。参考：Christie's 2004，第37、46页。

19 Late Ming dynasty *Binh Thuan* shipwreck *Swatow* bowl with chrysanthemum decoration (c. 1600). Diameter 10.5 cm, height 5.5 cm. Ref.: Christie's 2004, pp.37, 46.

20 明万历沉船漳州窑瓷碗。 四只，包括一只"平顺号"沉船碗（左下）。蓝色与灰乳色底釉。直径分别为18厘米、17厘米、13厘米和11.5厘米，高度分别为7厘米、6厘米、5厘米和4.5厘米。参考：Tan 2007，第122页；Christie's 2004，第48页。

20 Four late Ming dynasty (Wanli period) *Swatow* shipwreck bowls including one *Binh Thuan* shipwreck bowl (bottom left). Underglaze blue with a greyish milky glaze. Diameter 18 cm, 17 cm, 13 cm and 11.5 cm; height 7 cm, 6 cm, 5 cm and 4.5 cm. Ref.: Tan 2007, p.122 and Christie's 2004, p.48.

21 明代青花瓷碗。 1984 年出土于泰国来兴府来兴山顶墓。直径 18 厘米，高 8 厘米。

21 Ming dynasty blue and white bowl. Unearthed in 1984 at the Tak hilltop burial site in Tak province, Thailand. Diameter 18 cm, height 8 cm.

22 明代沉船漳州窑青花碗和小罐。 青花小罐饰以小鹿图案，直径 5.5 厘米，高 6 厘米。参考：Tan 2007，第 144 页；Harrisson 1979，第 81 页，插图 153。

22 Ming dynasty blue and white *Swatow* shipwreck bowl and jarlet with deer design. Diameter 5.5 cm, height 6 cm. Ref.: Tan 2007, p.144 and Harrisson 1979, p.81, plate 153.

23 明代漳州窑红绿彩碗。 直径 14 厘米，高 6 厘米。

23 Ming dynasty *Swatow* bowl with red and green enamels. Diameter 14 cm, height 6 cm.

24 明代漳州窑青花瓷盘。饰以凤凰花卉图案。直径 18 厘米。参考：Tan 2007，第 98 页，插图 71；Harrisson 1979，第 67 页，插图 167。

24 Ming dynasty blue and white *Swatow* ware, decorated with a phoenix standing in a garden. Diameter 18 cm. Ref.: Tan 2007, p.98, plate 71 and Harrisson 1979, p.67, plate 167.

25 明代漳州窑裂塔彩盘。直径 38 厘米，高 8.5 厘米。参考：Crick 2010，第 378-379 页；Harrisson 1979，第 111 页，插图 223 和 224。

25 Ming dynasty "Split Pagoda" polychrome *Swatow* platter. Diameter 38 cm, height 8.5 cm. Ref.: Crick 2010, pp.378-379 and Harrisson 1979, p.111, plate 223-224.

26　明代漳州窑红绿彩釉浅盘。瓷盘饰有雕刻图案。雕刻图案与釉彩相结合的瓷器处理工艺不常见。红色和绿色珐琅可能是后期上釉。直径 33 厘米，高 7 厘米。参考：Harrisson 1979，第 119 页，插图 235；Tan 2007，第 164 页。

26　Ming dynasty polychrome *Swatow* platter with light green glaze and incised. A combination of incised design with overglaze colors is uncommon. The red and green enameling may have been applied at a later stage. Diameter 33 cm, height 7 cm. Ref.: Harrisson 1979, p.119, plate 235 and Tan 2007, p.164.

27　明代漳州窑红绿彩釉浅盘。直径 35 厘米，高 7 厘米。参考：Harrisson 1979，第 110、118 页，插图 234。

27　Ming dynasty polychrome *Swatow* platter. Diameter 35 cm, height 7 cm. Ref.: Harrisson 1979, pp.110, 118, plate 234.

28 明晚期漳州窑青花罐。 两只，直径均为 6 厘米，高均为 5 厘米。参考：Tan 2007，第 146 页；Harrisson 1979，第 82 页，插图 164。

28 Two Late Ming blue and white *Swatow* jarlets. Diameter 6 cm, height 5 cm. Ref.: Tan 2007, p.146 and Harrisson 1979, p.82, plate 164.

29 明晚期沉船青花碗。 瓷碗饰以菊花图案，附有沉积物。直径 14.5 厘米，高 8 厘米。参考：Brown 2009，第 136 页。

29 Late Ming dynasty blue and white shipwreck bowl with chrysanthemum decoration and encrustations. Diameter 14.5 cm, height 8 cm. Ref.: Brown 2009, p.136.

30 明代沉船漳州窑红绿彩碗和红绿彩盘。绿色和红色釉上彩已经被侵蚀。碗直径 20.5 厘米，高 9 厘米；盘子直径 26 厘米，高 4 厘米。参考：Christie's 2004，第 78 页；Tan 2007，第 177 页。

30 Ming dynasty polychrome *Swatow* shipwreck bowl and plate. Overglaze green and red enamels are eroded. Diameter of the bowl 20.5 cm, height 9 cm; diameter of the plate 26 cm, height 4 cm. Ref.: Christie's 2004, p.78 and Tan 2007, p.177.

31 清康熙时期"头顿号"沉船碗（1690 年）。直径 11.5 厘米，高 5.5 厘米，碗上有 1992 年阿姆斯特丹佳士得拍卖会 969 号拍品标签。参考：Christie's 1992，第 128-129 页。

31 Qing dynasty (Kangxi period) *Vung Tau* shipwreck (1690) bowl. Diameter 11.5 cm, height 5.5 cm, with the lot 969 sticker from the *Christie's* auction 1992 in Amsterdam. Ref.: Christie's 1992, pp.128-129.

销往西方的中国外销瓷
Chinese Export Porcelain to the West

克拉克瓷
Kraak Porcelain

32 明万历克拉克瓷盘。中国出口葡萄牙和荷兰的外销瓷。直径 32 厘米。参考：Avitabile 1992，第 44 页，插图 65。

32 Late Ming dynasty (Wanli period) *Kraak* plate. Exported to Portugal and the Netherlands. Diameter 32 cm. Ref.: Avitabile 1992, p.44, plate 65.

33 明晚期"万历号"沉船双鹿克拉克瓷盘（约 1625 年）。景德镇双鹿图案青花瓷，双鹿之间绘有桃和灵芝图案。预计船载货物中约有 37 000 件青花瓷，但发掘过程只有 7 434 件登记在案。此盘为第 199 号登记（共登记 2 674 件）双鹿盘。直径 22 厘米，高 3.8 厘米。参考：Sjostrand 2007，第 212、213 页（序列号 1985）。

33 Late Ming dynasty *Kraak* twin deer plate from the *Wanli* shipwreck (c. 1625). Blue and white porcelain from Jingdezhen with a two deer decoration including a peach and a lingzhi fungus between the deer. Its ceramic cargo consisted of estimated 37,000 blue and white pieces, but only 7,434 could have been registered during the excavation. This piece is no.199 of the 2,674 registered twin deer plates. Diameter 22 cm, height 3.8 cm. Ref.: Sjostrand 2007, pp.212–213 (serial number 1985).

34 明万历克拉克碗。瓷碗饰以蚂蚱站立岩石的图案。直径 15 厘米，高 5 厘米。

34 Late Ming dynasty (Wanli period) *Kraak* bowl ("Klapmut") with a grasshopper on a rock design. Diameter 15 cm, height 5 cm.

清康熙和雍正时期的景德镇青花瓷
Kangxi & Yongzheng Period Blue and White Porcelain from Jingdezhen

35 清康熙青花盘。瓷盘饰以"修长侍女"（荷兰称为"修长伊莉莎"）图案。"修长侍女"和"嬉戏男童"是康熙时期外销瓷的常见图案。直径 15 厘米，高 3 厘米。

35 Blue and white Kangxi period dish with "Long Eliza" decoration. The "Long Eliza" and the "dancing boy" are very common decorations of the Kangxi period export porcelain. The name is the translation of the Dutch "lange Lijzen". Diameter 15 cm, height 3 cm.

36 清康熙青花壶。瓷壶饰以"修长侍女"图案和荷兰银镶嵌。直径9厘米，高17厘米。参考：Kerr 2011，第85页，插图116。

36 Blue and white Kangxi period jug with "Long Eliza" decoration and Dutch silver mount. Diameter 9 cm, height 17 cm. Ref.: Kerr 2011, p.85, plate 116.

37 清康熙银镶嵌青花盐罐。瓷罐饰以"修长侍女"图案。直径6厘米，高14厘米。

37 Blue and white Kangxi period Dutch silver-mounted salt cellar with "Long Eliza" decoration. Diameter 6 cm, height 14 cm.

38 清康熙青花汤盘。边缘饰以荷兰银镶嵌和中国万字纹。直径21厘米，高5厘米。

38 Kangxi period blue and white soup plate with Dutch silver mount and "swastika" (Chinese "wan") rim decoration. Diameter 21 cm, height 5 cm.

39 清康熙青花瓷盘。直径 21.5 厘米,高 3.5 厘米。参考:Avitabile 1992,第 86 页,插图 154。

39 Kangxi period blue and white dish. Diameter 21.5 cm, height 3.5 cm. Ref.: Avitabile 1992, p.86, plate 154.

40 清康熙带盖青花小瓶。器型柔和,饰以开光花卉纹。直径 6.5 厘米,高 15 厘米。参考:Christie's 1992,第 48、49 页。

40 Kangxi period small blue and white vase and cover, slightly moulded and painted with bands of petal-panels of flower sprays. Diameter 6.5 cm, height 15 cm. Ref.: Christie's 1992, pp.48-49.

41 清康熙时期"头顿号"沉船青花带盖瓷瓶。该瓷器是佳士得拍卖会第 62 号拍卖品。盖子直径 8.5 厘米，瓶体带盖高度 20 厘米。参考：Christie's 1992，第 22-23 页（第 62 号拍卖品）。

41 Kangxi period blue and white deep beaker with cover from the *Vung Tao* Shipwreck. This piece is Lot 62 of the auction. Diameter of the cover 8.5 cm, height including cover 20 cm. Ref.: Christie's 1992, pp.22, 23 (Lot 62).

42 清康熙青花八角碟。直径 11 厘米，高 2 厘米。

42 Kangxi period blue and white octagonal saucer. Diameter 11 cm, height 2 cm.

43 清康熙青花瓷碟。瓷碟饰以"修长侍女"和"嬉戏男童"图案。直径 11 厘米，高 2 厘米。

43 Kangxi period blue and white saucer with "Long Eliza" and "dancing boy" decoration. Diameter 11 cm, height 2 cm.

44 清康熙青花瓷碟。瓷碟饰以"嬉戏男童"图案，直径 10-12 厘米。参考：Kerr 2011，第 25 页，插图 20。

44 Kangxi period blue and white saucer with "dancing boy" decoration. Diameter: 10-12 cm. Ref.: Kerr 2011, p.25, plate 20.

45 清康熙青花瓷杯碟。杯碟饰以松鹿图案。杯子直径 8 厘米，高 4 厘米；碟直径 12.5 厘米，高 2 厘米。

45 Kangxi period blue and white cup and saucers with deer design. Diameter of the cup 8 cm, height 4 cm; diameter of the saucer 12.5 cm, height 2 cm.

46　清康熙青花瓷盘。直径 21.5 厘米，高 3 厘米。参考：Avitabile 1992，第 101 页，插图 186。

46　Kangxi period blue and white plate. Diameter 21.5 cm, height 3 cm. Ref.: Avitabile 1992, p.101, plate 186.

47　清康熙时期"蓝菊"沉船青花瓷杯和两只碟（约 **1710 年**）。杯子直径 7.5 厘米，高 4 厘米；左碟直径 11 厘米，右碟直径 11.5 厘米。

47　Kangxi period blue and white cup and two saucers from the *Blue Chrysanthemum* shipwreck (c. 1710). Diameter of the cup 7.5 cm, height 4; diameter of the left saucer 11 cm, diameter of the right saucer 11.5 cm.

48　清康熙青花瓷盘。瓷盘饰以"修长侍女"图案。直径 22 厘米，高 3 厘米，口沿呈花瓣形。参考：Avitabile 1992，第 116 页，插图 230。

48　Kangxi period blue and white plate with "Long Eliza" decoration and moulded rim. Diameter 22 cm, height 3 cm with some rim fritting. Ref.: Avitabile 1992, p.116, plate 230.

49 清雍正时期"金瓯号"沉船青花杯碟和巴达维亚瓷沉船杯（一只）碟。 茶碟直径 12 厘米；杯子直径 7 厘米，高 4 厘米；贴有苏富比拍卖行标签。参考：Ganse 2008，第 56 页。

49 Yongzheng period *Ca Mau* shipwreck blue and white saucers and cup, and one Batavia ware shipwreck cup and saucer. Saucers with diameter 12 cm; cups with diameter 7 cm, height 4 cm, with the *Sotheby's* auction sticker. Ref.: Ganse 2008, p.56.

50 清雍正青花茶壶。 直径 10.5 厘米，高 13 厘米。参考：Jörg 1986，第 70 页，插图 57。

50 Yongzheng period blue and white teapot. Diameter 10.5 cm, height 13 cm. Ref.: Jörg 1986, p.70, plate 57.

51 清雍正青花瓷盘。 直径 21.5 厘米，高 3 厘米。

51 Yongzheng period blue and white plate. Diameter 21.5 cm, height 3 cm.

五彩瓷
Famille Verte (*Wucai*) Porcelain

52 清康熙五彩八角瓷盘。直径 24 厘米，高 3.5 厘米。参考：Jörg 2011，第 42 页，插图 31。

52 Kangxi period *Famille verte* **octagonal plate.** Diameter 24 cm, height 3.5 cm. Ref.: Jörg 2011, p.42, plate 31.

53 清康熙五彩瓷盘。瓷盘折沿有起伏波纹。直径 22.5 厘米，高 3.5 厘米。

53 Kangxi period *Famille verte* **plate with moulded rim.** Diameter 22.5 cm, height 3.5 cm.

54 清康熙五彩啤酒杯。直径 10.5 厘米，高 14.5 厘米。

54 Kangxi period *Famille verte* **tankard.** Diameter 10.5 cm, height 14.5 cm.

55 清康熙五彩瓷盘。直径 21.5 厘米,高 3.5 厘米。

55 Kangxi period *Famille verte* plate. Diameter 21.5 cm, height 3.5 cm.

巴达维亚瓷
Batavia Ware

56 清乾隆巴达维亚茶杯和茶碟(约 1750 年)。瓷器饰以竹子图案,来自荷兰"哥德马尔森号"沉船。碟子直径 12 厘米;杯子直径 7.5 厘米,高 3.5 厘米;贴有 1986 年拍卖的原始标签。参考:Jörg 1986,第 67 页,插图 46。

56 Qianlong period *Batavia* ware teacup and saucer with bamboo design from the Dutch VOC *Geldermalsen* shipwreck (c. 1750). Diameter of the saucer 12 cm; diameter of the cup 7.5 cm, height 3.5 cm, with the original stickers from the 1986 auction. Ref.: Jörg 1986, p.67, plate 46.

57　清乾隆巴达维亚粉彩瓷茶杯和茶碟。杯碟饰以开光粉彩莲花纹饰。碟直径 12 厘米；杯子直径 7.5 厘米，高 4 厘米。参考：Madsen 2011，第 124 页，插图 4.94C。

57 Qianlong period *Batavia* ware teacup and saucer with *Famille rose* lotus flower in panels. Diameter of the saucer 12 cm; diameter of the cup 7.5 cm, height 4 cm. Ref.: Madsen 2011, p.124, plate 4.94C.

58　清乾隆巴达维亚粉彩姜罐。瓷罐施以粉彩釉，饰有少量金饰加彩，可能为后期在荷兰添加。直径 17 厘米，高 24 厘米。

58 Qianlong period *Batavia* ware Ginger Jar with *Famille rose* enamel, with little gold decoration added probably in the Netherlands. Diameter 17 cm, height 24 cm.

中国伊万里瓷器
Chinese Imari

59　清雍正中国伊万里瓷盘（约 1730 年）。直径 23 厘米，高 2 厘米。参考：Chan 2012，第 104 页。

59 Yongzheng period *Chinese Imari* plate (c. 1730). Diameter 23 cm, height 2 cm. Ref.: Chan 2012, p.104.

60 清雍正中国伊万里瓷盘（约 1730 年）。直径 22.5 厘米，参考：Madsen 2011，第 110 页，插图 B；上海市历史博物馆，2019，第 73 页。

60 Yongzheng period *Chinese Imari* plate (c. 1730). Diameter 22.5 cm. Ref.: Madsen 2011, p.110, plate B and Shanghai History Museum 2019, p.73.

61 清乾隆中国伊万里剃须盘（约 1760 年）。直径 29.5 厘米，高 6.5 厘米。

61 Qianlong period *Chinese Imari* barber shaving bowl (c. 1760). Diameter 29.5 cm, height 6.5 cm.

62 清乾隆中国伊万里瓷盘（约 1750 年）。直径 22 厘米，高 2.5 厘米。

62 Qianlong period *Chinese Imari* plate (c. 1750). Diameter 22 cm, height 2.5 cm.

63 清乾隆中国伊万里牛奶罐（约 1750 年）。高 15.5 厘米。

63 Qianlong period *Chinese Imari* covered milk jug (c. 1750). Height 15.5 cm.

64 清乾隆中国伊万里无盖巧克力罐（约 1750 年）。高 13 厘米。

64 Qianlong period *Chinese Imari* Chocolate Pot without lid (c. 1750). Height 13 cm.

65 清乾隆中国伊万里瓷盘（约 1740 年）。直径 22 厘米，高 2.5 厘米。

65 Qianlong period *Chinese Imari* plate (c. 1740). Diameter 22 cm, height 2.5 cm.

66 清乾隆中国伊万里瓷盘（约 1750 年）。瓷盘为荷兰"哥德马尔森号"沉船货物。红色釉上彩几乎完全被海水侵蚀。参考：Jörg 1986，第 75 页。

66 Qianlong period *Chinese Imari* plate from the Dutch VOC *Geldermalsen* shipwreck (c. 1750). The overglaze red is almost completely eroded. Ref.: Jörg 1986, p.75.

67 清乾隆无盖青花加彩壶（约 1740 年）。粉彩瓷釉是欧洲采用的一种在中国瓷底釉上进行二次装饰的工艺（加彩）。直径 8 厘米，高 11 厘米。

67 Qianlong period clobbered blue and white jug without lid (c. 1740). The *Famille rose* enamels are a secondary decoration applied in Europe above the Chinese underglaze blue (clabbering). Diameter 8 cm, height 11 cm.

68 清乾隆青花加彩瓷碗。瓷碗加施欧洲釉彩，直径 14.5 厘米，高 7 厘米。参考：Ganse 2008，第 116 页。

68 Qianlong period clobbered blue and white bowl ("Amsterdam bont") with European enameling. Diameter 14.5 cm, height 7 cm. Ref.: Ganse 2008, p.116.

209

69 清雍正金属镶嵌青花加彩碟（约 1730 年）。 瓷碟很可能是在法国被加施欧洲釉彩并被加上黄铜底座。直径 11 厘米，含底座高 11 厘米。

69 Yongzheng period ormolu-mounted and clobbered underglaze blue saucer (c. 1730). This saucer got European enameling and a European bronze mount possibly from France. Diameter 11 cm, height 11 cm (with mount).

粉彩瓷
Famille rose (*fencai*) porcelain

70 清乾隆釉下青花开光粉彩马克杯（约 1780 年）。 瓷杯开光内施以粉彩，饰有枝叶和"满大人"开光图案。"满大人"装饰描述中国人生活场景。直径 11.5 厘米，高 14.5 厘米。参考：Madsen 2011，第 109 页。

70 Qianlong period underglaze blue porcelain mug with sprouts and *Mandarin* decoration in one reserve in *Famille rose* enamels, moulded lotus flowers (c. 1780). The term *Mandarin* refers to the depiction of scenes with Chinese people. Diameter 11.5 cm, height 14.5 cm. Ref.: Madsen 2011, p.109.

71　清乾隆青花粉彩花口盘（约 1760 年）。瓷盘饰以河景，口沿施以釉下蓝彩。直径 22.5 厘米，高 2.5 厘米。

71　Qianlong period *Famille rose* plate with river scene decoration and underglaze blue rim (c. 1760). Diameter 22.5 cm, height 2.5 cm.

72　清乾隆青花粉彩汤匙托盘和瓷杯（约 1780 年）。瓷器饰以"满大人"纹饰，口沿施以釉下蓝彩。汤匙托盘长 12.5 厘米，宽 11 厘米，杯子直径 6 厘米，高 6 厘米。

72　Qianlong period *Famille rose* spoon tray and cup with *Mandarin* decoration and underglaze blue rim (c. 1780). Length of the spoon tray 12.5 cm, width 11 cm; diameter of the cup 6 cm, height 6 cm.

73　清乾隆青花粉彩茶壶（约 1790 年）。瓷壶饰以粉彩"满大人"四开光纹饰，带四处粉彩清朝装饰。壶盖有"锔瓷"修复痕迹，执手处有修复痕迹。直径 12 厘米，高 16 厘米。

73　Qianlong period underglaze blue porcelain teapot with *Famille rose Mandarin* decorations in four reserves (c. 1790). Cover repaired with staples, handles restored. Diameter 12 cm, height 16 cm.

74 清乾隆青花粉彩马克杯（约1790年）。瓷杯上饰有粉彩"满大人"纹饰，配有镶嵌金属手柄。直径11厘米，高14.5厘米。

74 Qianlong period underglaze blue tankard with *Famille rose Mandarin* decoration (c. 1790) with bronze mount handle. Diameter 11 cm, height 14.5 cm.

75 清乾隆粉彩瓷盘（约1750年）。瓷盘饰有玫瑰花卉和蝴蝶纹饰。直径22.5厘米，高3厘米。

75 Qianlong period *Famille rose* plate with rose and butterfly decoration (c. 1750). Diameter 22.5 cm, height 3 cm.

76 清乾隆青花粉彩瓷盘。瓷盘口沿饰有釉下蓝彩装饰。直径23厘米，高2.5厘米。

76 Qianlong period *Famille rose* plate with underglaze blue rim decoration. Diameter 23 cm, height 2.5 cm.

77 清乾隆青花粉彩瓷盘（约1760年）。瓷盘饰有河岸杨柳装饰，口沿施以釉下蓝彩。直径22.5厘米，高2.5厘米。

77 Qianlong period *Famille rose* plate with a Willow design river scene decoration and underglaze blue rim (c. 1760). Diameter 22.5 cm, height 2.5 cm.

78 清乾隆青花粉彩瓷盘（约1760年）。瓷盘饰有花卉和蝙蝠图案，口沿施以釉下蓝彩。直径22.5厘米，高2.5厘米。

78 Qianlong period *Famille rose* plate with flower and bat decoration, and underglaze blue rim (c. 1760). Diameter 22.5 cm, height 2.5 cm.

79 清乾隆粉彩瓷盘。销往法国的外销瓷。直径23厘米，高2.5厘米。

79 Qianlong period *Famille rose* plate, exported to France. Diameter 23 cm, height 2.5 cm.

80 清乾隆粉彩瓷盘。销往法国的外销瓷。直径 23 厘米，高 2.5 厘米。

80 Qianlong period *Famille rose* plate, exported to France. Diameter 23 cm, height 2.5 cm.

81 清乾隆两组粉彩瓷杯和瓷碟。瓷器饰有"满大人"纹饰，为景德镇烧制、在广州施加釉彩、销往英国的外销瓷。左杯直径 6.5 厘米，右杯直径 5.5 厘米；高度分别为 6.5 厘米和 6 厘米；左碟直径 12 厘米，右碟直径 12.5 厘米。

81 Two Qianlong period *Famille rose* cups and saucers with *Mandarin* decoration. Jingdezhen porcelain enameled in Canton, exported to Great Britain. Diameter of the left cup 6.5 cm, diameter of the right cup 5.5 cm, height 6.5 cm and 6 cm respectively; diameter of the left saucer 12 cm, diameter of the right saucer 12.5 cm.

82　清乾隆粉彩瓷盘。瓷盘饰以"满大人"纹饰风格的"窗中小童"图案。为销往英国的外销瓷。直径 23 厘米，高 3 厘米。

82　Qianlong period *Famille rose* plate with the *Mandarin* "Boy in the window" decoration, exported to Great Britain. Diameter 23 cm, height 3 cm.

中国订单瓷器，纹章瓷和墨彩
Armorial & *Grisaille* Porcelain

83　清乾隆纹章瓷套装（1780—1790 年）。这套瓷器以釉彩绘上家族徽章珐琅，釉下蓝彩，南京式样口沿。大盘直径 21 厘米，高 4 厘米，可见"锔瓷"修复痕迹和两处釉裂细纹。小盘破损，直径 15 厘米，高 3.5 厘米。三只碟（其中两只破损）直径 12.5 厘米，高 3 厘米。两只无柄杯，直径 7.5 厘米，高 4.5 厘米，均有釉裂细纹。两只带柄杯（其中一只破损），直径 5.5 厘米，高 6 厘米。参考 Madsen 2011，第 55 页；Palmer 1976，第 118 页。

83　Qianlong period armorial service with a family coat of arm in enamels and with underglaze blue *Nanking* butterfly and hex cell rim (1780–1790). Big dish diameter 21 cm, height 4 cm with staple repair and two hairline cracks; one broken small dish with diameter 15 cm, height 3.5 cm; three saucers (two broken) diameter 12.5 cm, height 3 cm; two cups without handle, diameter 7.5 cm and height 4.5 cm, both with hairline cracks; and two cups with handle (one broken), diameter 5.5 cm, height 6 cm. Ref.: Madsen 2011, p.55 and Palmer 1976, p.118.

84 清嘉庆纹章瓷带盖菜盘，饰有瑞典家族徽章（约 1800 年）。瓷盘施以釉彩。长 25.5 厘米，宽 21.5 厘米，高 14.5 厘米。参考：Schiffer 1975，第 249 页，插图 667。

84 Jiaqing period armorial porcelain covered vegetable dish with enamels and a Swedish coat of arms (c. 1800). Length 25.5 cm, width 21.5 cm, height 14.5 cm. Ref.: Schiffer 1975, p.249, plate 667.

85 清乾隆墨彩茶叶罐和无盖牛奶壶。茶叶罐高度为 13 厘米，牛奶壶高度为 10 厘米。

85 Qianlong period *Grisaille* tea caddy and milk jug without lid. Height of the tea caddy 13 cm, height of the milk jug 10 cm.

后期青花瓷和南京式样瓷器
Later Blue and White and *Nanking* Ware

86 清乾隆南京式样青花瓷盘（1760—1780 年）。瓷盘饰以亭子和蝴蝶纹饰，卷轴状口沿。长 27 厘米，宽 18.5 厘米，高 2 厘米。参考：Madsen 2011，第 98 页，插图 4.62；Godden 1979，第 128-129 页和第 141 页。

86 Qianlong period *Nanking* blue and white porcelain platter with pavilion decoration and a butterfly and scroll rim (1760-1780). Length 27 cm, width 18.5 cm, height 2 cm. Ref.: Madsen 2011, p.98, plate 4.62 and Godden 1979, pp.128-129, 141.

87 清乾隆南京式样青花瓷盘（1780—1799 年）。瓷盘饰以凉亭花卉装饰，口沿饰有六角格纹和鱼子纹。长 33 厘米，宽 23.5 厘米，高 3 厘米。参考：Godden 1979，第 130 页。

87 Qianlong period *Nanking* blue and white porcelain platter with pavilion decoration and a flower, hex cell and fish roe rim (1780-1799). Length 33 cm, width 23.5 cm, height 3 cm. Ref.: Godden 1979, p.130.

88 清乾隆南京式样青花热水瓷盘（约1760年）。瓷盘饰以凉亭图案，口沿饰以鱼子纹。直径23厘米，高5.5厘米。参考：故宫博物院、上海博物馆，2015，第312-313页，插图137。

88 Qianlong period *Nanking* blue and white hot water dish with pavilion decoration and a fish roe rim (c. 1760). Diameter 23 cm, height 5.5 cm. Ref.: the Palace Museum 2015, plate 137, pp.312-313.

89 清乾隆南京式样青花瓷敞口盐瓶（1785—1799年）。瓷瓶饰以"双寺"和蝴蝶图案，口沿饰以墨点网格纹。长9厘米，宽7厘米，高4.5厘米。参考：Schiffer 1975，第196页，插图530；Godden 1979，第142页。

89 Qianlong period *Nanking* blue and white porcelain open salt cellar with the "Two Temple" decoration and the butterfly and diaper rim (1785–1799). Length 9 cm, width 7 cm, height 4.5 cm. Ref.: Schiffer 1975, p.196, plate 530 and Godden 1979, p.142.

90 清乾隆南京式样青花瓷贝壳盘（1780—1799年）。瓷盘饰以花卉，口沿饰以菱纹锦和鱼子纹。长15厘米，宽14厘米，高5厘米。参考：Godden 1979，第126页。

90 Qianlong period *Nanking* blue and white porcelain shell dish with flower decoration and trellis/swastika & fish roe rim (1780–1799). Length 15 cm, width 14 cm, height 5 cm. Ref.: Godden 1979, p.126.

91 清乾隆南京式样青花瓷酱汁船（1760—1780年）。 瓷器饰以花卉，口沿饰以菱纹锦。长 21 厘米，宽 10.5 厘米，高 8 厘米。参考：Schiffer 1975，第 198 页。

91 Qianlong period *Nanking* blue and white porcelain sauce boat with flower decoration and trellis/swastika rim (1760–1780). Length 21 cm, width 10.5 cm, height 8 cm. Ref.: Schiffer 1975, p.198.

92 清乾隆南京式样青花瓷盘（约 1760 年）。 瓷盘饰以"修长侍女和嬉戏男童"和蝴蝶图案，卷轴状口沿。直径 23 厘米，高 2.5 厘米。

92 Qianlong period *Nanking* blue and white plate with the "Long Eliza and dancing boy" decoration, and a butterfly and scroll rim (c. 1760). Diameter 23 cm, height 2.5 cm.

93 清乾隆青花瓷茶叶罐（1760—1780 年）。 瓷罐饰以"双寺图案"，直径 9 厘米，高 12 厘米，经过修复，无盖。参考：Godden 1979，第 146 页，插图 50。

93 Qianlong period blue and white tea caddy with the "Two Temple" design (1760–1780). Diameter 9 cm, height 12 cm with restorations and without cover. Ref.: Godden 1979, p.146, plate 50.

94 清乾隆时期"哥德堡号"沉船青花瓷碟（约 1745 年）。直径 16.5 厘米，高 3 厘米。参考：Arensberg 2009，第 65 页。

94 Qianlong period small blue and white dish from the *Götheborg* shipwreck (c. 1745). Diameter 16.5 cm, height 3 cm. Ref.: Arensberg 2009, p.65.

95 清乾隆青花瓷盘（约 1740—1750 年）。瓷盘饰以河景，口沿饰以菱纹锦。直径 22 厘米，高 3.5 厘米。

95 Qianlong period blue and white octagonal plate with river scene decoration and a blue trellis rim (c. 1740–1750). Diameter 22 cm, height 3.5 cm.

96 清乾隆青花瓷盘（约 1750—1760 年）。直径 23 厘米，高 2.5 厘米，口沿有飞皮。参考：Madsen 2011，第 82 页，插图 4.38B。

96 Qianlong period blue and white plate (c. 1750–1760). Diameter 23 cm, height 2.5 cm with rim damages. Ref.: Madsen 2011, p.82, plate 4.38B.

97　清乾隆青花瓷盘（1760—1780 年）。 瓷盘饰以河景图案。直径 22.5 厘米，高 2.5 厘米。

97　Qianlong period *Nanking* blue and white plate with river scene (1760–1780). Diameter 22.5 cm, height 2.5 cm.

98　清乾嘉时期南京式样青花瓷杯、碟和糖罐（1780—1820 年）。 瓷罐带龙形手柄和桃形盖，饰有寺庙、阴影菱纹锦、矛头纹和铃铛坠图案，在英国完成镀金。直径分别为 6 厘米、14 厘米、10 厘米；高分别为 7 厘米、3 厘米、13 厘米。

98　Qianlong and Jiaqing period *Nanking* blue and white cup, saucer and covered sugar box with dragon shaped handles, a peach lid, temple decoration, shaded trellis, spearhead and dumbbell rim (1780–1820). Gilding is added in UK. Diameter 6 cm, 14 cm, 10 cm; height 7 cm, 3 cm, 13 cm.

99 清乾隆侍女塑像。两尊，其中一尊饰釉下蓝彩斗篷，另一尊饰粉彩装饰。高度均为 18 厘米。参考：Jörg 1986，第 100 页，插图 95。

99 Two Qianlong period female figurines. One with underglaze blue cape, one with *Famille rose* decoration. Height 18 cm. Ref.: Jörg 1986, p.100, plate 95.

100 清乾隆南京式样青花瓷茶壶（约 1780 年）。瓷壶饰凉亭图案。直径（不含手柄）11 厘米，高 15 厘米。参考：Godden 1979，第 146 页，插图 49。

100 Qianlong period *Nanking* blue and white teapot with pavilion decoration (c. 1780). Diameter (without handle) 11 cm, height 15 cm. Ref.: Godden 1979, p.146, plate 49.

101　清乾隆南京式样青花大瓷盘（1760—1780 年）。瓷盘饰以双孔雀、岩石和花卉图图案，口沿饰以花卉蝴蝶图案。长 33.5 厘米，宽 24.5 厘米，高 3 厘米。参考：Godden 2004，第 31 页。

101　Qianlong period *Nanking* blue and white platter with two peacock, rock and flower decoration, and a flower and butterfly rim (1760–1780). Length 33.5 cm, width 24.5 cm, height 3 cm. Ref.: Godden 2004, p.31.

102　清乾隆南京式样青花有盖海碗（1780—1799 年）。瓷碗饰以宫殿场景图案，口沿饰以蝴蝶、鱼子纹以及矛头纹。莲花形手柄和石榴盖钮。长 30 厘米，宽 18 厘米，高 19 厘米，有胎裂纹。

102　Qianlong period *Nanking* blue and white tureen (1780–1799) with a palace scene, butterfly and fish roe decoration, spearhead rim, lotus-shaped handles, and a pomegranate-shaped lid knob. Length 30 cm, width 18 cm, height 19 cm with cracks.

海上丝绸之路的 **陶瓷**
The Ceramics of the Maritime Silk Road

103 清乾隆南京式样青花瓷咖啡壶（1780—1799年）。瓷壶饰以凉亭、六角格纹和鱼子纹图案，配有欧洲金属镶嵌。直径 13 厘米，高 24 厘米。

103 Qianlong period *Nanking* blue and white coffee pot (1780–1799) with pavilion, hexagonal cells and fish roe decoration, and European metal mounts. Diameter 13 cm, height 24 cm.

104 清乾隆南京式样青花瓷八角碟（1785—1799年）。瓷碟饰以凉亭图案，口沿饰以蝴蝶、墨点网格纹和回字纹。瓷盘破损成两块，有"锔瓷"修复痕迹。直径 22.5 厘米，高 4 厘米。参考：Madsen 2011，第 85 页，插图 4.41。

104 Qianlong period *Nanking* blue and white octagonal dish (1785–1799) with pavilion decoration and butterfly, diaper and scale rim, broken in two pieces and repaired with metal staples. Diameter 22.5 cm, height 4 cm. Ref.: Madsen 2011, p.85, plate 4.41.

105　清乾隆菲次休青花八角盘（约 1780 年）。 瓷盘饰有阴影菱纹锦和铃铛坠图案。直径 16 厘米，高 2.5 厘米。参考：Madsen 2011，第 99 页。

105　Qianlong period *Fitzhugh* blue and white octagonal serving dish with shaded trellis and dumbbell rim (c. 1780). Diameter 16 cm, height 2.5 cm. Ref.: Madsen 2011, p.99.

106　清嘉庆南京式样青花带盖海碗，带八角托盘（约 1800 年）。 瓷碗饰以花园和柳树图案。直径（不含狗形手柄）14 厘米，高 13.5 厘米；托盘直径 20 厘米，高 3.5 厘米。

106　Jiaqing period *Nanking* blue and white porcelain tureen with octagonal base with garden and willow decoration (c. 1800). Diameter (without dog shaped handles) 14 cm, height 13.5 cm, diameter of the base 20 cm, height 3.5 cm.

广东式样瓷器
Canton Ware

107 清嘉庆广东式样椭圆镂刻瓷盘（约 1820 年）。瓷盘饰以凉亭图案。长 28 厘米，宽 24 厘米，高 4 厘米。参考：Schiffer 1975，第 175 页；Madsen 2011，第 86 页。

107 Jiaqing period oval pierced *Canton* plate with pavilion decoration (c. 1820). Length 28 cm, width 24 cm, height 4 cm. Ref.: Schiffer 1975, p.175 and Madsen 2011, p.86.

108 清道光广东式样瓷盘（约 1830 年）。瓷盘饰以仓促画作的凉亭图案，口沿饰以云雨纹，器型略微呈八角形。直径 22 厘米，高 4 厘米。参考：Schiffer 1975，第 169 页，插图 454；Madsen 2011，第 86 页，插图 4.43；Nagel 1999，第 237 页。

108 Daoguang period *Canton* dish with hurriedly painted pavilion decoration and rain & cloud border–slightly octagonal (c. 1830). Diameter 22 cm, height 4 cm. Ref.: Schiffer 1975, p.169, plate 454; Madsen 2011, p.86, plate 4.43; Nagel 1999, p.237.

109 清道光广东式样带盖糖罐（约 1830 年）和清嘉庆广东式样马克杯（约 1820 年）。糖罐饰以仓促画作的凉亭团，马克杯饰以凉亭图案，口沿饰以云雨纹。瓷罐直径 9 厘米，高 8.5 厘米。马克杯直径 9 厘米，高 11 厘米。参考：Schiffer 1975，第 95 页，插图 295 和第 128 页，插图 350。

109 Daoguang period *Canton* covered sugar bowl with hurriedly painted pavilion decoration (c. 1830) and Jiaqing period *Canton* mug with pavilion decoration and rain & cloud border (c. 1820). Diameter of the box 9 cm, height 8.5 cm. Diameter of the mug 9 cm, height 11 cm. Ref.: Schiffer 1975, p.95, plate 295 and p.128, plate 350.

玫瑰奖章式样瓷器（广彩）
Rose Medallion (*guangcai*)

110 清同治玫瑰奖章式样（广彩）马克杯（约 1862—1875 年）。瓷杯为景德镇烧制，在广东施加釉彩。直径 8 厘米，高 11 厘米。参考：Schiffer 1975，第 128 页，插图 350。

110 Tongzhi period *Rose Medallion* (*guangcai*) mug (c. 1862–1875). Jingdezhen porcelain with enameling from Canton. Diameter 8 cm, height 11 cm. Ref.: Schiffer 1975, p.128, plate 350.

111 清同治玫瑰奖章式样带盖糖罐（约1862—1875年）。高14厘米。参考：Schiffer 1975, 第96页。

111 Tongzhi period *Rose Medallion* covered sugar bowl (c. 1862–1875). Height 14 cm. Ref.: Schiffer 1975, p.96.

112 清同治玫瑰奖章式样茶壶，配有蟹钮（约1862—1875年）。直径12厘米，高15厘米。参考：Schiffer 1975, 第193页, 插图520。

112 Tongzhi period *Rose Medallion* teapot with a crab knob (c. 1862–1875). Diameter 12 cm, height 15 cm. Ref.: Schiffer 1975, p.193, plate 520.

113 清光绪玫瑰奖章式样瓷盘（约1900年）。直径22厘米。盘底"Made in China"或"China"标记已被海水侵蚀掉，因此无法准确断代。1891年后出口至美国的玫瑰奖章式样瓷器都标记了原产国。参考：Schiffer 1975, 第29页。

113 Guangxu period *Rose Medallion* plate (c. 1900). Diameter 22 cm. The "Made in China" or "China" mark underneath has been erased to disguise the age. *Rose Medallion* exports to the U.S. after 1891 had to be marked with their origins. Ref.: Schiffer 1975, p.29.

销往亚洲国家的晚期外销瓷
Late Chinese Export Ceramics to Asian Countries

114 清乾隆地方瓷窑青花瓷盘（约1750年）。瓷盘来自荷兰东印度公司"哥德马尔森号"沉船，为出口至好望角的外销瓷。直径 19.5 厘米，高 4 厘米。参考：Jörg 1986。

114 Qianlong period (c. 1750) provincial blue and white plate from the Dutch VOC *Geldermalsen* shipwreck. Export ware to the Cape. Diameter 19.5 cm, height 4 cm. Ref.: Jörg 1986.

115 清嘉庆时期"黛安娜号"沉船青花瓷碗。直径 15.5 厘米，高 8 厘米，贴有佳士得拍卖行拍卖标签。

115 Jiaqing period blue and white *Diana* shipwreck bowl. Diameter 15.5 cm, height 8 cm with the sticker from the *Christie's* auction.

116 清道光时期"泰兴号"沉船青花瓷碗和釉面勺。中国德化出口印度尼西亚的外销瓷。瓷器釉面已经被海水腐蚀。贴有德国纳格尔拍卖行的标签。碗直径 11 厘米，高 4 厘米。勺子的长度为 11 厘米。参考：Nagel 1999，第 188、189、226 页。

116 Daoguang period blue and white *Tek Sing* shipwreck bowl and glazed spoons. Dehua export ware to Indonesia. The glaze is completely eroded. With the sticker of the *Nagel* auction. Diameter of the bowl 11 cm, height 4 cm. Length of the spoons 11 cm. Ref.: Nagel 1999, pp.188, 189, 226.

117 清代沉船青花盘，瓷盘饰以独特的凤凰图案。德化销往印度尼西亚的外销瓷。直径 18 厘米。参考：Nagel 1999，第 206 页；Avitabile 1992，第 103 页，插图 192。

117 Qing dynasty blue and white shipwreck dish with a stylised phoenix. Dehua export ware to Indonesia. Diameter 18 cm. Ref.: Nagel 1999, p.206 and Avitabile 1992, p.103, plate 192.

118 清代沉船青花瓷杯。四只，德化销往至印度尼西亚的外销瓷。直径 5 至 8 厘米，高 3.5 至 4 厘米，参考：Nagel 1999，第 194 页。

118 Four Qing dynasty blue and white shipwreck cups. Dehua export ware to Indonesia. Diameter from 5 cm to 8 cm, height from 3.5 to 4 cm. Ref.: Nagel 1999, p.194.

119 清道光青花汤匙（约 1830 年）。汤匙为"迪沙鲁号"沉船瓷器。长度 10.5 厘米。参考：The Desaru ship。

119 Daoguang period blue and white soup spoon from the *Desaru* shipwreck (c. 1830). Length 10.5 cm. Ref.: The Desaru ship.

120 清道光青花瓷盘（约 1830 年）。瓷盘为"迪沙鲁号"沉船瓷器。直径 25 厘米，高 4 厘米。参考：The Desaru ship；中国嘉德国际拍卖有限公司，2006，插图 1966。

120 Daoguang period blue and white dish from the *Desaru* shipwreck (c. 1830). Diameter 25 cm, height 4 cm. Ref.: The Desaru ship and China Guardian Seasons Auction 2006, plate 1966.

121 清道光青花瓷盘（约 1830 年）。瓷盘为"迪沙鲁号"沉船瓷器。直径 28 厘米，高 5.5 厘米，有修复痕迹。参考：The Desaru ship；中国嘉德国际拍卖有限公司，2006，插图 1968。

121 Daoguang period blue and white dish from the *Desaru* shipwreck (c. 1830). Diameter 28 cm, height 5.5 cm with restorations. Ref.: The Desaru ship and China Guardian Seasons Auction 2006, plate 1968.

122 从左至右：清代沉船酱釉茶碟，碟底未上釉；清代沉船酱釉小罐；清代沉船橄榄釉小罐，足底未上釉；清代沉船酱釉带盖小罐。中国销往印度尼西亚的外销瓷。尺寸分别为：直径9厘米；直径6厘米，高9厘米；直径7厘米，高10.5厘米；直径7厘米，高5厘米。参考：Nagel 1999，第246-247页，第250-251页，第243页，第253页。

122 Left to right: Qing dynasty brown glazed small shipwreck saucer with unglazed underside; Qing dynasty brown glazed small shipwreck jar; Qing dynasty olive glazed shipwreck jar with unglazed foot; Qing dynasty brown glazed small shipwreck pot with cover. Chinese export wares to Indonesia. Their sizes are: diameter 9 cm; diameter 6 cm, height 9 cm; diameter 7 cm, height 10.5 cm; diameter 7 cm, height 5 cm. Ref.: Nagel 1999, pp.246-247, 250-251, 243, 253.

123 清代沉船酱釉瓷瓶。中国销往印度尼西亚的外销瓷。高17厘米，参考：Nagel 1999，第308页。

123 Qing dynasty brown glazed tall shipwreck vase. Chinese export ware to Indonesia. Height 17 cm. Ref.: Nagel 1999, p.308.

124 清代青花碗。直径 18 厘米，高 7 厘米。参考：Bi 1991，第 180 页。

124 Qing dynasty blue and white ogee-shaped bowl. Diameter 18 cm, height 7 cm. Ref.: Bi 1991, p.180.

125 清光绪青花瓷盘。直径 15 厘米。

125 Guangxu period blue and white plate. Diameter 15 cm.

126 清晚期青花瓷盘。盘心饰有花篮、青花双圈，口沿为蓝色水墨纹。直径 20 厘米，高 2.5 厘米。参考：Nagel 1999，第 213 页。

126 Late Qing dynasty blue and white plate decorated with a flower basket, two rings and a wide blue band. Diameter 20 cm, height 2.5 cm. Ref.: Nagel 1999, p.213.

光绪仿康熙瓷和班加隆瓷器
Kangxi Revival and *Bencharong* porcelain

127 清光绪仿康熙风格金边青花盖碗（约 1890 年）。中国销往泰国的外销瓷。直径 10.5 厘米，高 12.5 厘米。参考：Chandavij 2015。

127 Guangxu period *Kangxi Revival* blue and white covered bowl with metal-bound rim (c. 1890). Chinese export ware to Thailand. Diameter 10.5 cm, height 12.5 cm. Ref.: Chandavij 2015.

128 清光绪仿康熙风格青花盖罐（约 1890 年）。中国销往泰国的外销瓷。直径 6.5 厘米，高 9.5 厘米。参考：Chandavij 2015。

128 Guangxu period *Kangxi Revival* blue and white covered bowl (c. 1890). Chinese export ware to Thailand. Diameter 6.5 cm, height 9.5 cm. Ref.: Chandavij 2015.

129 清光绪仿康熙风格金边青花盖碗（约 1890 年）。中国销往泰国或越南的外销瓷。直径 8 厘米，高 6 厘米。参考：Chandavij 2015。

129 Guangxu period *Kangxi Revival* blue and white cup with metal-bound rim (c. 1890). Chinese export ware to Thailand or Vietnam. Diameter 8 cm, height 6 cm. Ref.: Chandavij 2015.

130 清光绪仿康熙风格金边青花痰盂（约1890年）。中国销往泰国的外销瓷。直径10厘米，高7厘米。参考：Chandavij 2015。

130 Guangxu period *Kangxi Revival* blue and white spittoon with metal-bound rim (c. 1890). Chinese export ware to Thailand. Diameter 10 cm, height 7 cm. Ref.: Chandavij 2015.

131 清晚期顺化青釉青花小托盘。中国销往越南的外销瓷。长15.5厘米，宽9.5厘米，高1.5厘米。

131 Late Qing dynasty *Bleu de Hué* blue and white miniature tray. Chinese export ware to Vietnam. Length 15.5 cm, width 9.5 cm, height 1.5 cm.

132 清晚期无盖班加隆珐琅五彩缸。瓷缸饰以佛教神像图案。中国销往泰国的外销瓷。班加隆是泰语，意指五种颜色。直径6.5厘米，高度4厘米。参考：Robinson 1982。

132 Late Qing dynasty *Bencharong* enameled "Toh prik" jarlet without cover and the "Thepanom" decoration (Buddhist minor deity). Chinese export ware to Thailand. *Bencharong* is Thai and means five colors. Diameter 6.5 cm, height 4 cm. Ref.: Robinson 1982.

海峡中国瓷
Straits Porcelain

133 清晚期中国双喜青花大花瓶。中国销往英属海峡殖民地的外销瓷。直径 17 厘米,高 43 厘米。参考:Ho 2008,第 120–121 页。

133 Late Qing large Chinese blue and white baluster vase with the double happiness character. Chinese export to the British Straits Settlements. Diameter 17 cm, height 43 cm. Ref.: Ho 2008, pp.120–121.

134 清晚期青花盖罐。中国销往英属海峡殖民地的外销瓷。直径 9 厘米,高 11.5 厘米。参考:Ho 2008,第 120–121 页。

134 Late Qing blue and white covered bowl ("kat-mau"). Chinese export to the Straits Settlements. Diameter 9 cm, height 11.5 cm. Ref.: Ho 2008, pp.120–121.

135　清晚期青花茶壶。中国销往英属海峡殖民地的外销瓷。直径 10 厘米，高 8.5 厘米。参考：Ho 2008，第 120-121 页。

135　Late Qing dynasty blue and white teapot. Chinese export to the Straits Settlements. Diameter 10 cm, height 8.5 cm. Ref.: Ho 2008, pp.120-121.

136　清晚期青花瓷盘。中国销往英属海峡殖民地的外销瓷。直径 15 厘米。参考：Ho 2008，第 120-121 页。

136　Late Qing dynasty blue and white plate. Chinese export to the Straits Settlements. Diameter 15 cm. Ref.: Ho 2008, pp.120-121.

137　清光绪或宣统粉彩峇峇娘惹瓷盘（约 1908 年）。瓷盘饰以凤凰和牡丹图案。中国销往英属海峡殖民地的外销瓷。盘底盖"Wang Shen-shu"红印。直径 22.5 厘米，高 3 厘米。参考：Ho 2008，第 53、118 页；Kerr 2006，第 97 页，插图 214c。

137　Guangxu or Xuantong period rose pink enameled phoenix and peony *Peranakan* plate (c. 1908). Chinese export to the Straits Settlements, with the red "Wang Shen-shu" chop mark on the reverse side. Diameter 22.5 cm, height 3 cm. Ref.: Ho 2008, pp.53, 118 and Kerr 2006, p.97, plate 214c.

第六章 亚洲其他国家陶瓷
Chapter 6 Ceramics of Other Asian Countries

日本陶瓷
Japanese Ceramics

138 日本江户时期有田青花瓷盘（1670—1720年）。 日本销往荷兰的外销瓷，瓷盘具有中国克拉克瓷风格。直径 21.5 厘米，高 3.5 厘米，釉面已被海水侵蚀。

138 Edo period Japanese Arita porcelain plate with underglaze blue decoration in the Chinese *Kraak* style (1670–1720). Japanese export porcelain to the Netherlands. Diameter 21.5 cm, height 3.5 cm with eroded glaze.

139 日本江户时期有田青花瓷盘（1670—1720 年）。瓷盘具有中国克拉克瓷风格。直径 21.5 厘米，高 3 厘米。参考：Jörg 2003，第 225 页，插图 285 和第 230 页，插图 291；Schiffer 1986，第 62 页；Shono 1973，插图 120.t。

139 *Edo period Japanese Arita porcelain plate with underglaze blue decoration in the Chinese Kraak style (1670–1720)*. Diameter 21.5 cm, height 3 cm. Ref.: Jörg 2003, p.225, plate 285 and p.230, plate 291; Schiffer 1986, p.62 and Shono 1973, plate 120.t.

140 日本江户时期伊万里瓷盘（1700—1730 年）。瓷盘施以釉下蓝彩和釉上红彩。直径 28.5 厘米，高 5 厘米。另一类似瓷器收藏于维也纳霍夫堡宫皇家珍宝馆。参考：Hetjens-Museum 2000，第 49 页，插图 11。

140 *Edo period Japanese Imari porcelain charger with underglaze blue and overglaze red (1700–1730)*. Diameter 28.5 cm, height 5 cm. A similar item is part of the *Vienna Hofburg Imperial Treasury*. Ref.: Hetjens-Museum 2000, p.49, plate 11.

141 日本江户时期瓷盘。瓷盘施以釉下蓝彩和釉上彩。直径 20 厘米，高 2.5 厘米。

141 Edo period Japanese dish with underglaze blue and overglaze enamels. Diameter 20 cm, height 2.5 cm.

142 日本明治时期有田伊万里瓷盘（约 1900 年）。直径 21 厘米，高 3.5 厘米。

142 Meiji period Japanese *Imari* plate from Arita (c. 1900). Diameter 21 cm, height 3.5 cm.

143 日本明治时期有田伊万里瓷盘（1879—1897 年）。由有田的征士·魁车工厂烧制，带征士·魁车印章。直径 30 厘米，高 4 厘米。参考：Nielson（2）。

143 Meiji period Japanese *Imari* plate from the *Seiji Kaisha* factory in Arita (1879–1897). Diameter 30 cm, height 4 cm with the impressed *Seiji Kaisha* mark. Ref.: Nielson (2).

144 日本江户时期柿右卫门小瓷碟。直径 12.5 厘米，高 2 厘米。

144 Edo period *Kakiemon* small dish or saucer. Diameter 12.5 cm, height 2 cm.

145 日本深川瓷器厂生产的柿右卫门瓷花瓶（约 1920 年）。直径 12 厘米，高 15.5 厘米，盖有深川印章。参考：Nielson (2)。

145 *Kakiemon* vase by the *Fukagawa* porcelain factory (c. 1920). Diameter 12 cm, height 15.5 cm with *Fukagawa sei* mark. Ref.: Nielson (2).

146 日本自石川县九谷瓷糖罐。直径 11 厘米，高 13.5 厘米。

146 Japanese *Kutani* porcelain sugar box from the Ishikawa prefecture. Diameter 11 cm, height 13.5 cm.

147 日本明治时期萨摩小瓷盘。直径 13.5 厘米，高 2.5 厘米。

147 Japanese Meiji period small *Satsuma* plate. *Satsuma* ware is made of yellowish earthenware and has a crackled glaze. Diameter 13.5 cm, height 2.5 cm.

148 日本明治时期萨摩带盖瓷壶。直径 9 厘米，高 11 厘米。

148 Japanese Meiji period *Satsuma* covered jug. Diameter 9 cm, height 11 cm.

越南陶瓷
Vietnamese Ceramics

149 15世纪"会安号"沉船釉上彩巧克力底瓷碗。 该瓷碗是2000年旧金山和洛杉矶举行的巴特菲尔德会安珍品拍卖会1326件拍品中的第12号拍品。直径14.5厘米，高9厘米。参考：Butterfields 2000，第153页。

149 *Hoi An* shipwreck bowl with overglaze enamels and chocolate base (15th century). The bowl is number 12 of the 1326 lot of the 2000 *Butterfields* auction of the *Hoi An* hoard in San Francisco and Los Angeles. Diameter 14.5 cm, height 9 cm. Ref.: Butterfields 2000, p.153.

150 15世纪"会安号"沉船青花碗。 两只，左碗釉面已完全被海水侵蚀，直径8厘米，高5厘米，贴有拍卖标签；右碗直径8.5厘米，高5.5厘米，贴有越南政府部门条码。参考资料：Butterfields 2000；Stevenson, Wood 2011，第250页，插图201。

150 Two blue and white *Hoi An* shipwreck bowls (15th century). Bowl on the left with completely eroded glaze, diameter 8 cm, height 5cm with sticker from the auction; right bowl diameter 8.5 cm, height 5.5 cm with a barcode sticker from the Vietnamese authorities. Ref.: Butterfields 2000 and Stevenson, Wood 2011, p.250, plate 201.

151 16世纪巧克力底青花瓷盘。 瓷盘饰以花卉图案，有明显修复痕迹，直径 23.5 厘米，高 5.5 厘米。参考：Stevenson 1997，第 331 页，插图 281。

151 Blue and white plate with chocolate base and flower motive (16th century), and with major restorations. Diameter 23.5 cm, height 5.5 cm. Ref.: Stevenson 1997, p.331, plate 281.

152 16世纪釉下彩带盖瓷盒。 瓷盒施以釉下蓝、红、绿三色彩，来自 16 世纪的一艘沉船。直径 6.5 厘米，高 4.5 厘米。参考：Stevenson 1997，第 362 页，插图 339。

152 Underglaze blue, overglaze red and green covered box from a shipwreck (16th century). Diameter 6.5 cm, height 4.5 cm. Ref.: Stevenson 1997, p.362, plate 339.

泰国陶瓷
Thai Ceramics

153 西萨查纳莱釉下黑彩陶瓷碗（15 世纪至 16 世纪中期）。直径 19 厘米，高 8 厘米。参考：Brown 2000，插图 XXXa；Brown 2009，插图 71.5。

153 Si Satchanalai (also called *Sawankhalok ware*) underglaze black bowl (15th to mid-16th centuries). Diameter 19 cm, height 8 cm. Ref.: Brown 2000, plate XXXa and Brown 2009, plate 71.5.

154 西萨查纳莱釉下黑彩双鱼陶瓷碗（15 世纪至 16 世纪中期）。直径 17 厘米，高 6.5 厘米。参考：Goepper 1977，插图 155。

154 Si Satchanalai (*Sawankhalok*) underglaze black bowl with fish motives (15th to mid-16th centuries). Diameter 17 cm, height 6.5 cm. Ref.: Goepper 1977, plate 155.

155　西萨查纳莱釉下黑彩带盖罐（15世纪至16世纪中期）。出口至印度尼西亚的泰国外销瓷。直径13厘米，高11厘米。参考：Übersee-Museum 1977，插图37；中国嘉德国际拍卖有限公司，2006，插图1946。

155　Si Satchanalai (*Sawankhalok*) underglaze black covered box (15th to mid-16th centuries). Thai export ware to Indonesia. Diameter 13 cm, height 11 cm. Ref.: Übersee-Museum 1977, plate 37 and China Guardian Seasons Auction 2006, plate 1946.

156　西萨查纳莱青绿瓷罐（14世纪至16世纪中期）。瓷罐有破损，可能在烧制过程中产生。直径7厘米，高7.5厘米。参考：Übersee-Museum 1977，插图67。

156　Si Satchanalai (*Sawankhalok*) bluish-green celadon jar (14th to mid-16th centuries). Damaged, possibly during the firing in the kiln. Diameter 7 cm, height 7.5 cm. Ref.: Übersee-Museum 1977, plate 67.

157 左：西萨查纳莱青瓷碗（14世纪至16世纪中期）。右：西萨查纳莱青瓷碗（约1460年）。瓷碗来自"皇家南海号"沉船，釉面已被海水腐蚀。左碗直径10.5厘米，高5厘米；右碗直径8.5厘米，高4.5厘米。参考：中国嘉德国际拍卖有限公司，2006，插图1930。

157 Left: Si Satchanalai (*Sawankhalok*) celadon bowl (14th to mid-16th centuries). Right: Si Satchanalai (*Sawankhalok*) celadon bowl with eroded glaze (1460) from the *Royal Nanhai* shipwreck. Diameter of the left bowl 10.5 cm, height 5 cm; diameter of the right bowl 8.5 cm, height 4.5 cm. Ref.: China Guardian Seasons Auction 2006, plate 1930.

158 素可泰釉下黑彩鱼纹盘残片（15世纪）。该瓷盘残片发现于西萨查纳莱的永河，直径18厘米。参考：Shaw 1987，第42页。

158 Sukhothai fragment of an underglaze black plate with fish motive (15th century). Found in the Yom River in Si Satchanalai. Diameter 18 cm. Ref.: Shaw 1987, p.42.

159 西萨查纳莱绿色青瓷钵（14 世纪到 16 世纪中期）。瓷钵内壁未上釉，直径 17 厘米，高 12 厘米。参考：Brown 2000，插图 XXXIIb。

159 Si Satchanalai (*Sawankhalok*) green celadon mortar bowl with unglazed interior (14th to mid-16th centuries). Diameter 17 cm, height 12 cm. Ref.: Brown 2000, plate XXXIIb.

160 西萨查纳莱沉船青瓷盘（14 世纪到 16 世纪中期）。瓷盘盘心有雕刻装饰，附有沉积物，直径 24.5 厘米，高 7 厘米。

160 Si Satchanalai (*Sawankhalok*) shipwreck celadon plate with incised decoration and encrustations (14th to mid-16th centuries). Diameter 24.5 cm, height 7 cm.

161 西萨查纳莱青瓷小罐（**14 世纪至 16 世纪中期**）。5 只，直径约 6 厘米，高约 6 厘米。参考：Brown 2009，第 75 页，插图 55。

161 Five Si Satchanalai (*Sawankhalok*) celadon jarlets (14th to mid-16th centuries). Diameter approx imately 6cm, height approx imately 6 cm. Ref.: Brown 2009, p.75, plate 55.

162 西萨查纳莱青瓷瓶（**14 世纪至 16 世纪中期**）。5 只，均有轻微破损或釉面腐蚀，直径约 7 厘米，高约 13 厘米。参考：Shaw 1987，第 59 页；中国嘉德国际拍卖有限公司，2006，插图 1944。

162 Five Si Satchanalai (*Sawankhalok*) celadon bottles (14th to mid-16th centuries). Diameter approx imately 7 cm, height approx imately 13 cm, with minor damages or eroded glaze. Ref.: Shaw 1987, p.59 and China Guardian Seasons Auction 2006, plate 1944.

163 棕釉双耳坛（14 世纪至 16 世纪中期）。直径 8 厘米，高 8 厘米。

163 Brown glazed jarlet with loop handles (14th to mid-16th centuries). Diameter 8 cm, height 8 cm.

164 缅甸釉下绿彩瓷碗（15 世纪）。直径 13.5 厘米，高 8.5 厘米。在仰光西南端迪地区的窑址发现了带有白色或不透明釉下绿色装饰的缅甸陶瓷。从其图案以及使用锡和铅釉来看，它可能受到伊斯兰陶瓷的影响。参考：Brown 2000，插图 XLVIII a。

164 Burmese underglaze green bowl (15th century). Diameter 13.5 cm, height 8.5 cm. Burmese ceramics with green decoration under white or opaque glaze have been found in kiln sites in the Twante district southwest of Yangon. Applying tin and lead glaze and the design patterns could have been influenced by Islamic ceramics. Ref.: Brown 2000, plate XLVIII a.

Chapter 7 European Ceramics
第七章 欧洲陶瓷

欧洲"青花瓷"
European "Blue and White"

165 德国韦斯特瓦尔德带锡盖单柄啤酒杯（1770—1850年）。直径 10 厘米，不含盖高 20 厘米。

165 German stoneware tankard with tin cover from the Westerwald (1770−1850). Diameter 10 cm, height 20 cm (without cover).

166 荷兰代尔夫特白锡釉陶折沿盘（1660—1680 年）。瓷盘为仿制中国明朝晚期克拉克盘。直径 38 厘米，有修复痕迹。参考：Schaap 2003，第 30-31 页；Frégnac 1976，第 169 页。

166 Large Dutch faience charger from Delft (1660–1680). Imitation of Chinese late Ming dynasty *Kraak* plate. Diameter 38 cm with restorations. Ref.: Schaap 2003, pp.30–31 and Frégnac 1976, p.169.

167 德国法兰克福白锡釉陶瓷盘（约 1680 年）。瓷盘折沿饰以八开光图案，围绕盘心纹饰，直径 29.5 厘米，高 5 厘米，有修复痕迹。参考：Heilbronn 1992，第 48-49 页。

167 German faience platter ("Buckelplatte") from Frankfurt with eight humps around a Chinese center scene (c. 1680). Diameter 29.5 cm, height 5 cm, with restorations. Ref.: Heilbronn 1992, pp.48–49.

168 荷兰带盖白锡釉陶瓶（1760—1770 年）。 陶瓶饰以两位中国侍女游园图案，可能属于五件式瓷罐橱柜饰品。高 33 厘米，宽 14 厘米，有修复痕迹和釉裂。参考：Aronson 2011，第 65 页；Schaap 2003，第 48-49 页。

168 Dutch faience covered baluster vase with two Chinese women in a garden (1760–1770). Probably formerly part of a five-vase garniture. Height 33 cm, width 14 cm, with restorations and chips. Ref.: Aronson 2011, p.65 and Schaap 2003, pp.48–49.

169 荷兰代尔夫特白锡釉陶盘（18 世纪）。 直径 16 厘米，边缘破损。

169 Dutch faience plate from Delft (18th century). Diameter 16 cm, with rim damages.

170　荷兰白锡釉陶折沿盘（约1800年）。 陶瓷盘饰以花园图案，直径32厘米，边缘破损。参考：Van Dam 2004，第197页；Frégnac 1976，第303页，插图467。

170　Dutch faience charger with garden scene (c. 1800). Diameter 32 cm, with rim damages. Ref.: Van Dam 2004, p.197 and Frégnac 1976, p.303, plate 467.

171　荷兰代尔夫特白锡釉陶孔雀盘（约1750年）。 德布洛波特白锡釉陶工厂生产。直径22.5厘米。参考：Van Dam 2004，第196页，插图148；Schaap 2003，第72-73页。

171　Dutch faience "Peacock" plate from Delft, *De Blompot* faience factory (c. 1750). Diameter 22.5 cm. Ref.: Van Dam 2004, p.196, plate 148 and Schaap 2003, pp.72-73.

172　英国伦敦白锡釉陶青花盘（约1750年）。 直径26厘米，高3厘米。

172　English blue and white faience plate from London (c. 1750). Diameter 26 cm, height 3 cm.

173　德国拜罗伊特白锡釉陶带盖单柄啤酒杯（1728—1739年）。 装饰图案为仿照中国青花风格绘制的欧洲风景画。直径 11.5 厘米，高 15 厘米（不含锡盖）。参考：Freunde des Historischen Museums Bayreuth 2006，第 86 页，插图 94。

173　German faience tankard with tin cover from Bayreuth (1728–1739). The decoration shows a European landscape painted in Chinese style-imitating blue and white porcelain. Diameter 11.5 cm, height 15 cm (without tin cover). Ref.: Freunde des Historischen Museums Bayreuth 2006, p.86, plate 94.

174　法国圣阿芒白锡釉陶花鸟盘。 直径 22 厘米，高 3 厘米。

174　French faience plate with the "rock and bird" pattern from St. Amand. Diameter 22 cm, height 3 cm.

175　法国鲁昂白锡釉陶盘（18 世纪）。 盘上饰以蓝色花篮，棕色盘底。长 32 厘米，宽 24.5 厘米，高 3 厘米。

175　French faience platter from Rouen "Forge les eaux & cul noir", with blue flower basket and a brown back decoration (18th century). Length 32 cm, width 24.5 cm, height 3 cm.

176　法国纳维尔康熙风格白锡釉陶青花盘（18世纪）。 直径33厘米，高5厘米，有修复痕迹。

176　French blue and white faience platter from Nevers in the *Kangxi* style (18th century). Diameter 33 cm, height 5 cm with restorations.

177　荷兰代尔夫特白锡釉陶盘（18世纪下半叶）。 盘上饰以中国风荷兰海边景色，直径22.5厘米，高2.5厘米，边缘有缺口，且有一道长12厘米的釉裂。

177　Dutch faience plate from Delft with a Dutch seaside landscape in Chinese style (second half of 18th century). Diameter 22.5 cm, height 2.5 cm, with chips to the rim and a 12 cm hairline crack.

178　英国伍斯特陶瓷厂软瓷茶碗和茶碟（1755—1770年）。 茶碗和茶碟饰以釉下蓝彩手绘"修长侍女"图。碟直径11厘米；杯直径6.5厘米，高4厘米。碗碟边缘各有一个缺口，带有伍斯特陶瓷厂的新月标记。

178　English soft-paste porcelain teabowl and saucer with underglaze blue hand painted "Long Eliza" decoration from Worcester, *Worcester Porcelains* (1755–1770). Diameter of the saucer 11 cm; diameter of the cup 6.5 cm, height 4 cm. The saucer and the bowl have each one chip at the rim, with the *Worcester* crescent mark.

179　英国伍斯陶瓷厂特软瓷杯碟（1765—1785年）。 杯碟饰以采用转印技术纹绘的篱笆样式图案。碟直径12厘米；杯直径8厘米，高4厘米。杯碟均带有伍斯特陶瓷厂的新月标记。参考：Godden 2004，第156、400页。

179 English soft-paste porcelain cup and saucer with transfer printed "Fence" pattern from *Worcester* (1765–1785). Diameter of the saucer 12 cm; diameter of the cup 8 cm, height of the cup 4 cm, with the *Worcester* crescent mark. Ref.: Godden 2004, pp.156, 400.

180　英国伍斯特陶瓷厂软瓷茶叶罐（1770—1775年）。 瓷罐饰以"渔夫"图案。直径8厘米，高11厘米，盖子缺失。参考：Godden 2004，第407页。

180 English soft-paste porcelain tea caddy with the "Fisherman" pattern from *Worcester* (1770–1775). Diameter 8 cm, height 11 cm; lid is missing. Ref.: Godden 2004, p.407.

181　德国迈森陶瓷厂中国风釉下蓝彩杯碟（约1850年）。 碟直径15.5厘米；杯直径9厘米，高6厘米。

181 German porcelain underglaze blue cup and saucer with chinoiserie from Saxony, *Meissen* manufacture (c. 1850). Diameter saucer 15.5 cm; diameter cup 9 cm, height 6 cm.

257

182   德国迈森陶瓷厂蓝色洋葱瓷具套装（约 1880 年）。盘子直径 21 厘米；碟直径 13.5 厘米；杯直径 8.5 厘米，高 6 厘米。参考：Sterba 1989，第 151 页，插图 55。

182   German "Blue Onion" decor ("Zwiebelmuster") porcelain service from the *Meissen* manufacture (c. 1880). Diameter of the plate 21 cm; diameter of the saucer 13.5 cm; diameter of the cup 8.5 cm, height of the cup 6 cm. Ref.: Sterba 1989, p.151, plate 55.

183   德国迈森陶瓷厂花鸟瓷器套具（20 世纪）。18 世纪纹饰风格的现代版。参考：Sterba 1989，第 154 页，插图 58。

183   German porcelain service with the underglaze "rock and bird" decoration from Saxony, *Meissen* manufacture (20th century). Modern production of an 18th century decor. Ref.: Sterba 1989, p.154, plate 58.

184 奥地利维也纳瓷杯、碟和牛奶罐（1770—1780 年）。 瓷器饰以釉下蓝 "岩石和鸟" 纹饰，施以釉上彩和描金。碟直径 14 厘米；杯直径 7.5 厘米，高 4.5 厘米；罐高 14 厘米。参考：Museum 1983，226 页，插图 406。

184 Austrian porcelain cup, saucer and milk jug from Vienna with underglaze blue "rock and bird" decoration and overglaze colors and gilding (1770−1780). Diameter of the saucer 14 cm; diameter of the cup 7.5 cm, height 4.5 cm; height of the jug 14 cm. Ref.: Museum 1983, p.226, plate 406.

185 德国咖啡瓷壶（1783—1800 年）。 瓷壶饰以釉下蓝 "蜡菊" 纹饰。由图林根州劳恩斯坦的格赖纳家庭陶瓷厂制造。直径（不含把手）14 厘米，高 28 厘米，带釉下 "R" 标记。参考：Röntgen 2007，第 227 页。

185 German porcelain coffee pot with the underglaze blue "Strohblume" pattern from Rauenstein in Thuringia, *Familie Greiner und Friedrich Christian Greiner & Söhne* manufacture (1783−1800). Diameter (without handle) 14 cm, height 28 cm, with underglaze "R" mark. Ref.: Röntgen 2007, p.227.

186 德国巴达维亚风格瓷杯和瓷碟。马尔科利尼担任迈森陶瓷厂技术主管时期（1774—1814 年）烧制。碟直径 14 厘米；杯直径 8 厘米，高 4.5 厘米。

186 German *Batavia* ware style porcelain cup and saucer from the *Meissen* manufacture in Saxony, Marcolini period (1774–1814). Diameter of the saucer 14 cm; diameter of the cup 8 cm, height 4.5 cm.

187 德国瓷杯、碟子和奶油罐（1794—1887 年）。瓷器饰以釉下蓝"蜡菊"图案，由巴伐利亚州泰陶的 JGFS 陶瓷厂制造。碟直径 13.5 厘米；杯直径 7 厘米，高 7 厘米；罐高 13 厘米。

187 German porcelain cup, saucer and cream jug with the underglaze blue "Strohblume" pattern from Tettau, Bavaria, *J. Schmidt, G. Chr. F. Greiner, Ferdinand Klaus, Sonntag und Söhne* (1794–1887). Diameter of the saucer 13.5 cm; diameter of the cup 7 cm; height 7 cm; height of the jug 13 cm.

188 法国尚蒂利"小蓝枝"软瓷锡釉茶壶（约 1760—1800 年）。茶壶饰有橡果状盖钮。直径 10 厘米，高 18 厘米。

188 French soft-paste porcelain with "Brindille" pattern on a tin glaze from the *Chantilly* factory and an acorn shaped lid knob (c. 1760–1800). Diameter 10 cm, height 18 cm.

189 左：英国斯塔福德郡蓝色转印"柳树纹"珍珠色白陶盘（1815—1825 年），无标记；右：清嘉庆中国南京式样青花"柳树纹"瓷盘（约 1800 年）。 左盘直径 26.5 厘米，高 3 厘米；右盘直径 24.5 厘米，高 2 厘米。参考：Copeland 1980 年，第 37 页，插图 7 和第 42 页，插图 18；Godden 1979，第 132 页，插图 32。

189 Left: English pearlware plate with blue transfer print from Staffordshire with the blue "Willow" pattern, without mark (1815–1825); Right: Jiaqing period Chinese *Nanking* blue and white porcelain plate with the "Willow" design (c. 1800). Diameter of the left plate 26.5 cm, height 3 cm; diameter of the right plate 24.5 cm, height 2 cm. Ref.: Copeland 1980, p.37, plate 7 and p.42, plate 18; Godden 1979, p.132, plate 32.

190 左：英国蓝色转印"中国风景"珍珠色白陶分隔盘（约1820年）；右：英国蓝色转印"柳树纹"珍珠色白陶晚餐分菜盘（四分之一），带盖，可能为斯波德陶瓷厂产品（约1800年）。分隔盘直径15厘米，高3.5厘米；分菜盘长28厘米，高10厘米。盘底有裂缝和飞皮。参考：Copeland 1980，第36页，插图6。

190 Left: English pearlware divided dish with a blue Chinese landscape transfer print (c. 1820); Right: English pearlware lidded supper quadrant section with blue "Willow" pattern transfer print, probably *Spode Company* (c. 1800). Diameter of the dish 15 cm, height 3.5 cm; length of the supper quadrant 28 cm, height 10 cm; with a crack and chip on the base. Ref.: Copeland 1980, p.36, plate 6.

191 英国什罗普郡蓝色转印"双寺"描金瓷杯和瓷碟（1775—1790年）。考利陶瓷厂生产。碟直径14厘米；杯直径6厘米，高6厘米。参考：Godden 1979，第442页。

191 English porcelain cup and saucer with the underglaze blue "Two Temple" transfer print pattern and overglaze gilding from *Caughley Works* in Shropshire (1775–1790). Diameter of the saucer 14 cm; diameter of the cup 6 cm, height 6 cm. Ref.: Godden 1979, p.442.

192　英国什罗普郡蓝色转印青花软瓷碟（约 1785 年）。考利陶瓷厂生产。直径 16 厘米，高 4 厘米。参考：Copeland 2010，第 8 页。

192　English blue and white soft-paste porcelain blue transfer print saucer from *Caughley Works* in Shropshire (c. 1785). Diameter 16 cm, height 4 cm. Ref.: Copeland 2010, p.8.

193　英国斯塔福德郡"双寺"青花瓷器套具（1800—1816 年）。马森陶瓷厂生产。瓷器底部有伪中国款。直径分别为 20 厘米，16.5 厘米，14.5 厘米，9 厘米；高分别为 1.5 厘米，3.5 厘米，3.5 厘米，5.5 厘米。参考：Haggar 1977，插图 20 和插图 48；Godden 1979，第 531 页，插图 663。

193　English blue and white soft-paste porcelain service in the "Two Temple" decoration from the *Miles Mason* factory in Staffordshire (1800–1816), with a pseudo Chinese printed mark. Diameter 20 cm, 16.5 cm, 14.5 cm, 9 cm; height 1.5 cm, 3.5 cm, 3.5 cm, 5.5 cm. Ref.: Haggar 1977, plate 20 & 48 and Godden 1979, p.531, plate 663.

194 英国斯塔福德郡蓝色转印珍珠色白陶大盘（1815—1830 年）。特纳陶瓷厂生产。长 40.5 厘米，宽 31 厘米；陶盘纹饰灵感来自中国风景画图案。

194 English big pearlware blue transfer print platter from the *Turner* factory in Staffordshire (1815−1830). Length 40.5 cm, width 31 cm; inspired by a Chinese landscape decoration.

195 英国斯塔福德郡蓝色转印"修长侍女和嬉戏男童"珍珠色白陶汤盘（1815—1825 年）。斯波德陶瓷厂生产。直径 24 厘米，高 3.5 厘米。参考：Copeland 1980，第 143 页，插图 23。

195 English pearlware soup plate with the *Kangxi* style blue transfer print "Long Eliza and dancing boy" decoration, *Spode Company* in Staffordshire (1815−1825). Diameter 24 cm, height 3.5 cm. Ref.: Copeland 1980, p.143, plate 23.

196 英国斯塔福德郡蓝色转印"蚂蚱纹"珍珠色白陶盘（约 1815 年）。斯波德陶瓷厂生产。直径 24.5 厘米，高 2 厘米，带斯波德陶瓷厂标记。参考：Copeland 1980，第 143 页，插图 21。

196 English pearlware "Grasshopper" plate from the *Spode Company* in Staffordshire (c. 1815). Diameter 24.5 cm, height 2 cm, with the blue printed underglaze Spode factory mark. Ref.: Copeland 1980, p.143, plate 21.

197　德国梅特拉赫珍珠色白陶套具。唯宝陶瓷厂生产。饰以"India"和"Fasan"转印图案（约1860年）。咖啡壶直径13厘米，高20厘米；汤盘直径23厘米，高3.5厘米。

197　German pearlware service with the "India" and "Fasan" transfer print pattern from the *Villeroy & Boch* factory in Mettlach, (c. 1860). Diameter of the coffee pot 13 cm, height 20 cm; diameter of the soup plate 23 cm, height 3.5 cm.

198　荷兰代尔夫特现代青花陶盘。德·波切琳·弗莱斯陶瓷厂生产。该厂创立于1653年，19世纪已从生产白锡釉陶转向了生产英式白陶。直径25厘米，高3厘米。

198　Dutch modern underglaze blue white earthenware plate from *De Porceleyne Fles* in Delft. *De Porceleyne Fles*—established in 1653—turned already in the 19th century away from the faience production to the production of white earthenware in the English style. Diameter 25 cm, height 3 cm.

欧洲 "伊万里"
European *"Imari"*

199 荷兰代尔夫特伊万里风格白锡釉陶盘（约 **1750** 年）。直径 23.5 厘米，高 3 厘米。

199 Dutch faience plate in *Imari* style from Delft (c. 1750). Diameter 23.5 cm, height 3 cm.

200 左：清乾隆中国伊万里瓷盘，采用柿右卫门卷轴画设计（约 **1740** 年）；右：中国伊万里风格的英国珍珠色白陶盘，饰以所谓的柿右卫门"印度纸卷"样式设计（约 **1850** 年）。左盘直径 22 厘米，高 3 厘米；右盘直径 23 厘米，高 3 厘米。参考：Pietsch 1996，第 98 页。

200 Left: Qianlong period Chinese *Imari* plate with a scroll *Kakiemon* design (c. 1740); Right: English pearlware plate in Chinese *Imari* style with the so-called "Indian scroll" *Kakiemon* design (c. 1850). Diameter of the left plate 22 cm, height 3 cm; diameter of the right plate 23 cm, height 3 cm. Ref.: Pietsch 1996, p.98.

201　德国图林根州劳恩斯坦的伊万里风格"花鸟"茶壶（约 1900 年）。直径（不含手柄和壶嘴）10 厘米，高 12 厘米。参考：Trux, 2005, 第 87 页, 插图 75。

201 German fluted porcelain teapot with flower and bird decoration in the *Imari* style from **Thuringia, Rauenstein (c. 1900).** Diameter (without handle and spout) 10 cm, height 12 cm. Ref.: Trux, 2005, p.87, plate 75.

202　德国伊万里风格"蓝色洋葱"瓷盘（约 1850 年）。迈森陶瓷厂生产。直径 21 厘米。

202 German porcelain plate with the "Blue Onion" pattern in *Imari* style from the *Meissen* **manufacture (c. 1850).** Diameter 21 cm.

203　英国利物浦郡伊万里风格软瓷茶碟，饰以寺庙图案，釉下蓝彩、釉上红彩和金彩（约 1770 年）。直径 12.5 厘米，高 3 厘米。

203 English soft-porcelain *Imari* style saucer from Liverpool with temple design, underglaze blue, and overglaze red and gold (c. 1770). Diameter 12.5 cm, height 3 cm.

267

204 英国斯塔福德郡伊万里风格"日本篱笆"样式贝壳软瓷盘（约 1815—1820 年）。马森陶瓷厂生产。长 25 厘米，高 4 厘米。参考：Haggar 1977（插图 114）；Christie's 2003，第 17 页，插图 56。

204 English soft-porcelain *Imari* shell dish "Japan Fence" pattern from the *Miles Mason* factory in Staffordshire (c. 1815–1820). Length 25 cm, height 4 cm. Ref.: Haggar 1977, plate 114 and Christie's 2003, p.17, plate 56.

205 英国马森陶瓷厂伊万里风格"日本"样式软瓷瓷盘（约 1820 年）。瓷盘印有专利标志"中式硬陶，马森专利"。直径 23.5 厘米，高 2 厘米。参考：Christie's 2003，第 39 页，插图 129。

205 English soft-porcelain *Imari* plate with the "Japan" pattern from the *Miles Mason* factory in Staffordshire (c. 1820), with the "MASON'S PATENT IRONSTONE CHINA" pressmark. Diameter 23.5 cm, height 2 cm. Ref.: Christie's 2003, p.39, plate 129.

206 英国马森陶瓷厂伊万里风格"九头蛇"样式壶（约1825年）。瓷壶印有专利标志"中式硬陶，马森专利"。直径13厘米，高16厘米。参考：Christie's 2003，第29页，插图90和第42页，插图135。

206 English soft-porcelain *Imari* "Hydra" jug from the *Miles Mason* factory in Staffordshire (c. 1825), with the "MASON'S PATENT IRONSTONE CHINA" pressmark. Diameter 13 cm, height 16 cm. Ref.: Christie's 2003, p.29, plate 90 and p.42, plate 135.

207 英国马森陶瓷厂伊万里风格软瓷盘（1813—1829年）。直径24厘米，高5厘米，有修复痕迹。

207 English soft-porcelain *Imari* dish from *G.M. and C.J. Mason* in Staffordshire (1813–1829). Diameter 24 cm, height 5 cm with restorations.

208 左：英国斯塔福德郡科普兰陶瓷厂生产的伊万里风格软瓷盘（约1851—1885年）；右：英国德比陶瓷厂生产的伊万里风格珍珠色白陶盘，饰以蓝色转印纹饰，釉上红彩以及描金（1800—1825年）。左盘直径22厘米，高2厘米；右盘直径20厘米，高3厘米。

208 Left: English soft-porcelain *Imari* plate from the *Copeland* factory in Staffordshire (c. 1851–1885); Right: English pearlware plate with *Imari* style decoration with underglaze blue print, overglaze red and gilding from *Derby Porcelain Works* (1800–1825). Diameter of the left plate 22 cm, height 2 cm; diameter of the right plate 20 cm, height 3 cm.

欧洲"粉彩"和"五彩"
European "*Famille rose*" and "*Famille verte*"

209 德国图林根州劳恩斯坦手绘粉彩小咖啡壶（1783—1800年）。格赖纳家庭陶瓷厂生产。含盖高度16厘米。

209 German porcelain small coffee pot with hand-painted *Famille rose* decoration from Rauenstein, Thuringia, *Greiner Family* (1783–1800). Height 16 cm (with cover).

210 荷兰代尔夫特白锡釉陶盘（约1750年）。直径22.5厘米，高2.5厘米。

210 Dutch polychrome faience from Delft (c. 1750). Diameter 22.5 cm, height 2.5 cm.

211 英国斯塔福德郡彩釉陶杯碟（1805—1815年）。斯波德陶瓷厂生产。采用转印技术绘制釉下粉彩式样纹饰，口沿饰有釉上彩纹饰。直径分别为7.5厘米，14.5厘米；高分别为7厘米，3厘米。

211 English glazed earthenware cup and saucer with a Chinese *Famille rose* transfer print and enamel decoration from Staffordshire, *Spode Company* (1805–1815). Diameter 7.5 cm, 14.5 cm; height 7 cm, 3 cm.

212 英国伍斯特郡釉上彩粉彩瓷盘（1811—1840年）。张伯伦陶瓷厂生产。直径23厘米。

212 English porcelain plate with overglaze enamel *Famille rose* decoration from Worcester, *Chamberlain & Co.* (1811–1840). Diameter 23 cm.

213 德国"茶几"样式咖啡瓷壶和杯碟。 马尔科利尼担任迈森陶瓷厂技术主管时期（1774—1814 年）生产。"茶几"样式包括釉下蓝彩和釉上彩。咖啡壶装饰未完成，未施釉上彩。咖啡壶含盖高度 25 厘米，有一条长冲；碟直径 13.5 厘米；杯子直径 8 厘米，高度 4.5 厘米。参考：Sterba 1989, 第 90、91、127、128 页。

213 German porcelain coffee pot, cup and saucer with the "Tischchen" decoration from Saxony, *Meissen* manufacture, Marcolini period (1774–1814). The so-called *Meissen* "Tischchen" decoration consists of a combination of underglaze blue and overglaze colors. The coffee pot decoration is unfinished with missing overglaze colors. Height of the coffee pot with cover 25 cm, with a long hairline crack; diameter of the saucer 13.5 cm; diameter of the cup 8 cm; height 4.5 cm. Ref.: Sterba 1989, pp.90, 91, 127, 128.

214 英国斯塔福德郡中式"茶馆"样式瓷杯和瓷碟（1812—1835 年）。 拉斯伯恩陶瓷厂生产。瓷器为釉下转印绘制图案，并施以釉上彩。碟直径 14 厘米，高 3 厘米；杯子直径 9 厘米，高 5 厘米。参考：Davis 1991, 第 139 页。

214 English porcelain cup and saucer with blue chinoiserie "Tea-house" pattern transfer print and overglaze colors from *S. & J. Rathbone* factory in Staffordshire (1812–1835). Diameter of the saucer 14 cm, height 3 cm; diameter of the cup 9 cm, height 5 cm. Ref.: Davis 1991, p.139.

215 英国斯塔福德郡"窗中小童"样式瓷茶壶、瓷杯和瓷碟（1795—1800年）。 新霍尔陶瓷厂生产。该样式为第425号新霍尔样式。新霍尔陶瓷厂于1781年采用了真正的瓷膏"硬瓷"，生产了约20种中国粉彩"满大人"样式，其中有些与中国瓷器十分相像，难以区分（见图82）。茶壶宽度（包括壶柄和壶嘴）24厘米，高18厘米；茶碟直径13厘米，茶杯直径6.5厘米；茶杯高度7厘米。参考：Davis 1991，第80页。

215 English porcelain teapot, cup and saucer with the "Boy in the window" decor from *New Hall* in Staffordshire (1795–1800). It's called the *New Hall* pattern number 425. *New Hall* has introduced real (hard-paste) porcelain in 1781 and has produced about 20 different Chinese *Mandarin Famille rose* patterns which are sometimes difficult to distinguish from the original (see plate 82). Width (including handle and spout) of the teapot 24 cm, height 18 cm; diameter of the saucer 13 cm; diameter of the cup 6.5 cm, height of the cup 7 cm. Ref.: Davis 1991, p.80.

216 英国斯塔福德郡"小童戏蝶"样式瓷茶壶、瓷杯和瓷碟（1795—1800年）。 新霍尔陶瓷厂生产。该样式为第421号新霍尔样式。直径13厘米，高3厘米。参考：Davis 1991，第79页。

216 English porcelain teapot, cup and saucer with the "Boy with butterfly" decor from *New Hall* in Staffordshire (1795–1800). It's called the *New Hall* pattern number 421. Diameter 13 cm, height 3 cm. Ref.: Davis 1991, p.79.

217 英国斯塔福德郡"小童与斑点狗"样式瓷碟（1811—1833年）。希尔迪奇 & 索恩陶瓷厂生产。直径20厘米，高4厘米。参考：Davis 1991，第130页。

217 English porcelain plate with transfer print chinoiserie decoration "Boy with Spotted Dog" from *Hilditch & Son* in Staffordshire (1811–1833). Diameter 20 cm, height 4 cm. Ref.: Davis 1991, p.130.

218 德国卡尔斯鲁厄·马约利卡陶瓷厂生产的现代白锡釉陶大浅盘（1974年）。此样式瓷盘用以纪念1735年生产的安斯巴赫白锡釉五彩陶。德国安斯巴赫、福尔达的白锡釉陶制造商以及迈森陶瓷厂都从五彩瓷中汲取了灵感。冯·勒文芬克是一位特别擅长五彩纹饰的德国画家。直径35厘米，高5厘米。参考：Frégnac 1976，第147页。

218 German modern faience platter from *Karlsruher Majolica* commemorating the Ansbach *Famille verte* faiences from 1735 (1974). *Famille verte* has inspired the faience manufactures in Ansbach and Fulda, and the porcelain manufacture of *Meissen*—all in Germany. Von Löwenfinck was a German painter specialized in this decor. Diameter 35 cm, height 5 cm. Ref.: Frégnac 1976, p.147.

欧洲"中国白"
European "*Blanc-de-Chine*"

219 左：明晚期福建德化窑中国白瓷杯；右：德国迈森陶瓷厂"中国白"风格瓷杯（1740—1780 年）。左杯高 5 厘米；右杯直径 7 厘米，高 4 厘米。参考：Avitabile 1992，第 194 页，插图 414。

219 Left: Late Ming dynasty *Blanc-de-Chine* cup from the Dehua kiln in Fujian province; Right: German porcelain cup in *Blanc-de-Chine* style from *Meissen* manufacture (1740–1780). Height of the left cup 5 cm; diameter of the right cup 7 cm, height 4 cm. Ref.: Avitabile 1992, p.194, plate 414.

欧洲"柿右卫门"和"萨摩"
European "*Kakiemon*" and "*Satsuma*"

220 德国扇形边瓷盘和瓷壶，饰有日本柿右卫门风格图案。1774—1814 年卡米洛伯爵冯·马尔科利尼担任迈森陶瓷厂技术主管时期生产。直径 24.5 厘米，高 21.5 厘米。参考：Sterba 1989，第 87 页，插图 33。

220 German porcelain plate and jug with Japanese *Kakiemon* decoration and scalloped rim from Saxony, *Meissen*, Marcolini period (1774–1814). Camillo Graf von Marcolini was technical director in *Meissen* from 1774–1814. Diameter 24.5 cm, height 21.5 cm. Ref.: Sterba 1989, p.87, plate 33.

275

221 迈森陶瓷厂"皇家龙"瓷器套具。 1730 年，迈森陶瓷厂的技术主管约翰·约阿希姆·肯德勒受到奥古斯特二世收藏的一只日本瓷盘启发，对日本柿右卫门风格进行模仿，设计出了"皇家龙"装饰图案。参考：Pietsch 2006，第 95 页；Sterba 1989，第 166 页，插图 70。

221 German porcelain service with a red dragon decoration from Saxony, *Meissen*. The so-called "Reicher Drache" decor, imitation of the Japanese *Kakiemon* style, developed by the technical director of the *Meissen* manufacture Johann Joachim Kaendler in 1730, influenced by a Japanese plate of the August the Strong collection. Ref.: Pietsch 2006, p.95 and Sterba 1989, p.166, plate 70.

222 （奥地利）波希米亚州图恩–特普利茨的新艺术花瓶（1899—1905 年）。 萨摩烧风格，施特尔马赫陶瓷厂生产。直径 11 厘米，高 16 厘米。

222 Austrian porcelain Art Nouveau vase from Turn-Teplitz in Bohemia, *Riessner, Stellmacher und Kessel* manufacture (1899–1905) in *Satsuma* style. Diameter 11 cm, height 16 cm.

223 （捷克）波希米亚州图恩 – 特普利茨的白陶新艺术花瓶（1920 年）。安蓬陶瓷厂生产。直径 13 厘米，高 16 厘米。

223 Czech white earthenware Art Nouveau vase from Turn-Teplitz in Bohemia, *Amphora factory* (1920). Diameter 13 cm, height 16 cm.

图片来源 Pictures credits

Maps: By the author

Pic. 1.1: By the author, part of the author's collection

Pic. 1.2: By the author, part of the author's collection

Pic. 1.3: By the author, part of the author's collection

Pic. 1.4: By the author, part of the author's collection

Pic. 1.5: By the author, part of the author's collection

Pic. 1.6: By the author, part of the author's collection

Pic. 2.1: Unknown painter: https://commons.wikimedia.org/wiki/File:Lisboa-Museu_Nacional_de_Arte_Antiga-Retrato_dito_de_Vasco_da_Gama-20140917.jpg

Pic. 2.2: By the author, part of the author's collection

Pic. 2.3: By Dubbelgamer, CC0, https://commons.wikimedia.org/w/index.php?curid=68824044

Pic. 2.4: Wikimedia Commons: https://commons.wikimedia.org/wiki/File:Jan_Pieterszoon_Coen.jpg. With thanks to the Rijksmuseum Amsterdam

Pic. 2.5: From the Eugenius-atlas, or Atlas Blaeu, https://commons.wikimedia.org/w/index.php?curid=25689070

Pic. 2.6: With thanks to the Rijksmuseum Amsterdam, https://www.rijksmuseum.nl/en/collection/SK-A-4821 and Wikimedia Commons: https://commons.wikimedia.org/wiki/File:Floris_van_Dyck_002.jpg?uselang=de

Pic. 2.7: Johan Nieuhof: An embassy from the East-India Company of the United provinces to the Grand Tartar Cham Emperor of China, published in 1665 in Dutch and 1669 in English, part of the author's collection

Pic. 2.8: Portrait of the Kangxi Emperor in Court Dress, Palace Museum Collection, Beijing, China

Pic. 2.9: By the author, part of the author's collection

Pic. 2.10: Antoine François Prévost d'Exiles: *Histoire générale des voyages* with copper engravings by Jacques Nicolas Bellin, 1746-1759

Pic. 2.11: By Amsterdam Museum-http://hdl.handle.net/11259/collection.22584, CC0, https://commons.wikimedia.org/w/index.php?curid=86794199

Pic. 2.12: By the author, part of the author's collection

Pic. 2.13: By the author, part of the author's collection

Pic. 2.14: https://commons.wikimedia.org/wiki/File:Coat_of_arms_of_the_East_India_Company.svg

Pic. 2.15: Antoine François Prévost d'Exiles: *Histoire générale des voyages* with copper engravings by Jacques Nicolas Bellin, 1746-1759, part of the author's collection

Pic. 2.16: By Unknown author-http://www.richardrothstein.com/china-trade-hong-painting-rrmp016.html, Public Domain, https://commons.wikimedia.org/w/index.php?curid=9987830

Pic. 2.17: By J. F. Heland von-Sjöhistoriska museet, Public Domain, https://commons.wikimedia.org/w/index.php?curid=64647638

Pic. 2.18: Peter Tom-Petersen-Uploader was Niels Aage, https://commons.wikimedia.org/w/index.php?curid=7216938

Pic. 2.19: https://commons.wikimedia.org/wiki/File:Anonymous_The_Noord-Nieuwland_in_Table_Bay,_1762.jpg, Iziko William Fehr Collection (Castle of Good Hope)

Pic. 2.20: By the author, part of the author's collection

Pic. 2.21: By the author, part of the author's collection

Pic. 2.22: By the author, part of the author's collection

Pic. 3.1: By the author

Pic. 3.2: https://commons.wikimedia.org/wiki/File:Johann_Baptiste_Bouttats_-_An_Honourable_East_India_Company_flagship_returning_to_home_waters_in_triumph.jpg

Pic. 3.3: By the author, part of the author's collection

Pic. 3.4: Wikimedia Commons: https://commons.wikimedia.org/wiki/File:Louis_de_Silvestre-August_II.jpg

Pic. 3.5: copper engraving by Johann Friedrich Eosander, 1718

Pic. 3.6: Wikimedia Commons: https://commons.wikimedia.org/wiki/File:Van_Aken,_tea_party.jpg

Pic. 3.7: By the author, part of the author's collection

Pic. 4.1: By the author

Pic. 4.2: Brooklyn Museum, Gift of Frank L. Babbott, 35.677. Creative Commons-BY (Photo: Brooklyn Museum, CUR.35.677_interior.jpg) https://www.brooklynmuseum.org/opencollection/objects/44299

Pic. 4.3: Exhibit in the *Cinquantenaire Museum*-Brussels, Belgium, by Daderot, https://commons.wikimedia.org/w/index.php?curid=56315787

Pic. 4.4: Wikimedia Commons: https://commons.wikimedia.org/wiki/File:View_of_Delft,_by_Johannes_Vermeer.jpg. Thanks to Mauritshuis in The Hague

Pic. 4.5: By the author, part of the author's collection

Pic. 4.6: By the author, part of the author's collection

Pic. 4.7: By the author, part of the author's collection

Pic. 4.8: By the author, part of the author's collection

Pic. 4.9: By the author, part of the author's collection

Pic. 4.10: By Meissen Porcelain Factory-https://clevelandart.org/art/1986.10, CC0, https://commons.wikimedia.org/w/index.php?curid=77137034

Plate 1 to plate 223 in Part II: All photos of the collection are copyright of Thorsten Giehler

参考文献 References

Albert Amor Ltd.: *Dr. John Wall, 1708–1776: A Commemorative Loan Exhibition of Dr. Wall Period Worcester Porcelain*, London, 1976.

Aldridge, Eileen: *Porzellan*, Stuttgart und Zürich, 1970.

Andrade, Tonio: *Lost Colony: The untold story of China's first great victory over the West*, Princeton and Oxford, 2011.

Arensberg, Ingrid: *Ostindiefararen Götheborg Seglar Igen: The Swedish Ship Götheborg sails again*, Mölndal, 2009.

Aronson, Robert D.: *In the Eye of the Beholder: Perspectives on Dutch Delftware*, Amsterdam, 2011.

Avitabile, Gunhild and Graf von der Schulenburg, Stephan: *Chinesisches Porzellan*, Frankfurt, 1992.

Bai Ming: *The Traditional Crafts of Porcelain Making in Jingdezhen*（白明：《景德镇传统制瓷工艺》，南昌：江西美术出版社），Nanchang, 2002.

Bai Shouyi: *Chinas Geschichte im Überblick*, Beijing, 2009（白寿彝：《中国通史纲要》德文版）.

Barnes, Ian and Hudson, Robert: *Historical Atlas of Asia*, New York, 1998.

Beijing Cultural Relics Bureau and Editorial Committee of 'Appreciating Beijing Cultural Relics': *Porcelains of the Liao Song and Jin Dynasties*（北京市文物局、《北京文物鉴赏》编委会编：《辽宋金瓷器》，北京：北京美术摄影出版社），Beijing, 2006.

Beurdeley, Michel: *Porzellan aus China: Compagnie des Indes*, München, 1962.

Bi Keguan: *Chinese Folk Painting on Porcelain*, Beijing, 1991.

Bo Zhong: *Chinese Porcelain*（伯仲编：《中国瓷》，合肥：黄山书社）, Hefei, 2011.

Bramsen, Christopher Bo: *Peace and Friendship. Denmark's Official Relations with China 1674-2008*, Hong Kong, 2008.

Brown, Roxanna M.: *The Ceramics of South-East Asia: Their dating and identification*, Chicago, 2000.

Brown, Roxanna M.: *The Ming Gap and Shipwreck Ceramics in Southeast Asia*, Bangkok, 2009.

Burnet, Ian: *East Indies: The 200 year struggle between the Portuguese Crown, the Dutch East India Company and the English East India Company for supremacy in the Eastern Seas*, Sydney, 2013.

Butterfields: *Treasures from the Hoi An Hoard. Important Vietnamese Ceramics from a late 15th/early 16th Century Cargo*, Auction catalogue, San Francisco and Los Angeles, October 11–13, 2000, two volumes.

Calado, Rafael Salinas and Bart, Jan: *Faiança Portuguesa 1600-1660 Portugese Fayence*, Lisbon, Amsterdam, 1989.

Cao Qianli: *Identification of Porcelain from Han and Tang Dynasties*（草千里编：《汉唐瓷器鉴定》，杭州：浙江大学出版社）, Hangzhou, 2004.

Carswell, John: *Iznik Pottery*, London, 1998.

Carswell, John: *Blue & White: Chinese porcelain around the world*, London, 2000.

The Chalre collection: *Ceramic treasures of Southeast Asia*, http://ceramics.chalre.com/index.html.

Chandhavij, Bhujjong: *Blue-and-White Chinaware and Siamese Ceramics*, Bangkok, 2015.

Chaudhuri, Kirti Narayan: *The Trading World of Asia and the English East India Company 1660-1760*, Cambridge, 1978.

Chen Ieng Hin, Roy, Sit Kai Sin: *A Rota Marítima da Porcelana. Relíquias dos Museus de Guangdong, Hong Kong e Macau*, 2012.

Chen Mingliang: *Selections from Ancient Dehua Porcelain Treasured*（陈明良编：《德化窑古瓷珍品鉴赏》，福州：福建美术出版社）, Fuzhou, 2005.

Chicarelli, Charles F.: *Buddhist Art: An illustrated introduction*, Chiang Mai, 2004.

China Guardian Seasons Auctions: *Shipwrecks Treasure of South China Sea*, Auction catalogue, December 16, 2006 Beijing（中国嘉德国际拍卖有限公司：《嘉德四季——中国嘉德四季拍卖会，南海瓷珍，2006.12.16，北京》）.

Christie's: *The Vung Tau Cargo*, Auction catalogue, 7–4 April, 1992, Amsterdam.

Christie's: *The Binh Thuan Shipwreck*, Auction catalogue, 1–2 March, 2004, Melbourne.

Christie's South Kensington: *The property of the late Valerie Howard removed from 4 Camden Street*.

Collani, Claudia von: *Von Jesuiten, Kaisern und Kanonen: Europa und China - eine wechselvolle Geschichte*, Darmstadt, 2012.

Copeland, Robert: *Blue and White Transfer-Printed Pottery*, Oxford, 2010.

Copeland, Robert: *Spode's Willow Pattern and Other Designs after the Chinese*, London, 1980.

Corrigan, Karina, Campen, Jan van, Diercks, Femke, Blyberg, Janet C. (Ed.): *Asia in Amsterdam: The culture of luxury in the Golden Age*. Salem, Amsterdam, 2015.

Cox, Ian: *Royal Crown Derby Imari Wares*, London, 1998.

Crick, Monique: *Chinese Trade Ceramics for South-East Asia: Collection of Ambassador and Mrs Charles Müller*, Milan, 2010.

Cultural Affairs Bureau of the Macao S.A.R. Government (Ed.): *Mundo de Fantasia. Chinoiserie*, Macau, 2013.

Curatola, Giovanni (Ed.): *Persian Ceramics from the 9th to the 14th century*, Milan, 2006.

Van Dam, Jan Daniel: *Delffse Porceleyne: Dutch delftware 1620–1850*, Amsterdam, 2004.

Darwin, John: *After Tamerlane: The Rise and Fall of Global Empires*, London, 2007.

Davis, Howard: *Chinoiserie: Polychrome Decoration on Staffordshire Porcelain 1790–1850*, London, 1991.

De Jonge, C.H.: *Delfter Keramik*, Tübingen, 1969.

The Desaru ship: http://www.mingwrecks.com/desaru.html, accessed on 17.12.2017.

Van Dyke, Paul A.: *The Canton Trade: Life and Enterprise on the China Coast, 1700–1845*, Hong Kong, 2007.

Van Dyke, Paul A. and Mok, Maria Kar-Wing: *Images of the Canton Factories 1760–1822*, Hong Kong, 2015.

Editorial Committee of 'Appreciating Beijing Cultural Relics': *Porcelains of the Yuan dynasty*, Beijing, 2004.

Edwards, Hugh: *Weisses Gold aus blauer Tiefe*, München, 2001.

Farris, Jonathan Andrew: *Enclave to Urbanity: Canton, Foreigners, and Architecture from the Late Eighteenth to the Early Twentieth Centuries*, Hong Kong, 2016.

Fehérvári, Géza: *Pottery of the Islamic World in the Tareq Rajab Museum*, Hawally, 1998.

Feldbauer, Peter: *Die Portugiesen in Asien 1498–1620*, Essen, 2005.

Feng Hejun: *Pottery Figures*（冯贺军编：《你应该知道的 200 件古代陶俑》，北京：紫禁城出版社），Beijing, 2007.

Finlay, Robert: *The Pilgrim Art: The Culture of Porcelain in World History*, in: Journal of World History, Vol. 9, No. 2, 1998.

Frank, Andre Gunder: ReOrient: *Global Economy in the Asian Age*, Berkeley and Los Angeles, 1998.

Frégnac, Claude: *Europäische Fayencen*, Stuttgart, 1976.

Freunde des Historischen Museums Bayreuth e.V.: *Bayreuther Fayencen: Sammlung Burkhardt*, Bayreuth, 2006.

Freundeskreis Kunstgewerbemuseum e.V. Schloss Pillnitz: *Teichert-Werke Meißen. Keramik und Porzellan 1863-1945*, Dresden, 2003.

Fung Ping Shan Museum: *Green Wares from Zhejiang*（冯平山博物馆编：《浙江青瓷》，香港：冯平山博物馆）, Hong Kong, 1993.

Ganse, Shirley: *Chinese Porcelain: An export to the world*, Hong Kong, 2008.

Garnier, Derick: *Ayutthaya: Venice of the East*, Bangkok, 2004.

Gauß, Renate and Witter, Katharina: *Die Porzellanmanufaktur Rauenstein*, Kulturbund der DDR, Sonneberg.

Gawronski, Jerzy (Ed.): *Amsterdam Ceramics. A city's history and an archaeological ceramics catalogue 1175-2011*, Amsterdam, 2012.

Geng Baochang: *The Complete Collection of Treasures of the Palace Museum*（耿宝昌主编：《故宫博物院藏文物珍品全集》，香港：香港商务印书馆）, Hongkong, 2010.

Gerritsen, Anne: *Domesticating Goods from Overseas: Global Material Culture in the Early Modern Netherlands,* in: Journal of Design History, 10 August 2016.

Godden, Geoffrey A.: *Oriental Export Market Porcelain and its Influence on European Wares*, London, 1979.

Godden, Geoffrey A.: *Encyclopedia of British Pottery and Porcelain Marks*, London, 1986.

Godden, Geoffrey A.: *Godden's Guide to English blue and white porcelain*, Woodbridge, 2004.

Goddio, Franck: *Das Geheimnis der San Diego*, Zürich, 1996.

Goddio, Franck: *Weißes Gold*, Göttingen, 1997.

Gøbel, Erik: *Asiatisk Kompagnis Kinafart 1732-1833*, Denmark, 1978.

Goepper, Roger (Ed.): *Legende und Wirklichkeit. Frühe Keramiken aus Südostasien*, Köln, 1977.

Guerin, Nicol and van Oenen, Dick: *Thai ceramic art*, Singapore, 2005.

Gunn, Geoffrey C.: *History Without Borders: The making of an Asian World Region, 1000-1800*, Hong Kong, 2011.

Guratzsch, Herwig (Ed.): *Fayencen aus dem Ostseeraum: Keramische Kostbarkeiten des Rokoko*, München, 2003.

Haggar, Reginald and Adams, Elizabeth: *Mason Porcelain & Ironstone: 1796-1853*, London, 1977.

Harding, Richard, Jarvis, Adrian and Kennerley, Alston: *British Ships in China Seas: 1700 to the present day*, Liverpool, 2004.

Hardy, Alain-René and Giardi, Bruno: *Les craquelés Art Déco. Histoire et collection*, Paris, 2009.

Harrisson, Barbara: *Swatow*, Leeuwarden, 1979.

He Li: *Chinese Ceramics: The new standard guide*, London, 1996.

Heilbronner Kunst-und Auktionshaus Jürgen Fischer: *66. Fischer Auktion, Fayence-und Steinzeugsammlung Heinz Weck*, 28. März, 1992.

Hess, Catherine (Ed.): *The Arts of Fire: Islamic influences on glass and ceramics of the Italian Renaissance*, Los Angeles, 2004.

Hetjens-Museum, Deutsches Keramikmuseum (Ed.), Pantzer, Peter: *Imari-Porzellan am Hofe der Kaiserin Maria Theresia*, Düsseldorf, 2000.

Historischer Verein für Mittelfranken: *Ansbacher Fayence und Porzellan. Katalog der Sammlung Adolf Bayer*, Ansbach, 1963.

Ho, Wing Meng: *Straits Chinese Porcelain: A collector's guide*, Singapore, 2008.

Huang Chunhuai and Zheng Jinqin: *Chinese White*（黄春淮、郑金勤主编:《中国白——德化白瓷鉴赏》，福州：福建美术出版社），Fuzhou, 2005.

Impey, Oliver: *Chinoiserie: The impact of oriental styles on western art and decoration*, London, 1977.

Irvine, Gregory (Ed.): *Der Japonismus und die Geburt der Moderne: Die Khalili-Sammlung*, Leipzig, 2014.

Jahn, Gisela: *Meiji Ceramics: The art of Japanese export porcelain and Satsuma ware 1868-1912*, Stuttgart, 2004.

Jenkins-Madina, Marilyn: *Raqqa Revisited: Ceramics of Ayyubid Syria*, New York, 2006.

Jörg, Christiaan J.A.: *Porcelain and the Dutch China Trade*, The Hague, 1982.

Jörg, Christiaan J.A.: *The Geldermalsen: History and porcelain*, Groningen, 1986.

Jörg, Christiaan J.A.: *Fine & Curious: Japanese Export Porcelain in Dutch Collections*, Amsterdam, 2003.

Jörg, Christiaan J. A.: *Famille Verte: Chinese porcelain in green enamels*, Schoten, 2011.

Kerr, Rose (Ed.): *The World in Colors*, The Oriental Ceramic Society, 2006.

Kerr, Rose and Mengoni, Luisa E.: *Chinese Export Ceramics*, London, 2011.

Ketel, Christine: https://independent.academia.edu/ChristineKetel, *Identification of export porcelains from early 17th century VOC shipwrecks and the linkage to their cultural identification*, accessed on 29.04.2017.

Kimura, Jun (Ed.): *Shipwreck Asia: Thematic studies in East Asian maritime archaeology*, Adelaide, 2010.

Kjellberg, Sven T.: *Svenska Ostindiska Compagnierna, 1731-1813: Kryddor, Te, Porslin, Siden*, Malmö, 1974.

Klein, Adalbert: *Islamische Keramik*, Baden Baden, 1976.

Koh Antique: *Jepara shipwreck*: http://www.koh-antique.com/jepara/jepara%20wreck.htm, accessed 17 April, 2021.

Koninckx, Christian: *The First and Second Charters of the Swedish East India Company (1731-1766)*, Kortrijk, 1980.

Krabath, Stefan: *Luxus in Scherben. Fürstenberger und Meissener Porzellan aus Grabungen*, Dresden, 2011.

Krist, Gabriela and Iby, Elfriede (Eds): *Investigation and Conservation of East Asian Cabinets in Imperial Residences (1700-1900)*, Vienna, 2015.

Lawrence, Louis: *Satsuma. The Romance of Japan*, Tarzana, 2011.

Langer, Axel: *Blauer Lotos-weisser Drache: Blau-weisse Keramik aus Asien und Europa*, Zürich, 2006.

Li, Baoping:, *Batavian' Style Chinese Export Porcelain: Origins, Recent Finds and Historic Significance*, in: Buslig, Szonja, Nguyen Dinh Chien, Li: *The Ca Mau Shipwreck Porcelain 1723-1735*, p.23-30, Budapest, 2012.

Li Guangning: *Collecting and Appraising of Ancient Porcelain Fragments*（李广宁：《古瓷片的收藏及价值评估》全二册，北京：知识出版社），Beijing, 2002.

Lin Han: *Overseas Collections of Chinese Treasures. Export Ware*（林瀚：《海外珍藏中华瑰宝：外销瓷》，北京：北京工艺美术出版社），Beijing, 2011.

Li Jian'an: *Tianmu Kilns in Fujian*, in: Global Tea Hut, *Tianmu Bowls*, pp.26-32, May 2018.

Madsen, Andrew D. and White, Carolyn L.: *Chinese Export Porcelains*, Walnut Creek, 2011.

Miedtank, Lutz: *Zwiebelmuster: Zur 300jährigen Geschichte des Dekors auf Porzellan, Fayence und Steingut*, Leipzig 2001.

Miksic, John, N.: *Southeast Asian Ceramics: New light on old pottery*, Singapore, 2009.

Mostert, Tristan and van Campen, Jan: *Silk Thread: China and the Netherlands from 1600*, Amsterdam, 2015.

Munoz, Paul Michael: *Early Kingdoms. Indonesian Archipelago & the Malay Peninsula*, Singapore, 2006.

Museum für Kunsthandwerk Frankfurt am Main: *Deutsches Porzellan des 18. Jahrhunderts. Geschirr und Ziergerät*, Frankfurt, 1983.

Nagel Auktionen: *Der Schatz der Tek Sing*, 1999.

Nanjing City Museum, Ningbo Museum and China Maritime Museum in Shanghai: *China and the World. Shipwrecks and Export Porcelain on the Maritime Silk Road*（南京市博物馆、宁波博物馆、上海中国航海博物馆编：《China 与世界——海上丝绸之路沉船和贸易瓷器》，北京：文物出版社），Beijing, 2017.

Narantuya, Ts. and Shur, B.: *Masterpieces of Nomadic Mongolia*, Ulaanbaatar, 2010.

Nezu Museum: *Ko-Imari: A Catalogue of Hizen Porcelain from the Nezu Museum's Yamamoto*

Collection, Tokyo, 2017.

Nielson, Jan Eric: Gotheborg.com: http://gotheborg.com/dest/company.shtml, accessed on 29.04.2017.

Nielson, Jan Eric (2): *Japanese porcelain marks*: http://www.gotheborg.com/marks/fukagawa.shtml, accessed on 23 December 2017.

Nierstrasz, Chris: *Rivalry for Trade in Tea and Textiles: the English and Dutch East India Companies (1700–1800)*, Houndsmills, 2015.

Nyström, Johan Fredrik: *De svenska ostindiska kompanierna: historisk-statistisk framställning*, Göteborg, 1883.

Orientations: *Chinese Ceramics. Selected articles from Orientations 1982–2003*, Hong Kong, 2004.

Ostkamp, Sebastiaan: *The Dutch 17th-century porcelain trade from an archaeological perspective*, in: J. van Campen en T. Eliëns (Ed.): *Chinese and Japanese porcelain for the Dutch Golden Age*, pages 53–85, Zwolle, 2014.

Osterhammel, Jürgen: *Die Entzauberung Asiens: Europa und die asiatischen Reiche im 18. Jahrhundert*, München, 2010.

The Palace Museum Shanghai Museum: *Ming-Qing Export Porcelain from the Palace Museum and the Shanghai Museum*（故宫博物院、上海博物馆编：《故宫博物院、上海博物馆明清贸易瓷》，上海：上海书画出版社），Shanghai, 2015.

Palmer, Arlene M.: *A Winterthur Guide to Chinese Export Porcelain*, New York, 1976.

Picard, R., Kerneis, J.-P., Bruneau, Y.: *Les Compagnies des Indes Route de la Porcelaine*, France, 1966.

Pichelkastner, Eleonore: *Bruckmann's Fayence-Lexikon, Majolica, Fayence, Steingut*, München, 1981.

Pietsch, Ulrich: *Meissener Porzellan und seine ostasiatischen Vorbilder*, Leipzig, 1996.

Pietsch, Ulrich, Loesch, Anette and Ströber, Eva: *China, Japan, Meissen: Die Porzellansammlung zu Dresden*, Berlin, 2006.

Pietsch, Ulrich and Bischoff, Cordula: *Japanisches Palais zu Dresden: Die königliche Porzellansammlung Augusts des Starken*, Dresden, 2014.

Pitcher, Philip Wilson: *Fifty Years in Amoy: Or a history of the Amoy mission, China, Founded February 24, 1842*, New York, 1893.

Pluis, Jan: *De Nederlandse Tegel: Decors en benamingen 1570-1930*, Leiden, 2013.

Ptak, Roderich: *Die maritime Seidenstraße*, München, 2007.

Puga, Rogério Miguel: *The British Presence in Macau 1635–1793*, Hong Kong, 2013.

Qianling Museum: *Exotic Flavor of the Foreigners on the Silk Road*（樊英峰编：《丝路胡人外来风》，北京：文物出版社），Beijing, 2008.

Qu, Yongjian: *Dating and Connoisseur of Ceramic Sherds Unearthed from the Beijing city*（曲永建编：《北京出土瓷片断代与鉴赏》，北京：文物出版社），Beijing, 2011.

Reinhard, Wolfgang: *Die Unterwerfung der Welt. Globalgeschichte der europäischen Expansion 1415-2015*, Bonn, 2017.

Robinson, Natalie V.: *Sino-Thai Ceramics*, Bangkok, 1982.

Röntgen, Robert E.: *Deutsche Porzellanmarken von 1710 bis heute*, Regenstauf, 2007.

Rooney, Dawn F.: *Bencharong. Chinese Porcelain for Siam*, Bangkok, 2017.

The Royal Nanhai shipwreck site: http://www.sawankhalok.com/royalnanhai.html, accessed on 01.10.2017.

Savage, George: *Seventeenth and Eighteenth Century French Porcelain*, Feltham, 1969.

Schaap, Ella B.: *Delft Ceramics at the Philadelphia Museum of Art*, Philadelphia, 2003.

Schärer, Jürgen: *Verschiedene außerordendlich feine Mahlerey und vergoldete Geschirre, die jederzeit ihren Liebhaber gefunden*, Meissen, 1996.

Schiffer, Herbert, Schiffer, Peter and Schiffer, Nancy: *Chinese Export Porcelain. Standard patterns and forms, 1780 to 1880*, Exton, 1975.

Schiffer, Nancy: *Japanese Porcelain 1800-1950*, West Chester, Pennsylvania, 1986.

Schmidt, Ulrich (Ed.), Staatliche Kunstsammlung Kassel: *Porzellan aus China und Japan. Die Porzellangalerie der Landgrafen von Hessen-Kassel*, Berlin, 1990.

Schmitt, Eberhard, Schleich, Thomas and Beck, Thomas (Ed.): *Kaufleute als Kolonialherren: Die Handelswelt der Niederländer vom Kap der Guten Hoffnung bis Nagasaki 1600 - 1800*, Bamberg, 1988.

Shanghai History Museum: *White Gold. East and West Porcelain Capital-Jingdezhen-Meissen Porcelain*（上海市历史博物馆编：《白色金子，东西瓷都：从景德镇到迈森瓷器选》，上海：上海书画出版社），Shanghai, 2019.

Shanghai Maritime Museum and Fuzhou City Museum: *Out to the World. Treasures from the Wan Reef I Shipwreck*,（中国航海博物馆、福州市博物馆编：《器成走天下："碗礁一号"沉船出水文物大展图录》，北京：文物出版社），Shanghai, 2019.

Shanghai Museum: *Traces of the Trade. Chinese export porcelain donated by Henk B. Nieuwenhuys*（上海博物馆编：《海帆留踪：荷兰倪汉克捐赠明清贸易瓷》，上海：上海书画出版社），Shanghai, 2009.

Shanghai Museum: *The Baoli Era. Treasures from the Tang Shipwreck Collection*（上海博物馆编：《宝历风物："黑石号"沉船出水珍品》，上海：上海书画出版社），Shanghai, 2020.

Shaw, J.C.: *Introducing Thai ceramics, also Burmese and Khmer*, Bangkok, 1987.

Shono, Masako: *Japanisches Aritaporzellan im sogenannten Kakiemonstil als Vorbild für die Meißener Porzellanmanufaktur*, München, 1973.

Simonis, Ruth Sonja: *Microstructures of global trade. Porcelain acquisitions through private networks for August the Strong*, Staatliche Kunstsammlungen Dresden, arthistoricum.net, Heidelberg, 2020.

Sjostrand, Sten, Taha, Adi Haji and Sahar, Samsol: *Mysteries of Malaysian Shipwrecks*, Department of Museums Malaysia, 2006.

Sjostrand, Sten and Sharipah Lok Lok bt. Syed Idrus: *The Wanli Shipwreck and its Ceramic Cargo*, Malaysia, 2007.

Söndergaard Kristensen, Rikke: *Made in China: import, distribution and consumption of Chinese porcelain in Copenhagen c. 1600–1760* in: Post Medieval Archaeology 48/1, pp 151–181, 2014.

Staatliche Kunstsammlungen Dresden and VEB Staatliche Porzellan Manufaktur Meissen: *Meissener Blaumalerei aus drei Jahrhunderten*, Leipzig, 1989.

Staatliche Kunstsammlungen Dresden: *Die schönsten Porzellane im Zwinger. Katalog der Sammlung in Dresden*, Gütersloh, 1982.

Staatliche Kunstsammlungen Dresden and Pietsch, Ulrich: *Phantastische Welten. Malerei auf Meissener Porzellan und deutschen Fayencen von Adam Friedrich von Löwenfinck 1714–1754*, Stuttgart, 2014.

Staatliche Schlösser und Gärten Baden Württemberg: *Die blau-weißen asiatischen Porzellane in Schloß Favorite bei Rastatt*, Schwetzingen, 1998.

Sterba, Günther: *Meissner Tafelgeschirr*, Stuttgart, 1989.

Stevenson, John and Guy, John: *Vietnamese Ceramics: A separate tradition*, Chicago, 1997.

Stevenson, John and Wood, Donald: *Dragons and Lotus Blossoms. Vietnamese Ceramics from the Birmingham Museum of Art*, Seattle, 2011.

Tan, Rita C.: *Zhangzhou Ware Found in the Philippines: "Swatow" export ceramics from Fujian 16th–17th century*, Malaysia, 2007.

Tan, Heidi (Ed.): *Marine Archaeology in Southeast Asia: Innovation and Adaptation*, Singapore, 2012.

Trux, Elisabeth: *Schnellkurs Altes Porzellan*, Köln, 2005.

Übersee-Museum: *Keramik aus Thailand. Sukhothai & Sawankhalok*, Exhibition catalogue, 1977.

Ulrichs, Friederike: *Johan Nieuhofs Blick auf China (1655–1657): Die Kupferstiche in seinem Chinabuch und ihre Wirkung auf den Verleger Jacob van Meurs*, Wiesbaden, 2003.

Villeroy & Boch: *Villeroy & Boch, 1748–1998*, Mettlach, 2006.

Volker, T.: *Porcelain and the Dutch East India Company: As recorded in the dagh-registers of Batavia castle, those of Hirado and Deshima and other contemporary papers 1602–1682*, Leiden, 1954.

Watney, Bernard: *English Blue & White Porcelain: of the 18th Century*, London, Boston, 1979.

Watson, Oliver: *Ceramics from Islamic lands*, Kuwait national museum, Singapore, 2004.

Weber, Julia: *Copying and competition: Meissen porcelain and the Saxon Triumph over the Emperor of China,* in: Forberg, Corinna und Philipp W. Stockhammer (Ed.): *The transformative power of the copy,* Heidelberg, 2017, pp.331–373.

Wellington, Donald C.: *French East India Companies: A historical account and record of trade*, Lanham, 2006.

Wiesner, Ulrich: *Chinesische Keramik auf Hormoz*, Museum für Ostasiatische Kunst, Köln, 1979.

Wolf, Norbert: *Jugendstil*, München, 2015.

Wu Chunming (Ed.): *Early Navigation in the Asia Pacific Region. A maritime archaeological perspective,* Singapore, 2016.

Wu Ruoming: *The origins of Kraak Porcelain: in the late Ming Dynasty*, Weinstadt, 2014.

Xiong Liao and Xiong Huan: *Canon of Porcelain Decoration through the Ages of China*（熊寥、熊寰：《中国历代瓷器装饰大典》，上海：上海文艺出版社），Shanghai, 2005.

Yang-Chien Tsai, Simon: *Trading for Tea: A Study of the English East India Company's Tea trade with China and the related financial issues, 1760–1833*, Thesis at University of Leicester, 2003.

Yew Seng Tai, Patrick Daly, E. Edwards Mckinnon, Andrew Parnell, R. Michael Feener, Jedrzej Majewski, Nazli Ismail, Kerry Sieh: *The impact of Ming and Qing dynasty maritime bans on trade ceramics recovered from coastal settlements in norther Sumatra, Indonesia*, in: Archeological Research in Asia 21, 2020.

Zeh, Ernst: *Hanauer Fayence*, Hanau, 1978.

Zhang Bai: *Complete Collection of Ceramic Art unearthed in China*（张柏：《中国出土瓷器全集》，全16卷，北京：科学出版社），Volume 1–16, Beijing, 2008.

Zhang Wenge: *Xinjiang Earthenware Art*（张文阁：《新疆土陶艺术》，乌鲁木齐：新疆人民出版社），Urumqi, 2006.

Zhejiang Province Relict Office: *Longquan celadon of China*（浙江省文物局编：《中国龙泉青瓷》，杭州：浙江摄影出版社），Hangzhou, 2001.

Zhou Guangzhen and Zeng Guanlu: *Chinese Ceramic Cultural Sites. A Traveler's Handbook*（周光真、曾冠禄：《中国陶瓷文化旅游手册》，台北：五行图书），Taipei, 2004.

Zhou Shirong: *Changsha Ceramics*（周世荣：《长沙窑》，南昌：江西美术出版社），Nanchang, 2016.

Zhu Yuping: *China Three Colours*（朱裕平：《中国唐三彩》，济南：山东美术出版社），Jinan, 2005.